Return to Leipzig

Letters of War and Care

MARIA RITTER

Return to Leipzig: Letters of War and Care
© 2022, Maria Ritter. All rights reserved.

Austin, Texas

Published by PartnerPress.org, Carlsbad, California
978-1-944098-19-3 (paperback)
Also available in eBook edition

Publisher's Cataloging-in-Publication Data
provided by Five Rainbows Cataloging Services

Names: Ritter, Maria, author.
Title: Return to Leipzig : letters of war and care / Maria Ritter.
Description: Carlsbad, CA : PartnerPress.org, 2022. | Also available in ebook format.
Identifiers: LCCN 2022937642 (print) | ISBN 978-1-944098-19-3 (paperback)
Subjects: LCSH: Leipzig (Germany)--Biography. | Germany (East)--Biography. | Dresden (Germany)--History--Bombardment, 1945. | World War, 1939-1945--Psychological aspects. | Letters. | BISAC: BIOGRAPHY & AUTOBIOGRAPHY / Personal Memoirs. | HISTORY / Europe / Germany.
Classification: LCC CT1063 .R58 2022 (print) | LCC CT1063 (ebook) | DDC 920.043--dc23.

Contact: mariaritterphd@sbcglobal.net

Without limiting the rights under copyright reserved above, no part of this publication may be reproduced, stored in or introduced into a retrieval system, or transmitted in any form or by any means (electronic, mechanical, photocopying, recording or otherwise whether now or hereafter known), without the prior written permission of both the copyright owner and the above publisher of this book, except by a reviewer who wishes to quote brief passages in connection with a review written for insertion in a magazine, newspaper, broadcast, website, blog or other outlet in conformity with United States and International Fair Use or comparable guidelines to such copyright exceptions.

In memory of my mother
Helene Schnädelbach (née Wunderlich)
1903-1983

Contents

Untangled Wood i
Introduction iii
Opening Voices v
Prologue: Songs by the Fire 1
CHAPTER ONE: 2014 19
CHAPTER TWO: 2014 23
CHAPTER THREE 31
CHAPTER FOUR 39
CHAPTER FIVE 45
CHAPTER SIX 63
CHAPTER SEVEN 79
CHAPTER EIGHT 89
CHAPTER NINE: 2014 95
CHAPTER TEN 101
CHAPTER ELEVEN 105
CHAPTER TWELVE: 2011 109
CHAPTER THIRTEEN: 1947 119
CHAPTER FOURTEEN: The Thank You Letters… 123
CHAPTER FIFTEEN 139
CHAPTER SIXTEEN: August 2012 147
CHAPTER SEVENTEEN 169
CHAPTER EIGHTEEN 173
CHAPTER NINETEEN 181
CHAPTER TWENTY 189
CHAPTER TWENTY-ONE 197
CHAPTER TWENTY-TWO 203
CHAPTER TWENTY-THREE 217

CHAPTER TWENTY-FOUR	221
CHAPTER TWENTY-FIVE	231
CHAPTER TWENTY-SIX: 2020–21	239
Epilogue: Temple City, 2014	275
Conclusion	291
A Word of Thanks	293
Appendix	295
About the Author	303

Untangled Wood

A single bird flies high into the shed
above the silent crowd of open hearts.
The waves of sound soar to the highest beam,
and break in splinters with the final note.
A single bird chimes in with loudest shrieks
to join the mighty orchestra below.
A descant to the darker side in life,
to woe and tears, to timpani and brass.
A single bird finds home above the silent
crowd to nest amidst the tiny twigs of wood.
The melodies ascent with trills and dance,
with dreams and warmth of piccolo and flute.
They all join in, the shrieks, the woes, the
playful trills—a tapestry of life among the tangled trees.

— Maria Ritter, *Tanglewood* 1999

Introduction

Following the collapse of the Hitler regime and the fall of Berlin in 1945, my family found refuge for the time in Leipzig where my grandfather, Paul Schnädelbach, lived in his flat. He had taken us in after our devastating flight from the approaching Russian Front in January 1945 and the catastrophic bombing in Dresden in February 13/14th of the same year. He gave us shelter when we were homeless, and he shared his rationed food with the five of us. He held my hand when we went outside. During those years of displacement and hunger, surrounded by ruins, the adults lived with the ideological defeat, with deep shame, crushed faith, and devastation of a trashed nation while fearing the brutal revenge of the Russian occupation. More so, we all were hungry and cold during the winter. They called it *die Hungersnot*, the famine.

And then, a miracle happened. Starting in 1947, somewhere in America, a group of Sunday School class members of a Methodist church in the Los Angeles, California area began to send us CARE packages, one at a time—all in all 64 packages over the next six years. They contained food and clothes to keep us alive and warm, basic items such as flour, sugar, and milk powder as well as yarn, soap and even toys. Faithfully, mother, in return, wrote back many thank you letters, some in half English half German. Someone in that distant Sunday School class took the time to translate some of mother's letters into readable English. I remember my mother sitting at the table late at night, when we had gone to bed, "Dear Blanche, ..." These letters tell our story.

In our time of emails, twitters and texting, handwritten letters on paper seem so outdated like old clothes you keep in the closet for sentimental reasons. Over the years, I have been given family letters to keep, but for what?

Signs of reconciliation and human kindness arrived with each of these CARE packages despite the hate and the massive loss of lives on both sides of the firing line. Letters and packages of food and clothing led the way out of ruins, out of our fears, out of hunger, and out of our losses. They not only restored our lives, but they told us of a human capacity for compassion despite war and hate. How is that possible?

The included letter exchanges between members of the Sunday School class and my mother are first set into a personal and current family frame with reactions and historical reflections during times of anguish, war, death, political chaos, and survival for some of us. The letter exchange between my mother to her older sister, Hilde, tell the real, heartbreaking story of our life right after WWII. It was Hilde who shared her meager food rations with us by sending us the first food packages which saved our lives in Leipzig. Some of my translations of the letters are intentionally kept in somewhat broken English to retain the feeling of my mother's original writing and her effort to connect with gratitude. The overall frame of the book also retains a letter form – this time telling this important story to my children, grandchildren, and to all you dear readers.

The story begins with a Prologue: *Songs by the Fire*, recalling the visit of an American work team in 1951 to assist with the building of a children's home in Bad Bergzabern, Germany and ends with an Epilogue: *Artaban Revisited*, my visit in 2014 to the United Methodist Church in Temple City, California, whose Sunday School class members by the name of *Artaban* had sent us the care packages between 1947 and 1951. Gratitude is timeless and Artabans are still among us. My own observations and narratives are not meant to give a complete historical account of that time but rather add another voice to many other survivors while not forgetting the ones that have finished their journey among us. Each one has a story to tell and needs to be heard. Together they weave "a tapestry of life among the tangled trees." (Maria Ritter, 1999)

— Maria Ritter, 2021

Opening Voices

"How it all turned out quite differently. Germany has been pushed into deep misery by National Socialism and has ceased to be a world power. Hitler's maliciously initiated war caused the loss of millions of human lives. I, too, lost two sons in their prime time of life. Karl fell 1942 in Russia, Herbert on 04-16-1945 in Croatia. Lord, for Jesus' sake, help our German nation up again."
— *Paul Schnäedelbach, 1947*

"Most of all, how could simple generosity and empathy overcome the hurdles of hate, prejudice, and bitterness from strangers six thousand miles away? Remember, the millions of Jews and other unwanted persons killed, more millions lost and driven out? How could all this happen in a misguided nation that claimed history, religion, science, music, and culture as the cornerstones of its civilization, only to derail in the most barbaric way? Why did we not hear and talk about it all until many years later?"
— *Maria Ritter, 2022*

"The following collection of letters tells a story of human compassion, of survival, and the power of an insistent faith. Gratitude is timeless and the Artabans are still among us on their journey."
— *Maria Ritter, 2020*

"I have never owned anything like this—all was left behind in our home, or it burned. You have clothed us all. I have tears in my eyes, I cannot comprehend it. I must think of the verses in the Bible: … "and you have clothed me.""
— *Leni Schnädelbach, 1948*

RETURN TO LEIPZIG

"It is always a great joy when I hear from all of you. We have never seen each other, but I feel we know each other and understand each other in love. Your love and care have sustained me during many difficult hours of the last few years. What would have happened to us without your love? We all would have been severely ill or would have perished. But you carried us through these difficult years. Many times, a package from you arrived just at the moment when I asked God how he would help us today because there was nothing left in the pantry. Those experiences strengthened my faith."

— Leni Schnädelbach, 1950 in her letters to the Artaban Sunday School Class after receiving care packages.

"And then there is the human capacity for compassion despite our own suffering. Maybe one own's suffering is soothed by identifying with others' suffering and by sharing with others in empathy and compassion."

— Maria Ritter, 2021

"The doctor said, "You must weep three days." But I cannot weep, my tears have dried up since the Dresden night."

— Leni Schnädelbach, 1948

"The Artaban's mission and their records are a living document to tell the story."

— Maria Ritter, 2014

"I assumed that my *Return to Leipzig* documentation of war and care would only be of personal, family and historical importance to share and complete— just to pass it on to you, my children and grandchildren and place on your bookshelves. Now, the reality of another war with its dark reminders of brutality, terror and human suffering is here again. Let's hope for solidarity, reason, peace and care to prevail and heal."

— Maria Ritter, 2022

Prologue: Songs by the Fire

My dear readers,

Sometimes stuff just shows up without being searched for. To my surprise, I recently opened a folder which contained my own memories from a visit of an American Methodist work team during the summer of 1951. It was a left-over chapter from my book, *Return to Dresden, (2004)* and will find a better place here.

RETURN TO LEIPZIG

When the six college students and their pastor, Frank Williams, from Pasadena, California, arrived in Bad Bergzabern, Germany, to assist in completing the Children's Home, a new world opened for all of us. We were not quite ready for American visitors. Running hot water in the building had not yet completely installed, the bare walls inside and outside still needed paint, and the garden looked more like an unkempt and trampled field after the potato harvest last fall. A group of college students had volunteered through their Methodist churches back in the Los Angeles area to help rebuild a struggling and demoralized Germany after the war by their presence—one project at a time, one kind hand at a time, and one shovel full of dirt at a time. They spoke a different language and brought quite different customs with them such as openly expressing thoughts, feelings, and wishes. Most of all, they brought such joy and enthusiasm. They sang and prayed, worked with garden gloves to protect their hands, and they played games I had never seen before. And how they loved my mother! They called her 'Helen', even hugged her frequently! She spoke with her broken English, and they loved it. They tried their bits of German and we laughed and tried to imitate their accent. It was a magical experience and a healing time for all of us. Just the thought of American visitors coming to our home, not soldiers, was so exciting and comforting.

Over the years, a special friendship had developed between our family and 'Papa Zurbuchen', a Methodist minister in the German church in Los Angeles, California who had taken on the plight of many of us in post-war Germany. He just helped us and many other families, organized Care packages and included signs of love such as personal notes and pictures. 'Papa Zurbuchen' was the one who had sent mother 400 Marks for a piano and had insisted that she spent all of it on a good instrument instead on furniture which we desperately needed. Mother had just laughed about such a gift but accepted it and bought a used, brown, up-right piano. It rarely was without a player in the years to come. Music was back in our home. It would take a few more years though before I got my turn.

I will tell you about their visit and how I remembered that summer of 1951.

*　*　*

PROLOGUE: SONGS BY THE FIRE

"The Amis[1] are coming next week. I don't know how this will all work out," my mother said to me shortly after we had moved into the small house next to the Children's Home in July of 1951.

Worry had painted deep lines on her forehead, her mind on needed food, limited beds and running water. We still needed electricity, wheelbarrows, enough shovels and building supplies. During the past months, Mother had received several letters from a Rev. Frank Williams somewhere in America, the address had said Pasadena, California, with an offer to bring a work team of College students to help complete the Children's Home project. Mother had accepted the plan, and now they were to arrive next week.

Letters from America were always so welcome in our house. The colorful striped envelopes with airmail stickers and different stamps promised a signal from a different part of the world. More so, the packages during the past years had been filled with food, clothing, and toys. Coffee and cigarettes, the most valuable of all the goods sent, had been traded on the black market when we still lived in East Germany and had paid for real food or music lessons. These Care packages had saved our lives during the years of famine following the end of the war. Some of the items in those packages had been so strange and puzzling to us, such as egg powder, Spam in a can, hard candy with red stripes on the outside and a soft peppermint filling on the inside. The packages also contained raisins, nuts, cocoa powder, and Lipton's noodle soup. I have never forgotten the taste of the steaming soup and can still see the thin, short noodles floating in the yellow broth. Even now, we still did not know how to throw that brown, egg shaped ball they had sent along and called it 'football'; it just would not roll and bounce like our balls outside on the street. I did treasure the bride doll in her white dress and her veil I had received one day, and the paper doll model by the name of Rita Hayworth. She wore a fancy, blue swimsuit and remarkably high heeled shoes that gave her a very shapely figure. I added to her wardrobe by cutting out dresses and skirts from used wrapping paper I could find. Unfortunately, I had to leave the dolls behind in Leipzig when we fled across the border to the West of Germany in 1949. My favorite red and green checkered skirt I had received a few years ago barely fit me now since I had

---

[1] 'Amis' means 'Americans' for short

grown too much. I loved the skirt because it opened into a full turning wheel when I twirled around.

Mother had faithfully written back to all the senders of these CARE packages, some were members of an Adult Sunday School class in Monrovia and Temple City, California, and thanked them in her broken English for their kindness and much needed help. One time, she wrote back,

> Dear Mr. and Mrs. Sawyer,
>
> "Thank you, we became your box," ... not knowing the word 'received' would have been a better choice. When we found out what she had written, we all laughed.
>
> She said, "I'm sure, they understood what I meant," and smiled. "Gratitude does not need an explanation in any language." Of course, she was right.
>
> "We will need to take two wagons to the train station for all their luggage." Mother said to us.
>
> "How many Amis are coming?"
>
> "I think six and Pastor Williams."
>
> "Do they speak German or English?" I wanted to know.
>
> "They want to learn German here, you may have to help them," was the answer.

I could hardly wait until school was out that day and anxiously looked forward to their arrival. There was no question in my mind who these Amis were, arriving at the train station. You could tell by their bright clothes and hats, not to mention them chewing gum while they greeted us warmly. I noticed right away that they did not shake our hands as was our custom. They just stood there and looked at us and we stared at them. Rev. Frank Williams only shook my mother's hand and then introduced each one of the students. There was Bill who was very tall, his teeth decorated the widest grin. He wore a baseball cap slightly tilted. Then there was Dean and Bob who immediately tried their German with *"Guten Tag"*[2] while chewing gum with an open mouth. Doris had curly, red hair and seemed on the quiet side. Sally was standing back near the

---

[2] Good Day or Hello

PROLOGUE: SONGS BY THE FIRE

luggage. Marty was so beautiful wearing bright pants and a matching head band, and then, there was Sylvia, a tall, young black woman. Her shiny hair combed in a stylish way; her bright eyes twinkled. I was quite shocked at her sight since I had never seen or met a black woman before. I had to stare at her, her broad smile met mine quickly. Mother said later, she looked like a gazelle, so graceful and so pretty.

The Amis had arrived in town. They smiled, and they loved us from the first day. I knew it, although I could not understand what they were saying to each other or to us.

Bergzabern, 1951. The American Work Team.
Front row: Maria, Gerhard, visitor from DDR.
Second row: Sylvia, Sally, (Erna?) Doris, Mother, Marti
Back row: Dean, Bill, (?) Bob, Horst Wunderlich (covered)

Life in our home changed in a hurry. Like a refreshing breeze blew out a long stuffy winter season. The students and their pastor moved into the empty children's home with their suitcases and duffel bags, sleeping on cots that my mother had organized from somewhere. Thank God, the water pipes had been connected and the electricity was finally on. No more candlelight at night. Hot water, though, still had to be prepared in the kitchen and be carried up to the bathtub for a comfortable bath. Wooden floors were still missing in most of the bedrooms.

The Amis did not complain. Instead, their chatter and laughter could be heard all around the home. They made plans immediately to organize their work activities and organize the tools and building supply necessary for landscaping around the Children's Home. My cousin, Horst, arrived, too. As a young, aspiring architect student, he was to take over the work plans and supervise their efforts. I was amazed about his English skills while I was trying to pick up some expressions and vocabulary such as, "Well… OK… Hello… Good morning… and, Thank you."

We all ate together at the long table in the dining room next to the large kitchen in the basement of the Children's Home. How relaxed they seemed at the table. I was not allowed to rest my elbows on the table while eating, and here was Bill hanging over his plate close to his mouth, spoon and the soup plate, his elbow resting on his left knee. He even kept on talking while chewing his food. Their manners were so different, even funny, when they ate with their forks in their right hand while putting the knife on the rim of the plate. And I was really surprised when they said grace before the meal without closing their eyes and bowing down in prayer. They just sat there and looked at each other while reciting a table grace,

> ….be our guest
> …bless this food
> … their hands
> … us be grateful.
> Amen.

"We've decided to only speak German during mealtimes," Rev. Williams said to my Mother.

"Anyone who forgets is to put *five Pfennige*[3] into this can." He pointed to the one on the table. During the next meal, it was so quiet you could have heard a pin drop.

Bob said, "*Dean, die Butter, bitte!*" (Please pass the butter!) That worked out fine.

---

[3] pennies

PROLOGUE: SONGS BY THE FIRE

"Danke!"[4]

"Ja, Ja!"

"Nein!"[5]

"Wunderbar!"

"Guten Morgen!"[6]

"Ich verstehe nix!"[7]

"Gesundheit!" They all burst out laughing.

After that, the silence returned with only the clatter of silverware on dishes and their noisy chewing of the food.

During their next morning's team meeting, they talked about this arrangement of language and the money fine one more time and decided to abandon the plan immediately. They were afraid of losing too much money, they said laughingly, but they were still willing to learn as much German as they could in other ways. After that, the table discussions were lively again.

Mother was amazed how much cold milk they drank during breakfast, lunch, and dinner. We never drank anything along with a meal. That did not seem necessary.

"It just fills up your stomach with liquid, and then you will be hungry soon after your meal," she said.

"I don't understand why they want to eat bread with each meal," she wondered aloud as she cleaned up the table.

"What I absolutely don't get at all is why they leave food on their plate. You see, they don't eat all the food they serve themselves. Why are they taking more than they can eat? Now, I have to throw it away."

She emptied a half full plate into a container in which she collected leftovers for the compost pile behind the house.

"Maybe I should get a piglet to eat all the leftovers. It's not right to throw away all this food, good meat and potatoes," she muttered.

I understood what she meant. Years of shortage and hunger had made food a special gift to us, not to be wasted, not even a few spoons of it. We were not

---

[4] Thank you

[5] No

[6] Good Morning

[7] I don't understand anything

allowed to leave any food on our plate, ever! And here came these Amis. They just stopped eating when they were full and went about their business outside of clearing the rocks and the dirt. They wore gloves when they worked outside. I only knew of wearing gloves during the wintertime. Some of the students were even happy doing the dishes, chatting with my mother while the others joked with each other and sprayed each other with the water hose outside. It was a hot summer day anyway.

They loved my mother. They hugged her in the morning and hugged her at night before bedtime. They called her "Helen". They liked her cooking and said it tasted *wunderbar!* We did not show such affection openly or offered compliments to each other, nor did we call adults by their first name without being related or being invited to. The Amis, however, did not follow our rules of formal interactions with hand shaking, bowing before elders, and a curtsy required from us girls. They just stood there with their hands in their pockets, jingling their loose change and said "Hi." Their warm smile or broad grin, and their curiosity about our life and history loosened us up. So, we smiled back and laughed.

I noticed that they helped my mother every day. The women cleaned up the kitchen with her, they scrubbed the floors. Marty loved to go with my mother to the open market and helped her carrying bread, milk, vegetables, and other goodies. In response, mother opened her heart to their smiles and touching love. I heard her teach the students some German songs. The Amis had moved into our home and our hearts.

I was still attending school in the mornings, waiting impatiently for the start of our summer vacation, and was eager to return home each day to watch their work progress. The dirt piles and the rubble slowly moved into their designated corners. The shovels and the wheelbarrows were loaded, pushed, and dumped. Dust clouds were flying all around them, sweat settled on everyone's face. The Amis not only drank milk with their meals but also water all day long. I never saw such thirsty people in my life. Occasionally, they stopped unloading their wheelbarrows and chatted with each other and laughed. Hard work and laughter, no beer bottles and trash littered around like the local workers had done during the construction time of the Home. On rainy days, they rested inside the Home, wrote letters back to California, went to town shopping, or did their laundry. They even prayed and read the Bible. Bill and Dean assumed that the women on the team would do their laundry, too, but that was declined immediately by them.

"You can do your own laundry," they quipped at the men in the group one afternoon outside.

I was surprised at their decisive response when they pulled up the large wash tub next to the house. They put their dirty work clothes into the cold water and had to scrub it on the metal wash board just like my mother had to do. They laughed about that, too. Maybe at home they had washing machines with warm water. But not here, in Bergzabern. Bill had the hardest time with his laundry. He had never washed his own clothes before and had no idea how to wring out a bulky mass of wet pants by hand. In desperation he finally threw the whole stuff over the cloth line, fastened it with wooden cloth pins where it hung there in a lump, dripping for hours, waiting for the sun to do the drying. I did see Marty one day when she washed some of the men's shirts, a favor for Rev. Williams.

"Just once!" she said smiling at me.

Sylvia's hair care was a fascinating activity. She poured a special pomade she had brought from America on her black hair, which made it shiny and straight; it smelled like coconut. Then she took her pink curlers and carefully rolled one strand of hair after the next until her head was covered with rolls and pins. She finally placed a scarf over the whole array of rollers and walked around like that all day, even slept at night with it on. I wondered if she was sleeping while sitting up. The next day she combed out her hair in perfect waves and even curls. She had done all this by herself without a hairdresser! I also watched her putting on make-up, lip stick and rouge. This was not done by Methodist women and girls in Germany; it bordered on sin and worldliness. All the women shaved their legs and their arm pits. They used deodorant. I had no idea that women in America did all this every day!

"The girls shouldn't walk around town with curlers in their hair!" my Mother muttered under her breath. "You don't do that here."

I noticed that Doris even wore pants while working, blue seer sucker ones, cotton pedal pushers, the ones that covered her knees and half of her calf, and black and white saddle shoes. She looked so comfortable and could easily move around while working. None of our women in town ever wore pants, not even in the wintertime; that was reserved for men only. Doris did not seem to mind when people stared at her as she walked through town, curlers, pants, and all. Bob purchased a pair of *Lederhosen*[8] on one of their shopping trips to Karlsruhe, complete with suspenders which he wore proudly. People in town snickered when he was walking by,

"Oh, this Ami in *Lederhosen!*" they said and shook their heads.

His pants needed no washing from then on. The more dirt and grease spots on them, the more authentic the look. My brother Gerhard had secretly wished for a pair of *Lederhosen* and one day, the Amis returned from a sightseeing trip and had purchased a pair for him. He was so surprised and so happy and did not mind when they called him, "Gerhard Lederhosen Schnädelbach," his last name pronounced freely as "Snadlback." They took pictures of each other with their camera and laughed some more, using the word 'cheeeese' for everyone to pose.

Their work effort was paying off day after day. Not only did the work team members level the grounds for a playground but also designed and dug out a fishpond on the side of the Home. The pond was to be part of a garden with a beautiful view toward the green hills, complete with gold fishes and a bench. A low wall had been completed, holding up the grounds of the play area. Its large sandstone boulders marked the borders of the property and provided a place to sit while watching any activities on the open playground. One day, I saw my mother sitting there with Frank Williams. They talked for a long time, but I could not understand what they were saying. I figured my mother was telling him about our family's history because she sat bent over with her handkerchief in her hands wiping away many tears while he listened. I was surprised that he wanted to know about us as a family. He just sat there listening to her broken English and her broken heart.

"We'll have a big sports festival tomorrow," Gerhard and I announced to our American visitors.

"All the classes compete in many track and field events. There'll be races and soccer games. The festival will be held down on the soccer field, right down the hill. All the school classes will compete with each other, and the winners will receive special ribbons; our grades in physical education for the school year will be determined."

---

[8] Leather pants

PROLOGUE: SONGS BY THE FIRE

All the Amis got excited. They loved sports.

"It's our national past time," Rev. Williams had said to my Mother one night during dinner time.

They had told us about their sports in their country, especially the football games in the fall season, and one sport called 'baseball' which they tried to explain to us on paper. I never got it right. I had seen the Amis standing on the new playground swinging a thick stick, standing in a crouched position while someone else threw a hard ball at that person holding the stick. They hit that ball right over the new wall, straight into the meadow where it disappeared. Then they yelled and cheered on the player who was running a large circle. Mother worried about the windows when she saw what was going on outside. Gerhard and I ran out into the dense grass, joined by our dog, Ria, and started fetching the ball. By the time my brother and I retrieved it, I had forgotten where they were in the game with their rules. All the Amis loved to run around the bases which had been marked by some wooden board; they ran so hard as if their lives depended on it. Then they slapped each other on the back or on their open hands and yelled again something that sounded like "Yeeeeah!" As we watched their game, Mother came out of the kitchen and started to watch them too. She said to me,

"I remember a similar game called *Schlagball* we used to play when I was a teacher in Leipzig. I forgot all about it until now. Except, we used a different ball."

I was still puzzled about the rules of their game.

"Come on, Helen. You are up hitting the ball."

They coaxed her up to the plate and Dean threw a ball at her which she promptly hit out to the bases. She stood and laughed as everyone watched the ball fly and disappear in the grass.

"Yeah, Helen!" they screamed even louder. "Run over here!"

She ran as fast as she could. Her apron was fluttering in the wind. Her eyes sparkled. She chuckled catching her breath at the base. They clapped their hands and yelled again, "Good eye, Helen, yeah!"

"I had forgotten all about it," she said to me later and smiled. Happy memories of play and cheers from happier times began to warm her heavy heart.

The next day all our American visitors went to the school's sports day. Thank God it did not rain in the morning, the soccer field would have been a muddy field. The grounds were overgrown with weeds by this time of the year, the dry soil dusting the air. All the school kids and teachers were assembled. On one side of the field, the sprint races were conducted for the various age groups; the teachers even used a gun to signal the start. It startled me every time. Frau Weber, our physical education instructor, and other teachers stood at the finish line with a stopwatch in their hand. They entered each person's running time by minutes and seconds into their record books, and grades were given accordingly. On the other side of the field, white charcoal lines marked a long jump field area, next to high jump equipment for the older students. A mattress was placed on the ground so that the courageous jumpers would land safely. Soccer games followed in the afternoon. Our visitors loved it all and wanted to know how to play the games. Our soccer balls were round and bounced well not like the Amis' plum shaped footballs they carried around while running in one direction.

Maria with Sylvia (left) and Marti (right) in Bergzabern, 1951

As soon as our visitors appeared, the sports festival shifted its attention. The Amis were a total sensation, especially Sylvia. Many people in my town had never seen a black person before in their life. Maybe they had seen a black

PROLOGUE: SONGS BY THE FIRE

American soldier at the end of the war, but not a woman. We knew there were black people in Africa, but a woman right here in Bergzabern! The kids followed her around all day long, stared at her, touched her, watched her every move. She looked so interesting—so foreign to us. Her warm smile disarmed them all. She did not mind all their looks, nor their touch. I was so proud that she was in my company and that she stayed in our home. Sylvia even put her arm on my shoulder as she walked with me around the sports field. It was a special day!

As the weeks passed, the Amis must have missed their home cooking although they never complained openly. The bread was not white and soft, the rolls too crispy and hard. They wanted to eat hot oatmeal for breakfast, and talked about their bacon, ham, and eggs at home. I had no idea you could eat bacon, eggs, and potatoes for breakfast. That combination would have been a fancy supper.

It must have been during the later weeks of their stay when they asked,

"Where can we find hamburgers?"

We shook our heads not knowing where that would be. Mother could not help them either.

"We have a city in Northern Germany by that name of Hamburg,"

They shook their heads.

"All we need are some soft buns, the rest we'll be able to organize quite nicely," they replied. "We'll have a cookout this Saturday night and fix hamburgers and hot dogs for all of us."

They got excited about it as they discussed the shopping plan for the various ingredients. Marty and Dean went down to Pfaffmann's bakery and looked over the rolls in the store. All the rolls were either too crisp on the top or the wrong shape for what was needed. They shook their heads,

"Nein, nix good for hamburgers!"

Finally, they asked the baker to make special, soft rolls for them on Saturday. Buying mustard and ketchup turned out to be more difficult than they thought. Both items were only sold in small, toothpaste like tubes. The mustard was much too spicy for them. The ketchup was too thick and looked like tomato paste to them. Mayonnaise was not available at all. Mother said, she knew how to make mayonnaise from scratch. They were glad to hear that and bought a bunch of eggs.

"We'll also have a campfire that night," Dean announced in the afternoon.

I could hardly wait for the day. They began their preparation early in the evening. The men started to make a fire for grilling the meat patties. I thought it to be much easier to cook the patties in the kitchen on the stove in a pan, but they would have none of it, and said the hamburgers and the wieners had to be grilled outside.

"Everything tastes much better if you cook it on an open fire."

A cloud of white smoke drifted high into the clear sky. I was sure the town's people could see it from far away. Mother was concerned about the Fire Department in town taking it as a wildfire. She was right. Not long after they started to grill the patties and the wieners, a red truck drove up the road. Thank God, the sirens were turned off. The firemen jumped off the truck to see what was causing such a smoke near the vineyards and the forest. My Mother walked up to them.

"The Amis are grilling hamburgers for us tonight."

Rev. Williams waved at them to come closer.

"Hi, es ist alles okay!"[9] he greeted them.

They shook their heads when they heard of grilling meat and chuckled. Then they stood by the grill for a while and watched the men cook. I guess they had wondered what the Amis were doing by the open fire. Cooking was a woman's job in their homes. The smoke was still drifting into the air. After their inspection of the grill and the smoke, they went to their truck, put on their helmets, and drove back into town. I had been so worried that we would be fined for a false alarm, but nothing happened.

The Amis cooked all the meat on a makeshift grill they had constructed from leftover bricks. They showed us how to put the meat on the open bun piled up with tomatoes, pickles, salad, cheese, raw onion, mustard, mayonnaise, and ketchup. Then they squeezed it together with their hands. I watched them as they bit into it, dripping all over themselves, smiling with their mouth wide open to get it in. As strange as it was, it tasted wonderful, so different—and messy, too! I was embarrassed to open my mouth that wide. This was totally against any table etiquette I had ever learned. Mother just chuckled and tried

---

[9] It's all fine

not to drip the food all over herself. Her apron caught the leftovers and Remo, our dog, enjoyed the smells, the company, and the droppings.

When it began to get dark, we brought our paper lanterns outside which we hung in the trees. The candlelight provided a soft, warm glow with shadows on branches and trunks. The campfire was in full swing now, no shortage of firewood that night. Marty and Sylvia talked about roasting marshmallows on sticks, but we did not know what they were talking about either. Mother had put some potatoes into the hot coal to roast them slowly.

The evening darkness had fallen all around us. The crackling of the fire mixed with the scraping rhythm of the crickets in the grass while the flames jumped high into the balmy summer night. Remo kept his distance. Suddenly, someone started singing:

> *Old Mac Donald had a farm, hea hea ho.*
> *And on his farm, he had a pig, hea hea ho -*
> *with an oink oink here, an oink oink there..*
> *... he had a cow...moo, moo here, moo, moo there...*
> *... he had a duck...quack, quack here, quack, quack there...*

This song went on and on, the list of animals on his farm grew longer and longer. Poor old Mac Donald needed a wife to help him with all these animals. It was fun. I mixed up the lineup of them all as we sang along. The Amis even clapped their hands as they sang to keep the rhythm. Sylvia's bright smile met my eyes.

They wondered if we knew *"Amazing grace how sweet the sound,"* so we could sing it together, but we had never heard of it. This song was one of their favorite hymns back home, they said, and began singing it. The slow phrases carried such feeling of sadness, the words gentle and full of promise.

By now, we all sat closer by the fire as the night air turned a bit nippy. Mother had brought out some blankets to sit on. Rev. Williams sat on one of the wooden crates. Bill just stood there chewing gum. I saw the glow of the fire in their eyes, their warm smile. The calmness of a peaceful night was among us.

"Do you know any spirituals?" my brother Klaus asked them. They nodded and began:

> *Swing low, sweet chariot, coming for to carry me home; ...*
> *I'm sometimes up, I'm sometimes down, Oh Yes, Lord.*
> *...coming for to carry me home...*

Sylvia sang out loud and clear,

> *Tell me why the stars do shine,*
> *Tell me why the ivy twines,*
> *Tell me why the skies are blue,*
> *And I will tell you just why I love you...*

I did not understand the text but felt the kindness in all our singing. The Amis just sang all these songs by heart without text or scores in front of them. Their melodies and the text spoke of love and sadness, faith and longing, praise, and trust. Our hymns sounded to me more like drudging through a harsh life with strong, steady melodies except when the softer melodies came around at Christmas with angel voices, harps, and Holy Night.

The Amis chimed into another spiritual full of mourning and Hallelujah!

> *Nobody knows the trouble I have seen,*
> *nobody knows but Jesus ...oh, ...*
> *... glory, Hallelujah!*

That song had to be my favorite. They said it had been sung among the slaves in America as they worked in the cotton fields in the South many years ago. The slaves were waiting for the Lord to release them from their suffering and take them home to the Promised Land.

> *... Oh, yes, Lord!*

Our songs and silences were connected by a gentle, dancing fire with its deep, orange, and glowing ashes warming our hands, our faces and our hearts. Peace was among us and in us. I looked around the circle as we held hands for the last song of that night:

> *Kum ba ya, my Lord, kum ba yah...*
> *Someone's praying, Lord. Kum ba yah...*
> *Someone's crying, Lord...*

PROLOGUE: SONGS BY THE FIRE

Someone's singing, Lord.
Oh Lord, kum ba yah!

Our songs drifted softly into the air—all the way to America. I wondered that night if I would ever be so fortunate as to visit there one day, see their land, sing their songs, and even eat their hamburgers![10] Would I ever start on my own peaceful journey? Away from the "trouble I have seen...", war and shame?

Their visit had come to an end. Their garden projects completed which included a bench Dean Freudenberger had built and placed at a spot in the front yard to enjoy the view of the town, the meadows, and the vineyards. After a tearful good-by, the work team returned to America and told their congregations including the Artaban Sunday school class in Temple City, California, about their experiences in Bergzabern with us. We promised we would never forget!

Bad Bergzabern, Germany 1952

---

[10] Quoted hymns taken from The United Methodist Hymnal, Nashville, Tennessee, 1989.

Chapter One: 2014

My dear readers,

Yes, sometimes we are on a journey long before we know it. I noticed it when last year's Christmas had passed with lingering memories of a long and dreamy day. Late in the evening all the traditional trimmings in the Ritter's house in Larkspur were still in place, the live tree stood proudly in the center of the room and had been decorated at eye level by the kids with handmade and whimsical ornaments swaying in the breeze. The sounds of happy chatter around the table over Holiday brisket, German Spaetzle and Stollen had long ceased. Christmas Day had come and gone. All was quiet in the house, the children dreamt of toys and laughter, Penny slept curled up at their feet. We had sung the old familiar hymns and the Three Wisemen had arrived the evening before during the Christmas Eve pageant in their quaint village church, the children bearing gifts and reverence. While watching this yearly procession, my mind had wandered off to our trip to Egypt last year. I remembered the sight of camels trotting through the sand and bright stars in the dark blue sky high above the vast Sahara Desert. The Three Kings are always on a journey, year after year, seeking and giving, arriving among us and disappearing in the night.

I remembered how Christmas had been in Leipzig when I was a little girl. Christmas season was such a special time, an oasis of temporary and fragile peace during and after WWII, even if it was just for a night or a few days. After

CHAPTER ONE: 2014

the war was finally over and we had found a refuge at grandfather's flat, we waited eagerly for Christmas Eve. I counted the hours before darkness fell, waited for our mother to open the door to the one room in the house closed all day for secret preparation. The keyhole was covered; all I could hear was the faint sound of rustling paper and the pungent incense coming from one of the Räuchermännchen[1], those wooden figurines of pipe incense-smoking shepherds or woodsmen from the Erzgebirge you, too, know so well. Their holy smoke drifted through walls. keyholes, and door cracks.

After the Christmas Eve service, which always took too long for me, we rushed home while singing Christmas carols along the way. Finally, the sound of a silver bell invited us into the room. In the darkness I saw the fine silhouette of the fir tree with lit candles carefully clipped on its outer branches with silver ornaments and angel hair reflecting a warm shimmer. I noticed the presents on a table, my doll sitting on a chair wearing a new outfit, and books wrapped with a bow placed on top. The old familiar melodies played in my head, sweet and strangely intact. Grandfather, my mother and my three brothers stood at the piano singing all the verses to *"Ihr Kinderlein kommet"* and *"Stille Nacht, Heilige Nacht…."*

Tonight, however, wrapped in this bittersweet, nostalgic mood and feeling slightly homesick, I slowly drifted in and out of sleep. I felt empty and alone, so far away from where I used to be, more yearning than sad as if many memories were missing and could never be found again. Despite the heaviness of arriving sleep, the images of Christmases past would not vanish.

I heard myself ask, "Where are you, mother and father, who taught and instilled in me this sense of mystery and joy for life despite the hardship and losses we all endured during and after the war? Are you both asleep forever, or can you still speak in some way and visit among us by what you said, wrote in letters, and how you felt? Have you been quiet forever, or did I not listen to you in the hustle and bustle of life?"

Of course, there were no answers to my questions this Holy Night, but fleeting melodies, smiles, familiar stories, sweet aroma of this year's Stollen in the

---

[1] Small, carved figurines such as chimney sweeps, woodsmen, fishermen, shepherds, etc. for incense burning around the holidays.

air and the scent of blown out candles as the mystery of Christmas was upon us all.

Thank you all for coming with me on this journey,

A multitude of angels, nutcrackers, and smoky figures, 2019

Chapter Two: 2014

Her tone on my voice mail one day in April seemed joyful and eager.

"Hi, my name is Marcia. I found your telephone number on the internet. I remember your book, *Return to Dresden*, a few years back and your stories about your childhood. I have met you before, years ago, talking to you about our church in Temple City, California, and the connection to your family way back during WWII. Do you remember?"

"Of course, I do."

I began to think ahead of what might be coming; maybe an invitation to speak to a group of church people on my history and struggle to come to grips with the heaviness of my country people's crimes during the Nazi history and the effects of transgenerational trauma.

Instead, she went on, "We cleaned out the church archives for our church's 100th anniversary and came across a ring binder full of letters your mother wrote to our Sunday school class between 1946 and 1952. Would you be interested in them?"

What a surprise! It was like Christmas all over again.

"Of course, of course," I stammered.

I could not find any words. She had found the letters mother wrote to women like Blanche, Lillian, and Mrs. Boeck, members of a Sunday school class at the Community Methodist Church in Temple City in California by the name of 'Artaban' and 'Caravaners', strange names of a class that had no meaning to me as a child.

Following the collapse of the Hitler regime and the fall of Berlin in 1945, my family found refuge for the time in Leipzig where my grandfather, Paul

Schnädelbach, lived in his flat. He had taken us in after our devastating flight from the Russian Front in January 1945 and the bombing in Dresden in February of the same year. He gave us shelter when we were homeless, and he shared his rationed food with the five of us. He held my hand when we went outside. During those years of displacement and hunger, surrounded by ruins, the adults lived with the ideological defeat and devastation of a trashed nation while fearing the brutal actions of the Russian occupation. More so, we all were hungry and cold during the winter. They called it *Die Hungersnot*.[2]

Starting in 1947, somewhere in America, a group of Sunday School members of a Methodist church in the Los Angeles area began to send us CARE packages, one at a time—all in all, more than 64 packages kept arriving over the next six years. Their gifts contained food and clothes to keep us alive and warm. Faithfully, mother, in return, wrote back many thank you letters, some in half English half German. Someone in the Sunday school class took the time to translate some of mother's letter into readable English. I remember my mother sitting at the table late at night, when we had gone to bed, "Dear Blanche, …"

"Of course, I'd love to see them, when could we meet?" I answered Marcia. My mind was spinning.

"I will be in your area later this week and can bring them by," she offered.

I was so excited by the annunciation of a treasure that I counted the days.

"Thank you, thank you, Marcia. What a surprise."

As promised, Marcia arrived on Friday as promised and placed a full red ring binder in my hands. We greeted each other as if we had been friends for a long time.

"Here they are, I am sure you can have them."

My stammered thank you felt again like an uneven gesture of what I had received and now held in my hand. I could hardly wait to look. All letters had been skillfully placed into plastic sleeves. I recognized my mother's handwriting right away and the photos of our family dated 1948 and beyond. One greeting card even had my signature on it, clearly printed with a pencil.

We sat at the table and shared stories of our families, going back to years of suffering and the kind response by church members in Temple City so many years ago, which spoke of a deep compassion despite the violence of war and

---

[2] Famine.

CHAPTER TWO: 2014

the destruction and losses on all sides of the firing line. What had been their motivation to reach out and help us in 1947? How did they find my homeless and lost family among the millions of survivors in war torn Europe? And how did my mother respond to their kindness? And how did she describe our life at that time?

I knew at that moment that I had received a late Christmas gift. Reading the notes and letters in that folder would give me many real answers to the questions I had posed last December.

I opened the ring folder and noticed my hands shaking. A hand scribbled note on top of the ring binder reads:

> *Artaban 1948*
> *Caravaners 1950*
> *Assistance to post war German family*
> *Mrs. Leni Schnädelbach*

Followed by another note:

> *1948-52*
> *Correspondence*
> *Between the Artaban 1949 (Caravaners 1950)*
> *Class & the German family.*

It is not unusual for Sunday school classes in churches now and then to identify themselves by a name to express their Christian mission. Besides social gatherings such as potlucks and receptions, church folks meet for Bible study, prayer, and often look for a way to reach out to other people in need. It is often called a 'Mission Project'. In 1948, the Sunday School class in Temple City, California, chose the name, Artaban, and later in 1950, changed it to the Caravaners. I had wondered why they would choose such a name rather than, The Seekers, The Forum, or The Disciples. I did some searching and want to tell you the story of Artaban as told by Henry Van Dyke.

The Story
of the
Other Wise Man
by
Henry van Dyke

According to a well-known legend, *Artaban's gift*, the great Persian Wiseman, *Artaban*, planned on joining the other Three Wisemen in search of the New-born King who was to be born in the Hebrew land. A star in the sky would lead them to his birthplace.

In a great hurry he sold all his possessions, and with the money he bought three precious gems: a sapphire, a ruby, and a pearl. He said goodbye to his household and friends and set off to a gathering place of the caravan. As he rushed on his horse through the night, the beast suddenly spooked at the sight of a half dead man on the ground. It was a Jew, who was seriously injured and needed immediate help. Caught between compassion and missing his caravan, he prayed, "...I cannot pass by; I must help this unfortunate Jew."

Through the night, he nursed the poor man back to health with water, food, and comfort. The next day when he reached the meeting point, the caravan had left for the sacred journey. In gratitude, the Jew revealed to him that the Newborn King was to be born in Bethlehem. He knew this from his scripture. In his excitement, Artaban sold one of his gems to finance his own caravan and hurried on toward Bethlehem.

When he arrived, a woman holding a child told him that the Three Wisemen had already been there and left town. The same night, Mary, Joseph, and the baby had disappeared, maybe they had moved to Egypt, she said. As she described the visit of the magi in Bethlehem, a swarm of soldiers overran the town to kill all the newborn children to eradicate any future baby King. Artaban reached for his second gem to bribe the army captain so they would leave the woman alone. He prayed, "Here, I am late again, I shall follow you to Egypt. Where will I find your face?"

Artaban continued his journey and traveled for a long time thinking how much suffering, grief, and sadness there is in this world. Wherever he went, he met never-ending cries for help, but also experienced moments of joy when he offered kindness and compassion. "When will there be comfort for your people?" he prayed.

He helped the poor, comforted the grief stricken, fed the poor, visited the lonely, talked to children, and cared for lost animals. He remembered the smiles on people's faces whenever he was exhausted.

Thirty-three years later, tired, and gray haired, he still searched for the One he wanted to find. An old wise man on the way told him to hurry to Jerusalem to meet a prophet of great might who had done many wondrous deeds for others.

As he arrived in Jerusalem, he got caught in a frenzy of shouting and wailing, announcing the crucifixion of the prophet who claimed to be the King. Artaban

RETURN TO LEIPZIG

wept bitter tears of regret, being too late again. But he had one gem left and rushed to offer it for the prophet's release. Someone in the crowd pulled on his garment. A Persian woman knelt beside him begging to save her. Her father had died, and she was to be sold into slavery the very day. Out of pity and compassion, he handed her his last gem to buy her freedom, full knowing that he had nothing left to bring to the King.

"I must be unworthy, to bring him my gift," he muttered.

While he wept, an earthquake struck. Thunder and lightning lit up the whole sky. A slate of roof hit the old man and he fell to the ground. It was then, that Artaban saw someone near him, "Lord." he uttered, "but when did I see you hungry and fed you? When did I see you thirsty?" I looked for you for thirty-three years and not one time did I see your face."

Artaban clearly heard a voice saying, "Truly I say to you, all that you ever did for your needy brothers and sisters, you did for me." Comforted and relieved, he finished his journey.[3]

So, here was the explanation for the '*Artaban*' class in action. More so, their deeds spoke louder than their spoken faith. They agreed with the appeal of the CARE organization to help where they saw a dire and human need, to speak peace where there had been war, and to feed the hungry; plain and simple, they did not worry about the timeliness, the bureaucracy, the fairness, the money, or the return rate. No revenge, no humiliation, no hesitation? How could that be?

In our time of emails, twitters and texting, handwritten letters on paper seem so outdated like old clothes you keep in the closet for sentimental reasons. Over the years, I have been given family letters to keep, but what for?

* * *

Not long ago, rummaging through my desk, I discovered another late Christmas gift under a pile of papers. I opened a folder with letters my mother wrote to her older sister, Hilde, starting in 1945, roughly the same time the Care

---

[3] Artaban's Gifts—A story. Is here loosely summarized based on a text found and translated from the Russian in Christo-Zhizn Nasha, compiled by Ye.N. Sumarokov, reprinted by the Russian Orthodox Youth Committee, New York. The full text in, *The Story of the other Wise Man*. By Henry Van Dyke. New York. Harper & Brothers Publishers, 1896.

CHAPTER TWO: 2014

packages arrived in Leipzig. The collection is titled: *Letters of your Mother from 1945 to 1951*.

Hilde's daughter, Inge, had saved them and given them on to my brother, and he thought I should keep them. I realized the voices from the past in their letters had been right in my house, including grandfather's diary, but I had not listened in the hustle and bustle of the daily rush especially during the Holidays. I created my own loneliness and disconnect. The letters had been there all the time. Now, I want to hear what mother, Hilde and Blanche thought and felt and wanted to share with us. As if at the time, when these letters were written, we children were not allowed to really know about the hardship, the grief, and the terror of the world. It was more like, do not notice, do not hear, and do not remember. That way we children would be somewhat protected, and the hardship would eventually forgotten.

While the intentions of our mother and teachers may hold true, we did discover the inner strength, the tenacity, and resilience of women and men, who far away in America, despite the contradictions of love and hate, blame and guilt, created a compassionate place in their midst to hear the needs of strangers. They began to respond with kindness. For sure, there is more to learn about mother, Hilde, and Blanche whose letters will speak one by one. It will be quite a journey.

Chapter Three

My dear readers,

Today is Memorial Day, once called Decoration Day, to remember all those men and women who died in our nation's wars. It is a sad day of remembrance and reflection, but a welcomed time off from work. The day was officially proclaimed as a holiday by General John Logan in1868, then a national commander of the Grand Army of the Republic when flowers were placed on the graves of the Union and Confederate soldiers at Arlington National Cemetery in Washington, D.C. After WWI, the holiday began to honor all who died fighting in wars. More wars would follow and the mourning among the families never stops. Some people have forgotten the meaning of this day. I think that the day is for remembering all the persons who have died in wars, and not just those who have lost their lives here in this country. Maybe it is to remind all of us to ask again and again, Why War?

Today, I remember both of our fathers who died somewhere during the last few months of WWII in Germany, fighting a bitter battle against the Russian Front and the Allied forces. Both soldiers have no graves to visit and grieve, nor decorate them with flags, plaques, or blooming plants. Over the years, The Red Cross could not report to us exactly where and how they had died. As you know, both men were ordered to go to war in 1939. They were to fight for their Fatherland and to defend the country from the Bolshevists, the Communists, the Allied Forces as well as protect their country from internal enemies. They died a senseless death with so many other men and women whose names are edged on plaques, church walls, cemetery memorial and gravestones everywhere here and in Germany. Those monuments are reminders that each life has value and, at the same time, urge us to heed war. We know the confrontations between nations and ethnic groups will never cease, but we can stem the tide by creating islands of community with acceptance, tolerance, forgiveness and understanding. Most of all not to create enemies in our minds and in our lives as a release for hate, humiliation, and revenge.

As I told you before, I found some of the answers to my questions when I looked at my own grandfather's, Paul Schnädelbach's, diary, started in 1938 in Leipzig with an inserted postscript written later in 1947. These paragraphs below speak volumes about his perception of the events leading up to WWII. I am sure he spoke for most of the people around him. Listen for the upbeat mood, his assurance of God's blessings on the German nation, and his sense of trust in the government in the late 1930s.

What will I find when I begin to unfold the fragile, yellowish papers with its envelopes intact, look at the list of items sent, each one neatly written down and meticulously accounted for? What will I find out about my mother's struggle to survive and her insistence on life and hope? Most of all, how could simple generosity and empathy overcome the hurdles of hate, prejudice, and bitterness from strangers six thousand miles away? Remember, the millions of Jews and other unwanted persons killed, more millions lost and driven out? How could all this happen in a misguided nation that claimed history, religion, science, music, and culture as the cornerstones of its civilization, only to derail in the most barbaric way?

I suspect that the Nazi leaders used their grandiose over-identification with military heroes and the geniuses of the last few centuries in music, art, and literature as a ground for a righteous superiority to eliminate whatever was unwanted and create a pure world of superiority. The obsession with the old Germanic mythology and the military hero worship became beguiling ideas to lift the German nation up after the humiliating experiences of losses in World War I. A pure and cleansed nation would become the world power, and nothing and no one would stop the strive of a united nation.

After the collapse in 1945, neither unending grief nor mountains of shame could ever suffice as a silent atonement. Maybe as survivors, we deserved the hunger and the suffering. I accepted this fact as a fitting punishment. All I had to do was to look at the faces of the people around me to validate my conclusion. Little did I understand the bigger historical and psycho-social aspects of

CHAPTER THREE

the defeat of the German nation after WWI and the deep-seated humiliation of the German soul, which opened the door for Hitler to seek revenge and power. Hate and an elated delusional self were going to lead the way toward horrific destruction all around. Sacrifices were expected and ordered. Even now, I do not claim to have all the answers to this evil and shameful time in history, but it was the world my parents and grandparents found themselves in. Some of us survived to tell the story.

Here is a sample of grandfather, Paul Schnädelbach's diary.

> Leipzig, February 24, 1938
>
> "It has been five years on January 20 since Hitler came to power. It is amazing what, with God's blessing, has been accomplished and achieved in those five years. Germany has regained its military defense sovereignty and has become a respected world power. It was possible to return the Saarland back to the Reich after France had occupied it for the last 15 years. Germany had signed friendship treaties with Italy, Japan, and Poland. These days, it was able to dissolve the rivalry with our brother nation, Austria, and most importantly, the mass of unemployment persons has been pushed back from 6 million to ½ million. Adolf Hitler, the savior, provided by God to us Germans, has accomplished great things. May the Lord God allow us to keep him for quite some time"!

Grandfather inserted the following paragraph two years after WWII was finally over in 1947. I have wondered why he inserted his thoughts between his entries from 1938 and 1940.

> Postscript. April 15, 1947
>
> "How it all turned out quite differently. Germany has been pushed into deep misery by National Socialism and has ceased to be a world power. Hitler's maliciously initiated war and caused millions of human lives lost. I, too, lost two sons in their prime time of life. Karl fallen 1942 in Russia, Herbert on 04-16-1945 in Croatia. Lord, for Jesus' sake, help our German nation up again."

RETURN TO LEIPZIG

Maybe he added this paragraph so much later although he began to see the beginning of the end but could not write down his thoughts more honestly and openly. Anything you put in writing could be confiscated by party officials or spies even after the war and could be used against you. A desperate prayer was the only response he could utter to his God. In his following entry, you hear a quite different man speaking and boasting in the glory of a successful German political strife under the Fuehrer.

Let us go back at his diary in 1940:

> Leipzig, August 27, 1940
>
> "Two and a half years have passed without me writing anything down. So much happened during that time! What usually would take a decade has happened in a rush this last year.
>
> First, we celebrated our 40th wedding anniversary on April 3, 1939. To avoid too much commotion, we celebrated this day with our children in Breslau. Over Pentecost the same year we traveled to Budapest. Gretchen enjoyed very much to have her parents with her, and we had some nice days of rest and relaxation. Adam (her husband) is doing a good job there; the Lord blesses his word.
>
> In the meantime, Austria has become a part of Great Germany in March 1938, causing great joy and enthusiasm. In the same year, the Sudetengau was incorporated into Germany, a transaction that was arranged by Mussolini and signed by Hitler, Daladier, and Chamberlain in Munich. The remaining part of Czechoslovakia joined Great Germany as a protectorate. Germany grew enormously that year, but our enemies, England and France would not rest. They wanted to encircle Germany by signing treaties with Russia, Rumania, Sweden, Norway, and others. Hitler's excellent diplomacy was able to thwart this plan with one strike. What no one had deemed possible is that Hitler accomplished to sign a treaty with Russia, which produced some marvelous political and economic benefits. That quickly took the wind out of the sails of our opponents and especially England's three-months attempt to gain a treaty aimed sharply against Germany.

CHAPTER THREE

Of our enemies, only Poland remained in place to hang their hopes on in order to defeat us. It was unnatural that, according to the peace treaty of Versailles, the border of this nation was cut straight through German territory. Thereby East Prussia was separated from the motherland and the so-called corridor was an open wound for Germany. The resident ethnic Germans had to suffer a horrible martyrdom. They were pestered and raped by the cocky Poles in every which way. Hitler attempted with well-intentioned negotiations to eliminate the condition, which in time would become intolerable. He requested only a narrow strip through the corridor, wide enough for an Autobahn and a train track to establish a connection between the Reich and East Prussia. In return, he would relinquish the other territory that was separated from Germany. But Poland's megalomania, provoked by England's promises, caused the generous offer to be ignored. The response was increased military armament. At the same time an outrageous persecution of ethnic Germans occurred in Poland. Hitler could not stand it any longer, and as a result, the military invasion and the Polish campaign began on September 1, 1939. It all happened with tremendous speed. In only 18 days the big-mouthed Pole was thoroughly beaten and destroyed! Simultaneously, the Russians pushed from the East; subsequently, the country was divided and disappeared from the map. Germany not only acquired the territory it had lost in what amounted to a robbery in 1919, but also gained great increase in Polish territory. Since our enemies' plan to weaken Germany through Poland failed, they were seeking other ways. Through Norway, Sweden, and Denmark they tried to get a hold of Germany in the North. But Hitler beat them to it. On April 5, 1940, our troops marched into Denmark and occupied the land without battle. Simultaneously, our Navy took important harbors in Norway, which of course did not happen without a fight, but supported by the Luftwaffe, our troops were able to overcome all resistance. It became clear that Norway took sides with England. That is why the campaign was fought to the end until every Englishman was driven out of there.

Now something new happened, totally unexpected. Holland and Belgium who were expected to be neutral had quietly become secret allies of France, their armament clearly aimed at Germany. The allies were planning an advance through Belgium into the Rhur area. Hitler got wind of these plans and so it was Hitler again who beat them to it with a surprise invasion of Holland on May 10, 1940. In an indescribable, triumphal march, the strongest fortresses of Holland and Belgium were quickly broken down and the battle carried on toward France. Victories were achieved like the world had never seen before; as a result, Paris was occupied, and France asked for a truce with our generals. It should also be mentioned that our ally, Italy, joined our ranks and dealt, particularly in England, and harsh blows in Malta, Gibraltar, and the Mediterranean Sea.

Of our sons, Herbert (my father) was drafted to the Wehrmacht immediately at the end of August 1939 to join a construction battalion in Poland, while Karl was called up for training in Naumburg/Sa. in April 1940. In my firm, nine young men were drafted, who encountered heavy fighting and four salesgirls were drafted to a work in factories."

June 26, 1941

"The war continues and has been broadened by Russia's entry. With Japan and Italy Hitler established the Three Power agreement for mutual assistance. If a new state would join the ones already engaged in war, the three powers would be committed to assist each other. This Three Power Agreement was eventually joined by Hungary, Rumania, Slovenia, and finally also Yugoslavia. But soon after a military clique toppled the government (Tito?) and provoked Germany with encroachments and persecutions of German Nationals and insults of the German ambassador. England and especially Russia had a hand in these affairs. Under the cover of their friendship pact with Germany, Russia secretly continued its game of Bolshevism. It also succeeded in having Yugoslavia break its alliance instantly. This led immediately to another military campaign in the Balkans.

Germany and Italy led the invasion and in 21 days, this poor country was razed from the map. Now we faced Greece, which had taken sides with England and was at war with Italy. Here, too, it was a clean sweep and in a short time the last Englishman was driven out. It produced an immense cache of weapons, ammunition and prisoners, and the Balkans were

CHAPTER THREE

> liberated by the Axis powers. The final base was Crete where the English and the Greeks established themselves. But, here too, was no stopping. This island, too, was completely purged of the enemy.
>
> And now, since Sunday, June 22, the war against Russia is raging. In this war Finland, Hungary, Rumania, and Slovenia are on our side, also a volunteer corps from Spain. The sympathies of all Europe except England are on our side, because nobody trusts the Russians, and all are afraid of the Bolshevists."

* * *

It is extremely hard not to notice his enthusiasm and his pride in the great success of the Hitler regime with its arrogant power and quick actions. It almost seems like he was describing a chess game with logical steps and alliances. I am struck by how he reports these historical events like a distant observer in full support of a justified revenge toward external and internal provocation. He reveals nothing but pride underneath a hatred belief in the service of justified defiance and self-defense. Above all, he reveals his deep fear of the Russians, a paranoid terror, which I still remember and even feel in my bones to this day.

I am writing with tears ... and sadness ... and shame for his words and opinions ... the year I was born.

Chapter Four

My dear readers,

Today is Father's Day, a special day to remember my father, grandfather to some of you readers. Herbert Schnädelbach, a minister in the German Methodist church stationed in Breslau since 1939. As you know, he never made it back from the war, even though we all waited for years to see him walking up to our house. He must have been killed about three weeks before the end of this insane and irreversible mess of a war, given this neutral name, WWII.

You can find his photo in the faded frame that stands in my office on the sideboard. The little flower wreath and the ribbon have been placed there next to the picture as long as I can remember—your Oma must have put it there as a sign of her unending love.

RETURN TO LEIPZIG

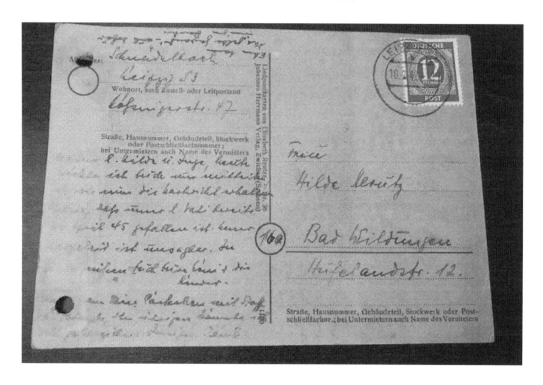

The above postcard, sent to mother's older sister, Hilde Wunderlich/Alrutz, has always been attached to our father's picture as long as I can remember. Here is the text:

> Frau Hilde Alrutz
> Bad Wildungen
> Hufelandstrasse 12
>
> Postmarked: Leipzig February 10, 1947
>
> Meine liebe (dear) Hilde und Inge,
>
> I only want to tell you today that we received the news that our dear Vati already fell in April 1945. Our heartache is without words. With grief we send greetings, Yours Leni and children.
>
> Thank you for your package with the fabric …. thank you. Just now, the yellow cloth has arrived. Many thanks…

CHAPTER FOUR

The other side of the postcard had this verse and message:

> What my God will, that'll be at all times,
> His Will is the Best!
> Nuremberg, around 1554

I have several letters that my father wrote during the later years of the war to friends and to our mother. On top of all the letters in the folder that my mother's sister Hilde kept, the following one must have been special for her, and it will be a guide on this journey of retrieval.

As you read on, you will also find a letter from my father, a brief comment about the military actions in October 1944 in Croatia, and his hope to hear from family members to be assured of our safety. Distributing propaganda flyers of asking people to trust in God in a world of demonic forces is a desperate attempt to keep sanity while living in a delusion.

RETURN TO LEIPZIG

> October 4, 1944
>
> Dear Hilde,
>
> I received your letter dated September 5th after we returned from a longer military mission. We had to move a Croatian military station that had been abandoned by them. Eighty percent of the people in the area have returned. They were to join the 'Bandits' following the betrayals of their officers. Yes, our situation here becomes more and more tense by the day. I was so happy to hear from Leni, Liddy, and Paulus that Friedrich has survived his ordeal. Now we are hoping that all will go well here for the many Volksdeutschen.[4]
>
> You might be interested in the enclosed flyer translated in Croatian that I helped to distribute to the local people. "Do not throw your trust (in God) away."
>
> Greetings to Inge and my heartfelt greetings to you,
>
> Herbert
>
> Feld post, 44056 A[5]

This brief letter, written in fine handwriting, does not tell us much of his grim story of where he was and what he was doing. All mail sent to family and friends was thoroughly scrutinized. He surely knew of the Allied invasion and the Russian Front entrenching on the Eastern region of the civil war in Yugoslavia. He knew that we were safe for the time being as well as of the whereabouts of my aunt and uncles. Holding on to his faith seemed all he could do and that he did with a spiritual tenacity of a prophet.

Going back into history of WWII, he was ordered in 1939 to participate in the invasion of Poland. He served in the Army until 1940 when he was released following a facial injury, only to be re-enlisted in 1942. As a pastor in the Methodist church, he was not exempt from serving in Hitler's Wehrmacht[6]. When conducting church services, he wore his uniform under his clerical robe. Hitler's party officials sat in the congregation every Sunday to listen for any critical

---

[4] German citizens living in that area.

[5] Military mailing address

[6] army

CHAPTER FOUR

remarks of the regime or any signs of opposition. During his time in Breslau, his military service sent him to various POW camps to translate letter of prisoners since he was fluent in English.

Just recently, did I find a letter written by my father during a happier homestay from the Wehrmacht in Breslau, January 3, 1944, to his sister Liesel and brother-in-law, Erich Zahn in Dresden. He tells of a warm and loving family Christmas time. Since I have no visual memories of my father, the letter below describes his memories—he did know me and how we celebrated Christmas with songs and gifts. As you know, Christmas is still a very special time for us.

> Herbert Schnädelbach   Breslau, January 3, 1944 (excerpts)
>
> Dear Erich, dear Liesel,
>
> We are glad that you were both able to celebrate the holidays without interruption as far as we could tell. It is a continuous hoping and begging to God that the terror of the enemies finally will be stopped, especially the beautiful Dresden—it would be unthinkable if the city would become the focus of the hate of our enemies.
>
> Let me though tell you about our Christmas holiday time. We were so grateful that we could be together despite the fifth year of this war. All the church services were attended well.
>
> Most of all, our four children celebrated the holidays and as long as the tree and the Christmas gift table were there. Gerhard will sing Christmas songs until Easter it seems, and our little girl sings along without all the words especially the special song, "Heit is der Heilge Ohmd, ihr Leit...”[7] She twittered it all day long. Christmas Eve was the highlight for us all with gifts and Christmas Eve service at 6'clock downstairs. Püt (Herbert) loved his ¾ violin the best. He will get lessons so he can make music with Klaus together on the piano.
>
> Maria's main interest provided a toy store. She did both, shopping and consuming and during the eve pretty much emptied the store and even tasted gingerbread cookies, apples and whatever was in reach. Her little stomach was by now too full followed by symptoms of the 'Christmas illness' when everything came back out. In the meantime, she feels better

---

[7] Today is the Holy Christmas Eve, you all....

> and continues to taste goodies again. The highlight of the evening was the puppet theater that Leni had put together with storytelling and an attentive audience.
>
> They are a happy bunch, and we are grateful that all four are healthy and safely go to their beds. Before that we have a short devotional time reading the Christmas story. Whenever the name 'Maria' is part of the text, our little Maria perks up and thinks it's about her and says, "Yesss1"
>
> May God protect them in this new year.
>
> We wish you all the best for the new year especially good health. As a country, we all just have one wish: Victory and Peace.
>
> With warm greetings from all of us,
> Herbert and Leni

Christmas is still so special to all of us. Songs and stories, gifts and food, candles ...

Chapter Five

Dear Readers,

I hope it will be helpful to step back in time to the final months of World War II (WWII) when my mother wrote to her sister Hilde in February and March of 1945, the time we all lost contact with our father. Her detailed descriptions of our life following our flight from Schlesien (Silesia) and the bombing of Dresden in February 1945 need no further explanation but will set the stage for the first Care packages that arrived in 1946.

The following postcard was written to my mother's sister, Hilde Alrutz, by her mother, my grandmother, Lydia Wunderlich, as she waited for our arrival from our flight from Breslau, Silesia at the end of January 1945.

POSTKARTE[8]

Frau Mathilde Wunderlich
16 Sontra/Krs. Rothenburg a.d. Fulda
N.S.... Seminar

January 30, 1945

My dear Hilde,

Your letters and card arrived together yesterday. Many thanks. Leni is not here yet; we expect her any day. We spoke to her on the phone ten days ago. She thought they were still safe, but if it becomes necessary, they will come with the trek, because they cannot leave

---

[8] postcard

> by train. That trip will take days. And all in this cold weather! I am so worried. She used to write a card every day, not any more for several days now. I hope they do not leave too soon. We will try to call again. Gerhard Freund has invited her to Eibenstock. Lydia must have left Liegnitz, which is being evacuated. Where is Hildegard? Lydia works in a refugee community center from 6 a.m. till evening. Most of the refugees have arrived from Breslau.
>
> Your brother, Friedrich, is doing fine. He does not write where he is located, but he recently visited Aunt Karoline. I am glad Paulus came to see you. Bless his heart! Friedrich's new No. is 58620. His military position is about the same.
>
> God bless you!
> Love, Mutter

Let me continue with a letter my mother's oldest sister Lydia, who lived with my grandmother, Lydia Wunderlich, in Dresden wrote to her niece, Inge Alrutz, on February 9, 1945, shortly after our arrival from our flight out of Silesia. The letter is written on small papers with a dull pencil and in the old Sűtterlin font. I can hardly read it. Aunt Liddy (Lydia) is writing the first part of the letter while waiting at a dentist's office...

> Fräulein Inge Alrutz
> 16 Fritzlar/ Hessen
> Marienburg
>
> Dresden, February 9, 1945
>
> Dear Inge,
>
> Many thanks for checking on us. I am eager to give you the latest report while I am waiting at the dentist's office and have a bit time. The most important news: Aunt Leni (my mother) and her four children with Ruth (our au-pair girl) arrived at our house on Thursday, the 1st of February, at 4 o'clock in the morning. You cannot say, they are well off, however, they arrived without major health issues. In all, for the first few days, we took 12 refugees into our flat. By now we have only Leni, the four children, and Ruth with us. Overnight, we grew to an eight-person household. For

CHAPTER FIVE

the last 14 days, I had already worked a lot in a refugee camp. We had to close all schools. By now the camps have been closed, too, and our normal life can return.

With all this turmoil, I did not realize that you poor thing did not get a thank you note and some news from us. I am deeply sorry because the straw trivet you made is so cute. Did you use oat straw for that? We also made these crafts in school but used drinking straws instead. We are here the central location for pattern supplies and the main office always provides us with new ones. I must keep up with all that.

Finally, our Christmas package has finally reached you in Sontra and, you poor thing, could not even see it.

Now to a report from our refugees! They walked by foot for 16 kilometers despite a severe snowstorm; they had to leave everything behind. Leni joined a trek with a family of five she did not even know; a single, older woman came also along. A total of seven children, the youngest is 1 ½ years old, a 3-year-old ill child in the stroller, and all in all, two baby carriages and three sleds, all this pulled through a severe snowstorm; little Maria always walked bravely.

What indescribable terror and despair they must have experienced. Despite all this, they passed through Frankfurt/Oder by God's grace. They were on the road, starting on Monday morning and arrived here on Thursday. But thank God, all are now here, all of them suffer from colds and flu, Aunt Leni with a very bleeding and infected finger, which is excruciating painful because all her fingers frostbitten—but now they are 'at home'. The 'empty room' in our flat is now full because all of them want to sleep near each other. Our sleeper bed is there for Leni, the old bed frames from the attic with old mattresses for the two big ones, two beds for the little ones. The linoleum-covered table from the pantry serves as their washstand.

Sunday, February 11, 1945

In the meantime, much has changed again. The Russians are moving suspiciously closer and closer, and we are thinking all day long what to do next to bring mother and the children to safety. We do not see a solution since we don't have a car and there is no snow for the sleds. Where should we go anyway?

Outside Dresden around Moritzburg and Bühlau people are digging trenches for protection, but what good will that do? What will happen this coming week? You are definitely better off in midst the bombing raids than we are here, knowing of the Russian atrocities to come over us. May we remain protected from evil!

I am sending get-well wishes for your skin problems. I am also troubled by painful eczemas in my hands from all the washing and disinfecting jobs I have been doing. Despite my cold, I just keep going. I am wondering if we will get new work orders tomorrow.

With warm greetings,
Your Aunt Liddy

Here is Grandmother Lydia Wunderlich describing the same events seen through her eyes.

Dresden, 9th of February 1945.

My dear Inge,

Just quickly a few words and many thanks for your letter. I am so sorry that you must suffer from that skin rash. Aunt Leni arrived here last Thursday, on February 1, early at 3:30 a.m. with her children and a few other people. They have suffered through a lot, had to walk 16 km (10

CHAPTER FIVE

miles) in a heavy snowstorm to get to the train station where they had to wait for hours, then by way of Königsfeld, Liegnitz, Frankfurt/Oder to get here in three days. We had 12 people in our apartment, now only six. All the children except the little one are sick now. Aunt Leni has a bad hand, but we are glad that they are here. They were only 29 km (18 miles) separated from the Russians. Hopefully, they don't come to us. Then where would we go? Here we have thousands of refugees from Silesia and the East. Liegnitz has also been evacuated. Lydia surely must have left. May God help us that the enemies do not come in any closer, God can provide more than we can ask or understand. We have no news at all from Neheim. Uncle Friedrich made a visit to Aunt Karoline. Maria (his wife) is still in Frankfurt. I wish you well. Even if we do not write a lot, we are thinking of you always. My vision is extremely poor, so pardon my scribble. Greet your mother. Now the Lessing Strasse has been destroyed, too. Mutti wrote me about your china, was it stored there?

With kind regards from your Oma [9]

---

[9] Dresden, 9th of February 1945
An Frl. Inge Alrutz
16 Fritzlar, Hessen, Marienburg

Meine liebe Inge,

Nur schnell ein paar Worte und vielen Dank für Deine(n) .....Es tut mir sehr leid, dass Du mit dem Ausschlag so geplagt bist. Tante Leni ist am letzten Donnerstag dem 1. Feb. früh ½ 4 Uhr mit ihren Kindern und anderen Leuten bei uns angekommen. Sie haben schwer durchgemacht, mussten zuerst im schweren Schneesturm 16 km laufen, bis sie an die Bahn kamen, dort stundenlang warten, dann über Königsfeld, Liegnitz, Frankfurt a.d. Oder in 3 Tagen hierher. Wir hatten 12 Personen in der Wohnung, jetzt noch 6. Nun sind alle Kinder bis auf die Kleine krank. Tante Leni hat wieder eine böse Hand, aber wir sind froh, dass sie da sind. Sie waren bloss noch 29 km von den Russen entfernt. Hoffentlich kommen sie nicht zu uns. Dann wohin? Hier waren viele tausende von Flüchtlingen aus Schlesien und dem Osten. Liegnitz ist auch geräumt. Lydia ist sicher fort von dort. Gott wolle helfen, dass die Feinde nicht weiter hereinbrechen, er kann über Bitten und Verstehen tun. Du kannst mit Deiner Mutter jetzt gar nicht zuhaus wohnen. Da ist sie gewiss traurig. Von Neheim haben wir gar keine Nachricht. Onkel Friedrich hat Tante Karoline besucht. Maria ist noch in Frankfurt. Und nun lass Dirs gut gehen. Wenn wir auch nicht oft schreiben, denken wir doch an Euch immerzu. Ich sehe sehr schlecht, darum das Gekritzel. Grüsse Mutti. Nun ist auch die Lessingstrasse kaputt. Mutti schrieb von Eurem Porzelan, war dieses dort untergebracht?

Sei herzlich gegrüsst von
Deiner Oma.

RETURN TO LEIPZIG

This was her last letter she, my grandmother Lydia Wunderlich, ever wrote full of concern and faithful longing. Therefore, it is placed in the footnotes below with her own words. Then silence fell like a heavy burning curtail.

Three days later, February 13/14, 1945, Dresden was severely firebombed and flattened by the RAF and the Allied Forces at a radius of 15 kilometers and beyond. We were right in the middle of it all, in grandmother's flat on Holbeinstrasse 28. Grandmother Wunderlich and her daughter, Lydia, were among the many dead in our hide out on Wintergartenstrasse 31 and the thousands throughout the city of Dresden. We four children and my mother were among the scared and spared survivors eventually to walk out of the burning city. Mother carried me for miles since I had caught on fire and could not walk.

That day, February 14, 1945, somewhere stationed in Croatia, my father wrote a gut-wrenching letter to my mother. He knew that we had arrived safely in Dresden at grandmother's home and worried all day and prayed at night when he could not sleep.

> My dear Leni and children,
>
> I am so extremely far away and must stand by while you are going through these horrific experiences …. Especially little Gerhard who is so fragile and our little Maria … I am so concerned about the effects of such traumata on their nerves and the lack of their healthy nutrition. Would it be better to leave the city in Dresden and wait it out somewhere in the countryside? But where will the Russian stop?
>
> (He wonders about his separation from us and our mother. He tries to remember the many years of love and family life and struggles to find meaning in his bitter destiny. Not to have been home with us for the past holidays remains a puzzle to him. He scrutinizes his mind.)
>
> Maybe God here, too, has thoughts of love even if we have not recognized them. (Psalm 73, 16-17). When I think back, some events come to my mind. The officers in Breslau wanted to do me evil, but God has meant it good with me.[10]

---

[10] He is referring to an incident in Breslau when he was scrutinized by the Nazi officers and refused to open his church membership registry and/or when he baptized a Jew in our home, which was against all rules of church and Nazi party.

CHAPTER FIVE

(He continues to talk about the hardship for us and many people fleeing in the deep winter with unspeakable suffering.)

Many of my comrades cried bitterly like children when various letters of their family members reached them here. Especially the very small children did not survive. I am so grateful that we did not expect another Matzel (baby).[11] How many of my comrades have no news of their loved ones and assume they did not flee in time and could not escape. I agree with you, better being bombed by the English forces than falling into the hands of the Russians soldiers especially the women and children .... I pray that you may receive kindness and friendliness and let me suffer instead of you. God is good and I pray the same every day.

During the last few days, I gained some insight into the calamities of the German people. You know how I am struggling with the thought of what might be happening to us all. It appeared to me that God does not give the victory to the most Christian nation but may have quite different ways of distinguishing nations and communities in the spirit of Jesus Christ. Both treat God differently. England was at the end in 1940, Russia in 1941/1942, both did not give up despite their dilemmas and now have changed in such a drastic way. It seems to me that God will test us to the very breaking point. If we give up now, we will be totally at the end. If we hold fast through it all, God will give us the victory. If I think about the nations that capitulated, I would rather be dead than a slave! Bolshevism has no future; it cannot be since life is more important than death. In any case, I keep feeling the task to continue to fight to my last breath in order to free our poor planet from these demonic powers. How I should participate to fight will be shown to me.

With Love, Herbert

---

[11] He is referring to a miscarriage my mother had in 1944.

RETURN TO LEIPZIG

Dresden, February 13/14th, 1945

Much has been written about the reasons for the bombing attack and I do not need to review all the historical facts and the intentions for you here. The destruction of Dresden as a center of art, culture, and history by the Allied Forces meant so much more than stem the Russians from advancing toward the river Rhein and staking out important territory for future occupation. Many other German cities had already been bombed and destroyed, but here it was February of 1945, and all that was left to conquer was Berlin, the city where Hitler and his henchmen were bunkered up.

At the time of the bombing attack, Dresden housed about 250,000 refugees, and we were in the middle of it following our flight from Silesia, seeking refuge at grandmother's house, just five kilometers from the center of town, on Holbeinstrasse 28. The obvious political strategic intent of the Allied forces was to bring the Third Reich and the German people to their knees. Besides these political and ideological goals, the Allies wanted to eradicate Germany's powerful presence in the region with its enormous expansion for power and control and destroy its culture. German human atrocities were countered by massive force, bombs, firestorms, invasion, and utmost counter destruction. Human lives did not count anymore, and victims had no faces, nor age, nor names. Numbers of casualties replaced their identity. The price had to be paid in human lives—a punishment well deserved for all the evil done.

Only lately did I recognize my own pain on a much deeper emotional level. Last year, I listened to a chamber concert in La Jolla, California, with Richard Strauss' 'Metamorphoses' on the program, composed for 23 strings. It is an elegy written during the early months of 1945 as a "memorial" following the

CHAPTER FIVE

bombing of the Munich Opera house and the destruction of Dresden's Semper Opera. Strauss' mournful lines played by strings echo some familiar melodies of J.S. Bach, 'Es ist vollbracht,'[12] and themes of Beethoven's 3rd Symphony, the 'Eroica'.

---

[12] Aria from J.S. Bach's St Matthew Passion. ... It is completed ...

During the pre-concert that evening, I learned from the lecturer introducing Richard Strauss' music that the underlying intent of both the Allied Forces and the Russian forces was most likely a united one, to bring Hitler to his knees and to end the Germanic culture once and for all by eradicating all and everything connected to Hitler and his strife for a pure Germanic cultural, economic superiority and united patriotism. This plan included the destruction of cathedrals, churches, museums, concert halls, opera houses, major historical buildings, schools and universities, music of treasured composers, art works, etc. and everybody in the way who would rescue any remains. I had never thought about this brutal cultural war more closely.

When I realized the fact that there had not only been a political but a global intent to destroy German cultural treasures, I was deeply touched and wept. We can lose belongings, family members, homes, and food, but to destroy centuries of cultural identity as a revenge for Hitler's and the Germans collusion with grandiosity, righteousness, and war, would mean no more cultural home and tradition. This destruction of treasured ideals and pillars of a cultural history are forms of sadistic and cultural warfare I had not understood before. Cultural eradication was exactly what Hitler had in mind with the Jewish people with their culture and history and now it was our turn to be destroyed and revenged.

A good example is the history of Hitler's propaganda and abuse of Richard Wagner's music (1813–1883) during the Third Reich, which was played at all major propaganda gatherings (Rienzi, Overture), and even in concentration camps, (The Overture to *Die Meistersinger von Nürnberg, 1867*). Wagner's music was used as the cornerstone of the pure German identity, associated with his Anti-Semitism, his grandiosity, themes of heroism and sacrifice for the German country. For many years, after WWII had ended Wagner's music was silenced, even in our home. The many marches and musical "Heil, Heil!" shoutings by the mighty choruses to the leaders of the German Reich served Hitler's psychotic, delusional identification with Wagner's music especially with the heroic figures deepened by his association with Winifred Wagner and her family in Bayreuth during the 1930s. In his clever and pathological justification to use music as propaganda, Hitler saw himself as a tragic hero, who like Wotan and/or Siegfried, in case of grandeur and tragedy would take the whole nation down with him, all the way to the bitter abyss of fire and ruins.

CHAPTER FIVE

Richard Wagner Festspielhaus, Germany

Within Hitler's political propaganda, little attention had been paid to the underlying human tragedies in Richard Wagner's operas such as our human strife for power at any price, greed, betrayal, tragic love, lying, conflicts, cheating, justified killings, lack of identity and death, leading eventually to destruction—not victory. Wagner's yearnings for an ending to suffering with redemption and sacrifice of and by the Feminine led him to a hope of a community of service and healing, reclaiming the Holy Grail, and a new beginning out the ashes after a cleansing fire (see the end, *Der Ring des Nibelungen*). The hovering deep seated evil around and within us yelled at the end of the Ring by Hagen's command, *"Zurück vom Ring,"* ("Get away from the Ring") will take on contemporary forms with a repeat of these epic struggles. And then, there are beginnings, out of the ashes.

Wagner claimed his own spiritual path expressed in the complexity and power of his music as well as in the drama of his last opera, *Parsifal*, 1882, with the last statement of "Erlösung dem Erlöser!"[13] that haunts us in new productions and soring voices on opera stages all over the world. What did he mean? At the end of his life, Wagner yearned for his own salvation through a young hero, such as the knight in Parsifal, fearless and a 'fool' to bring renewal to a corrupt society and to our human, internal struggle. The knight Parsifal embarks on a life journey, full of adventures, temptations, and suffering, and returns with reflection, wisdom, and compassion. The use of an adapted Eucharist ceremony has disturbed and puzzled many religious leaders and has been described as blasphemy, but the return to the balsam of the Holy Grail serves as a renewal and a revisit to the community of a faith until it may break apart again sometime in the future, and another cycle returns from deconstruction to renewal and refining.

Richard Wagner describes his own life journey in *Parsifal,* claiming his own insistence on salvation and the redemption to the needed redeemer. Maybe Wagner composed his own belief at the end of his life when he insisted on his own integrated theology, not unlike many other persons or artists who have taken the freedom to do so within their time and cultural setting. The public outrage and fascination with Parsifal remain his challenge for us listeners. In his own essay, "Kunst und Religion," which Wagner wrote two years before the first performance of Parsifal in 1882, he outlines his desire to rescue the artificial level of current religion by deepening it with true art, moving from beliefs into mythological symbols to a sensory-imagery presentation to allow for the recognition of a hidden deeper truth in the true art of music. The stage or theater becomes a place of strength, truth and a global spiritual experience of redemption, a journey of life from suffering to compassion.

Wagner's music stands like a beacon of light on the shore of the wild storms of life. His personal storms of life flooded the lands and left turmoil for generations to ponder. A turmoiled life can create a genius one through art and science, vision, and opposition, breaking boundaries and extending our horizons. May Wagner's music never let us rest in peace!

Only lately has Wagner's music been seen less Nazi-contaminated and intentionally de-Germanized in productions and is still performed and re-interpreted in contemporary presentations all over the world.

---

[13] "Redemption for the redeemer!"

CHAPTER FIVE

Bayreuth, Germany, Festspielhaus, 2017

Killing cultures and ethnic cleansing are as senseless as chopping down a tree and leaving the trunk standing. Regrowth will come for sure. These violent actions will induce suffering and with the re-emergence of new growth as insistence, the vicious cycles continue. The leaves and branches may be gone but the trunk stands as a gruesome memorial for all that walk by.

Martin Luther King, Jr. said," Darkness cannot drive out darkness: only light can do that. Hate cannot drive out hate: only love can do that."[14]

Another example besides the mournful music of Richard Strauss' *Metamorphosis* is the elegy by Albinoni (circa 1708), the Adagio in G minor for violin, strings and organ continuo as these pieces express deepest grief and touch our soul. They need no explanations. The latter elegy is attributed by Remo Giazotto to Tomaso Albinoni, an 18th century Venetian composer. Giazotto purportedly discovered a fragment of the original manuscript at the Saxon State Library in Dresden and completed its instrumentation. It is somewhat of a mystery where the manuscript really originated from and how it survived the end of WWII, but it is alive as a remnant of a wailing humanity in midst of the killing fields.

---

[14] —Martin Luther King, Jr., A Testament of Hope: The Essential Writing and Speeches, 1986, (2003) HarperOne

RETURN TO LEIPZIG

Adagio

Music serves as a fitting thread, an expression of emotions through melodies with or without words, a funeral music for so many, while some of us survived the bombing nights in Dresden on February 13/14th, 1945. Fragments of vivid memories are alive, not ever to fade with time.

CHAPTER FIVE

My mother described her elegy in words when she wrote the following letter.

> Donna by Heidenau, February 26, 1945[15]
>
> My dear Hilde,
>
> Since I will be unable to write down again everything that happened, I ask you to send this letter to Neheim. You probably know that Oma and Liddy are dead. It happened this way.
>
> Suddenly alarm, no pre-warning, we had just gone to bed. Everybody straight down to the basement. The radio wire urged to hurry. We barely made it down when the bombs started rattling.
>
> Schreiber's house burst in flames right away, as well as the small Burg Ecke at Wintergartenstrasse and Striesener Platz. Our house was rocking; we were all lying on the floor. Finally, the 'all clear' signal, upstairs, our house was not burning, our flat was a chaos, without windows and doors and what a firestorm! Protect our home, Oma and children to stay in the basement! One hour of desperate fighting. Raging firestorm outside. Peterman's house was burning and foremost Langes', which truly shocked us.—Then a new alarm. Quickly downstairs. We thought the world was coming to an end. The first raid was nothing compared to this one. The house rocked back and forth and caught fire; there wasn't a house that was not in flames.—Up and down the street. Smoke—smoke, off to the Grosse Garten! Not possible, fire everywhere, fire, fallen trees.—In a hallway, Wintergartenstrasse 31, our first protection. But that house was also burning, we all huddled together. Oma and Liddy tried one more time to go outside but quickly returned. I saw Maya and Inny outside, all very exhausted. Oma and Liddy laid down totally exhausted. Liddy said, we are all going to perish here. The fire came down the staircase, everything was in flames, the house door, everything. Oma gracefully suffered a heart attack, she looked so blue. Liddy suffocated; I saw it but could not help. Everyone suffocated or burned. I, myself, was only kept awake by the children asking, "Mutti, are you still alive?" With my last strength, early the next morning, I tried to rip the burning house door open. I succeeded. The

---

[15] This letter is also in Maria Ritter, *Return to Dresden*, 2004 p.83–84.

children out—Ruth out. Maria was fully ablaze, extinguished her with my coat—get out. Everybody else was dead.

Our house has burned down to the basement. I found mother's china and some silver spoons, everything else lost, all the suitcases and belongings burnt. A few days ago, I returned to Dresden. The house did not shake me up that much, but the hallway, full of rubble- Mother's and Liddy's grave! 120,000 official deaths, only Blasewitz is still standing, everything else a pile of rubble. Zwinger, etc. Palace—everything, everything destroyed. Incomprehensible. 3000 air crafts! We still do not know where to go, we are in emergency camps. Maria with third degree burns, getting better. The Grosse Garten in total chaos, particularly targeted, because there were so many people there, satanically! I wish we could leave Saxony, but where should we go?

Love, Leni

Dresden, Wintergartenstrasse 31
Grandmother Wunderlich and Liddy's grave under the rubble. Out of 17 people seeking shelter in this hallway during the firebombing of Dresden on February 14/15, 1945, 6 of us survived here.

I am so grateful to my mother for writing this letter to document her experiences and our survival. Without her courageous presence, her hands and

CHAPTER FIVE

her back, we would not have survived. My oldest brother Klaus at age at 10 ½ carried her burden with her.

In deep silence and gratitude……

Chapter Six

My dear readers,

I found among all these loose papers the following postcard written by my mother to her sister, Maria Lange-Wunderlich, also called Mariechen.

> The postcard is dated March 3, 1945
>
> Frau Maria Lange
> 10 Zschopau / Sa
> Krumhermersdorferstrasse
> bei Herrn Arthur Weigel
>
> My dear Mariechen,
>
> I am sure you have received our postcard and you know by now that we are safe and in one piece. Thank God! Again, it was terrifying! But the hospital is still standing. There are two unexploded bombs in the church building and the doors started on fire, but it was put out. J's home is uninhabitable, but not totally burned out. Last Wednesday, Sister Maria Austel brought us back here (Raschau), Maria is still very weak, but is starting to eat and walk. The wounds are slowly healing.
>
> How are you all? I am thinking of you often. It is not easy to be homeless if I begin to think back to Dresden! We have been taken in with much love, but we will most likely move to Zwoenitz because Mariechen Koerner has already six refugees as boarders.
>
> Greetings to you and your loved ones.
>
> God be with you!

> Have you received mail from anyone? I have no greetings from him. Yours, Leni, and children. Did you write to Friedrich?[16]

Dresden after the Fire bombing, February 1945

> Raschau, March 18, 1945
>
> My dear Hilde,
>
> I am sure all our news has you terribly upset. I am so sorry about that, but it is a horrible reality. Please do not worry so much about us. We have now arrived here in Raschau by Mariechen Freund after several detours and several stays in refugee camps. We have been welcomed here, but the house is too small for all of us so that we might not be able to stay for very long. Maybe there will be housing for us in Zwoenitz. The boys (Klaus, Herbert, and Gerhard) are doing well, and little Maria is now finally able

---

[16] Friedrich is mother's brother, Friedrich Wunderlich

to get up after much suffering and pain, pneumonia, and measles. Those horrible burn wounds are healing well. It is indescribable how this little girl went through all this with patience.

It is so kind of you to look for housing. But how should I get to you in midst of the ongoing bombings? I have no courage. I really would like to go to Bavaria.

I think because God has so wonderfully saved us despite misery, danger, and terror, I will trust Him to protect us in the future. It requires a lot of trust especially since there is little food here and the children are hungry. I must use all my inner strength to stay calm. There are no vegetables or beets only a few potatoes and bread.

I have not heard anything from Herbert (our father) for the last five weeks. His letters are for sure floating around but cannot find me due to our nomadic life.

Little Maria and I stayed a few days in the hospital in Chemnitz while the boys were already in Raschau. While there, we experienced severe bombings again, but miraculously, God protected us. Even the hospital was standing and intact. Two misfired bombs are lying in our church building so that nobody can live there anymore. Pretty much all is destroyed here. It looks like in Dresden where you can walk for hours passing by ruins and rubble. Our house back on Holbeinstrasse has burned down all the way to the basement. Your and my belongings and those of Friedrich (mother's brother) have burned down with our mother and sister, Liddy. We have truly lost everything. The same happened to Mariechen (mother's other sister). We met helpful people so that we now have again a change of clothes and socks and a few other belongings. My most precious possession, my children are alive. Thank God. Being alive is a miracle. We hardly can believe it.

My dear Hilde, we want to allow our mother to rest in peace. She would not have endured our refugee life without a home. As far as I could tell, God gave her a gentle death—a heart attack. Liddy also simply fell asleep and did not wake up again. Both did not struggle and suffer. I was there but could not help. I was so exhausted and half unconscious. Only the children's questions, "Mutti, are you still alive?" saved me. All this is terrible, but we should not get stuck there. Both mother and Liddy are

> better off than us—sometimes I envy them. Now we must stay close as sisters and brothers.
>
> Mariechen wants to try to find mother's estate, there were some possessions in her name.
>
> Warm greetings to you and Inge (her daughter).
>
> Your sister Leni and children
>
> PS. Mariechen visited me this week from Zschopau. She is so brave.
>
> Greetings from Mariechen Koerner. (The cousin we stayed with in Raschau, Erzgebirge, at the time).

* * *

I have very dark feelings about Raschau, living with mother's cousin in tight quarters and everyone worrying about food. We ate the peels of beets—my brother Gerhard looked for scraps in other people's trashcans. We were stuck there for the time being. It is hard to think about those months...

With even more tears I'll keep writing...

> December 11, 1945
>
> Dear Hilde,
>
> I just finished these lines to you when I received your letter dated November 18, 1945. What a great joy to hear from you. It seemed like you did not receive my letter from Raschau when I tried to tell you how we are doing.
>
> Langes (mother's sister Mariechen) now have a small apartment in Strehlen, Krusestr. 9. I have no idea how Kurt (Mariechen's husband) is doing. For some time, there was no hope for his recovery, but God can help in these hopeless moments....
>
> Warmest thanks for your birthday greetings. If my deepest wish would come true, with the return of my Herbert (our father), then all my suffering would be bearable. The children bring me joy, though. Klaus was

CHAPTER SIX

my best helper and on my side during the hardest hours of the last year[17], and I am so glad that he can be a child again. When he comes home from school, he rushes to the piano to play. I am so glad!

Mariele is a happy and sunny child, she looks just like her father. Her large scars are quite visible, but she is a joyful child. We are so grateful that we have a warm home.

Gerhard started school this fall. He is a sweet boy with a golden heart.

Greetings to your daughter, Inge, and all the best from all of us,
Leni and children

The Schnädelbach family is also sending greetings.

Leipzig, December 12, 1945

My dear, sweet Hilde,

Finally, your letter dated September 28 arrived and I hope that you also have received our mail. We have been separated for months now and I can see that you did not receive our last letter we sent. I am so pleased that we have a connection again and know of each other. Many thanks for your loving letter, how happy I am that you are alive and well. How fortunate that Inge has found another job, it is so difficult to find work. I know God will find a way for you, too.

As you know, starting in July, our family in Leipzig has welcomed us, and it has been so ever since. Our living quarters are tight, but with love one endures a lot. Klaus is attending the Oberschule[18], jumped one grade ahead, and makes good progress. Playing flute and piano brings him great joy; his piano playing is especially great. He can accompany my singing. Herbert is studying violin and he enjoys it. The little ones sing like larks. Through music, the horrible impressions and memories begin to vanish, and I am so relieved. By now, three-fourth of a year has passed since those terrifying events, and despite how bitter mother's and Liddy's

---

[17] Mother is referring to brother Klaus' calmness and courage to carry mother's purse across his shoulders during and after the bombing night in Dresden in February 1945 while she carried me out of the inferno.

[18] Like Junior High/Highschool

death weighs on me, I am relieved that both did not have to live through the struggles that followed. For sure, hunger and homelessness are the worst. May they rest!

Only our Vati is not home yet, and we have not heard a single word from him. There are rumors, but nobody knows any actual details. We keep hoping, even if the waiting is so hard.

Did Mariechen write you that her husband, Kurt, is deadly ill with suspicion of tuberculosis, and he has been laid off from his job? That is so difficult. Traudel is the only money earner in the family.

I am doing quite well. The church takes care of me, and by singing, I am earning some money. I am now a registered 'concert singer'. My old voice teacher helped dig out my voice I had previously lost with the carbon monoxide poisoning in Dresden. Now I am traveling with her as Alto soloist. Of course, I get homesick. You know what that is like, but since we feel so welcome here, all is easier to bear.

Our house in Breslau is stilled bombed out. Several families live in our flat. It is all so indescribable!

The Christmas season is now ahead of us. The children are so excited about it and us grownups want to "welcome the eternal light." It is the only thing that gives us a sense of steadiness and joy.

Dear Hilde, we also wish you a blessed Christmas season and celebrate with you and your daughter, Inge. Please give her my warmest greetings. God bless you both!

With much love and with the words of our own father's favorite Psalm, 23.

Yours, Leni and children

CHAPTER SIX

Grandfather's flat is on the 2nd floor, above the middle entrance, Leipzig, Lössniger Strasse 47. (2007)

Christmas time every year is still so special in our home. Below see the Schwibbogen …. with the Dresden scene, the Frauenkirche and the building nearby … rebuilt and remembered in my heart.

Schwibbogen, Dresden, Germany

RETURN TO LEIPZIG

January 6, 1946

Leipzig S3,
Lössniger. 47 1r

My dear Hilde,

Today, on your birthday, I am thinking of you with much love and best wishes. I hope you have received some of my letters to tell you that I am thinking of you every day and hope that the coming year will be much better for you. God may lead and guide you and give you strength for making a new home and finding work. God bless you, dear Hilde!

I was so happy to receive your letter with the pretty little book. Warmest thanks for your kindness, how special is every sign of connection we have with each other. I am not quite clear where you are living and working. Maybe in Kassel with Frau Oberin? Maybe one of your letters did not make it and I miss some information. I would like to join you there if I could start all over again at the Fröbel Seminary. Our sister, Liddy, would have joined us both, she would be so pleased that her work will continue with all the things she loved so dearly.[19]

Despite the hardship of the past year, we celebrated a peaceful Christmas, although without our Vati or any mail from him. The thought that no one can separate him from God's love is the only comfort I can find.

All four children were so happy. I am so grateful that we have a home here where we are safe and loved. My thoughts went to all the dear ones we have lost this past year. I could not stop thinking about them. They were the ones who celebrated the Holidays with us by sending warm greetings and much kindness every year.

I am so thankful that our little Marialein can be with us this Christmas. Oh, it would have been terrible if this sweet and sonny little girl would not have survived ... unthinkable! This child is a miracle to me if you look at her terrible scars on her legs. Klaus is attending upper grades in school and is very musical, he likes to play piano, even accompanies me when

---

[19] Mother is talking about the Pedagogical Seminary, Froebel Seminary, where all her sisters worked.

CHAPTER SIX

I sing. He sat at the organ last week for the first time, so excited to be there and he plays flute. Herbert started to play violin and piano. All four children bring me much happiness and throughout all these terrible experiences of fleeing and fire, none of them ever cried or complained. I have started to sing again, mainly in churches on Sundays with my former voice teacher as alto. This brings me much joy.

I would so much like to visit you. I heard from our sister, Mariechen, that her husband, Kurt, has been released from the hospital.

Dear Hilde, my heartfelt thanks for all your love you sent to all of us. I can feel it every day. Please do not worry too much about us. Blessings to you and Inge,

With warm greetings and love, Leni and children

Leipzig, March 27, 1946

My dear Hilde,

Your letter dated March 16 arrived today and a few days ago, the letter you wrote on March 1st. I had no idea you have had such hardship during the last months. I did not know you were in the hospital and all alone in your suffering. I am so sorry you were in pain for seven weeks as if there is not enough trouble all around us. Inge's letter did not arrive at all. You had to bear all this alone. I am so sorry. I hope that you are doing better and that you are happier.

Thank you so much for the cute apron you sent for Maria. She is so excited about it.

I just received a letter from our sister, Mariechen, with the devastating news that her daughter, Ingrid,[20] is in a hospital, near death, from a case of tuberculosis and meningitis. There is no hope and treatment left. What a devastating experience for all of them. There is so little we can do to help them, one tragedy after the next. May God be with them!

We also are not spared from serious worries. My Gerhard has tuberculosis, quite severely. Only last week did we receive this

---

[20] Ingrid or 'Inny' died in March 1946 at age 71/2.

devastating news. For me, another bitter pill to swallow in addition to all the other heart aches I have already. The other children are healthy. Since there is no treatment available for tuberculosis, very little hope is left. The deaconesses at Bethany Hospital are supportive and suggested a special Sanatorium where they work and where he may receive better food. This thought is giving me some hope. All this hardship without my Herbert!

Thank you for putting out a search notice for Herbert. During the last weeks, mail from POW in Yugoslavia actually did arrive with a return postcard. Maybe somehow a letter will reach us. I am trying to be hopeful, and God is giving me strength to carry these heavy burdens every day. Thank God!

Gerhard is suffering from malnutrition after all this terrible famine and hunger in Raschau which left him with a weak immune system. He is so skinny, but so bright and with so much musical talent.

Dear Hilde, nothing but worries and still there are God's gracious hands at work among us, he will give and do the right thing.

Christmas Pyramide

I am excited with you that you will restart pedagogical work in Bad Wildungen. I would like to join you right now. I have tried to apply at my previous employer, the City of Leipzig, but have not heard back. Could you please send me another copy of my transcripts and my work in Kollogrűn? All my papers have been destroyed by the fires. Thank

CHAPTER SIX

> God, there were copies in the local archives, but none of my work documentation between 1927–1929 at Fröbel Seminary.
>
> For today all my love to you and Inge,
>
> Yours, Leni and children

Mariechen's daughter, Ingrid, or "Inny", did die in May of 1946 from tuberculosis. I think she was seven years old. Mother talked about it, but it seemed that so many people had disappeared or had 'fallen' in the war with no tears left to weep over them. I do not remember if she went to Inny's funeral in Dresden. Traveling from one region to another was still strictly controlled by the local authorities. Her death notices just arrived with the traditional card with the black frame, and I did not want to think much about it. Death was all around us, but mother's prayers would have to suffice. We prayed for our father to come home soon from the war.

> Leipzig, May 13, 1946
>
> My dear Hilde,
>
> Finally, I am finding time to send you a letter. Time flies by so fast, never enough time for all the things I have planned. Foremost, my warmest thank you for both packages that have arrived—you have shared from your small portions! I feel so guilty how you send me from your food portions when I know that you have been ill and would need your share. Please, dear Hilde, do not sacrifice your food rationing, we will somehow manage here.
>
> I was so pleased to hear that you traveled to Frankfurt to visit brother Friedrich. They are lazy writing to us; any news just comes from other people. That is not very nice given our hard times. In times like that, a visit is so helpful and lifts our worries.
>
> Until yesterday, we had our brother Paulus here in Leipzig for 3 1/2 days for the Trade Show. He arrived with a special train. It was so wonderful to have him here. We spend all day, Friday. Together, talking and walking, on Saturday, he traveled to Dresden to see all the devastation. Of course, he visited with our sister, stopped at Holbeinstrasse, etc.

When he returned, he said, everything looks more devastating than he had ever imagined.

About five weeks ago, I took Herbert and Gerhard to a sanatorium in the Dresden area to treat tuberculosis. Herbert is more in danger of a full onset, while Gerhard is ill. The physicians were not too hopeful. Annelise Grütters, a pulmonary specialist, did the x-rays and assured me that due to the early diagnosis, treatment may be more effective. I am waiting for good news and hope for his recovery. It looks like I may be able to pick up Herbert in the near future, while Gerhard may have to stay longer to complete his recovery. Fortunately, I am receiving "Lebertran" for the children[21] and are assured that the nutrition in the children's sanatorium is quite sufficient. God is still helping although my courage is wearing thin.

I need to bring you up to date with Langes (their sister Mariechen and family). All is so incredibly sad; you cannot image the grief and sorrow in their home. I did not attend Ingrid's funeral, but stopped by a week later when I traveled with the boys to their sanatorium. Despite of all this loss, they are brave and calm. The sweet child is relieved from her pain and is at peace.

I am sure you are aware that Traudel, (Inny's's sister) wants to become a teacher. Both girls are so talented and have a wonderful attitude toward life. God is at work despite hardship and sorrow.

We want to finally make funeral arrangements for our mother and Liddy so they can be buried in a sacred place. We all must carry the expenses. Mariechen wants to make all the arrangements soon. A photo will be taken of the pile of rubble and ashes that cover their bodies. We plan to add their names on our father's tombstone, and I am sure all this is fine with you. We may receive some money from the insurance, but we will have to see because all the moneys are still frozen in the accounts.

I am so pleased to hear that you have made progress with reopening Fröbel Seminary. Congratulations! It is a pity you are not rehiring Frl. Schroeder. She is a capable and a hard worker, talented and organized. In the meantime, she accepted another job in an orphanage of the J. M.

---

[21] "Lebertran" is cod liver oil. It tasted yucky, but we had to take it anyway.

CHAPTER SIX

but would be able to change employment. I am sure you are aware that she was a Pg. (Parteigenosse)[22], only a nominally one. She is currently undergoing a rehabilitation process. We have been good friends.

I hope you are pleased you have a home in Bad Wildungen and return to some stability and calmness given these past years of hardship and illness.

We need to keep hoping and trust in God and feel his strength and protection every day. He can bring our Vati back. For today, May God be with you! Greetings to all that know me, especially your daughter, Inge!

In love, Leni

---

[22] "Parteigenosse" refers to a member of the Nazi Party.

With Lisa at the gravesite in Dresden, Johannisfriedhof 1985.

Leipzig, July 8, 1946

My dear Hilde,

I just received your letter with gratitude and joy. I wanted to write you sooner but could not find the time. I believe our thoughts have crossed and we have been thinking of each other. I believe you when you wrote how little time you have with the reopening of the Seminary which requires so much work and you know I am familiar with the intensity of the faculty members and their work ideas. I hope all will be completed soon. I am so pleased to hear that your daughter, Inge, is with you. I understand that it is hard for her, I remember when I was one of the "young ones." We were expected to work like the older teachers, but we were not allowed to speak up. I was also quite unhappy, but looking at it later, it was not very nice. Maybe Inge will adjust if she is accepting of the situation. Otherwise, it will be hard for her. I am so relieved that you two can be together.

I wished I had someone close to me. When Paulus was here, I could speak more openly with him. Not receiving letters from our mother is so painful. Dresden was my "Heimat" (home) and now it is so horribly destroyed and the thought of it brings me to tears.

I long for my own home although we are so welcome here and cared for. I also have friends and acquaintances here in town that care. Hanna Kupsch celebrated their silver wedding anniversary. I met their daughters, Clärchen and Hedi; they send greetings and asked about you.

Unfortunately, I heard from Gerhard that he is still losing weight, otherwise he is in good spirits. Herbert would be able to come home, he is much improved, but the staff worries about Gerhard becoming more homesick if his brother would be gone. So, they have kept him for the time being. I will travel there on his birthday (August 6th). We are looking forward to the trip. Klaus is a happy and calm boy; he likes tinkering and playing music. He is good at both activities. He can accompany me with Bach and Handel songs, so that we can make music together. No problem with his studies in school. An abscess on his foot has kept him home this week. Maria spends all day outside playing and comes home for meals on time.

Last week I gave some concerts around Streudal with performances in churches and good attendance. I even had some income, so it was worth it. My effort to work for the city did not pay off because I do not belong to the S.E.D. (Political, Socialistic Party). I must be honest; I am so tired and without energy to work with children. I really do not want to work

> there and therefore I am not so disappointed. I turned down a job for imprisoned women and girls.
>
> We can manage with our food supply only with God's help. Otherwise, it would not work at all. It is so sad that the children have no father, but we hope when Herbert returns that we will be able to have a home again. We still have not heard from him and hope so much for his return.
>
> Last June, I attended the Methodist Church Conference in Zwickau and met up with Dörffelts, Frau Wurzbaschen? and others. They asked about you and are sending greetings. Please do not let yourself be taken over by the Seminary work, stay human.
>
> I want to end this letter so it can be mailed soon.
>
> Warm greetings to both of you.
>
> Yours, Leni, Klaus, and Maria
>
> Thank you also for the photos of mother and sister Liddy. I actually have them—they were in my handbag Klaus carried bravely over his shoulders. Those, and a family picture of all of us, and a picture of Herbert are the only photos we saved.
>
> Many thanks for all your kindness. Our brother Friedrich has not written me at all. It saddens me, I am not sure what I should make of it...

Now, my dear readers take a breath and return to grandfather's diary.

Writing and reading with a heavy heart and document their experiences. Thank you coming along so far....

Chapter Seven

Grandfather, Paul Schnädelbach wrote these lines in his diary:

> Leipzig, September 2, 1946
>
> "Still no sign of life from Herbert. Leni and the children are still living with me. We have not heard anything from him since March 1945. Is he still alive or is he unable to write anything as a POW? God knows it all, but it is hard for his family to live with the unknown. Leni is receiving much support and help from friends as she lives through this very trying time. May the Lord continue to be her helper."

* * *

I found a postcard mother wrote on September 12, 1946, written with a pencil and on much faded paper. With help of a flashlight and a magnifying glass, I can decipher most of her message to her sister, Hilde.

> My dear Hilde,
>
> Many greetings to you and Inge from my successful concert tour. This time, I took Maria with me who keeps herself busy all day. Every day she drank milk! My two boys are in Dresden. We will return on Saturday. I enjoyed the family letter very much. Please greet all our friends. Unfortunately, we have not received any mail from Herbert.

RETURN TO LEIPZIG

> Many POWs are returning home, but not from this area. We are waiting painfully.
>
> Aunt Karoline sent me a package. Gudrun and Traudel spent a few days with me; it was so good to have them. Gerhard is beginning to feel better. Thank God!
>
> Yours, Leni and Maria

I do remember this concert trip quite well. Mother said later she was taking me along because I had been so homesick previous times, she had left the house before and traveled.

> Leipzig, October 21, 1946
>
> Dear Hilde,
>
> Thank you so much for all your mail and the packages. Everything arrived intact and I can use all of it. It sounds like you had a well-deserved vacation. Hopefully, you will have less illnesses in the future—it was terrible... I am so pleased you are better.
>
> I finally brought Gerhard home last week. He is doing so much better and has gained eight pounds. He is lively and in good spirits. It was time to come home, he still needs much care. He was much liked by all the people at the place there.
>
> Klaus is leaving tomorrow to Inge Priemer's farm for a vacation! Great!
>
> Overall, we are doing fine. I have quite some episodes of fatigue and exhaustion, maybe it is part of the course.
>
> I have tried to bring Herbert to the Thomas School[23]. He is scheduled for an entrance exam in November with Prof. Kanina (?). He has a small chance of being accepted. Greetings to you both and with this note that we are still alive.

---

[23] Mother is talking about enrolling Herbert into the famous St. Thomas Church school and boys choir going back to Johann Sebastian Bach's time (1685—1750).

CHAPTER SEVEN

> Warmly, Leni and children.
>
> Gerhard says thank you for your greetings to his birthday. I had sent them to him.

* * *

It is hard to comprehend now that my brother Gerhard at age seven lived in a Methodist Hospital Home staffed by deaconesses in Schwepnitz, North of Dresden, between March and October of 1946. Through mother's church connections, he and my older brother, Herbert, were sent to Schwepnitz to treat his symptoms of tuberculosis with the help of a better climate outside the coal-polluted city air of Leipzig and to receive a steadier nutrition. Gerhard only recently told me on the phone about his time there.

"I stayed in Schwepnitz with the Sisters (deaconesses)," he started, "but my presence had to be secretive. I was not to be there because I had no official local rationing card for food and if the Medical Director would have found out, they would have been in trouble, and I would have had to leave. When the doctor made his daily rounds, I had to hide in the cleaning closet with the brooms and pails. I came out when he had left."

He paused a while. "Since I had no food allowances, the Sisters shared their food with me every day. There were no other children there for me to play with and I had no toys. I remember a big pine tree outside I could see through the window. The tip of the tree looked like a little figure I called "Matzel." It had two legs and two arms and was black and blue. He became my playmate and I told stories about him to the Sisters. They found this entertaining, even crocheted a small doll for me, but it did not really look at all anything like my "Matzel" in the tree. Oh, I would also sing for them, and they let me stay up later in the evening. They also gave me some help with my writing and reading—there was no school…

The worst time came when brother Herbert left after his three months treatment time was over. Mother came to pick him up and we all went to the train station. I did my usual happy face and joyful skipping dance around them, but when the train left and I had to stay behind, I cried and cried and cried…"

A longer pause followed. I did not want to probe much further, not to trigger too much pain. He went on,

"There was a janitor and property manager on the grounds. One day I went there to his cottage and asked if I could play with his toys. He shushed me away, "You go play with your own toys! But I had none."

His voice began to quiver, and I wanted to respond and not leave him alone with his memories.

So, I said, "I remember well how I missed you, but also you were not there to argue with. I guess we squabbled at times, and I would not listen to your plans and directions. I sure was glad when you came back alive."

I remembered suddenly about his imaginary playmate. My older brothers teased him after he was back in Leipzig with us, and eventually Matzel disappeared.

He chuckled, "Then two years later (in 1948), I had to go to Pulsnitz for follow-up treatment at a sanatorium of the church. I stayed there for two months—that was not that bad. I shared a room with one of the Sisters…"

Loneliness and abandonment while being ill left him forever with deep emotional scars, his "worst experience" in a row of accumulated traumata. From then on and even now, his joyful and playful demeanor covers up a very painful and wounded soul. I am grateful to give him a voice. May he now rest in peace after much suffering and his death on January 23, 2015.

* * *

Now, back to our time during and after WWII. We waited eagerly each year for the Christmas Season to bring love, light and promises to us in the darkness. Yes, sometimes we had no electricity in the evenings due to rationing each day, but the candles brought the flickers of hope and comfort. We could see each other's faces.

> Leipzig, December 7, 1946
>
> My dear Hilde and Inge,
> This card and the picture are bringing you our warmest Christmas greetings. We are wishing you a blessed Holiday in this dark and gloomy time with the light that comes with the babe in the manger. Oh, if it would be light around us and among all of us! We are hoping for such a gift. We will be thinking of you at the Christmas tree and will remember all those

> who have died, although they will be in better hands, their absence still pains me a lot.
>
> The enclosed picture did not come out too well. Maria was moving too much and had to be retouched. At least, you have a picture of us currently. I also hope you received our package. I would have liked to send you something else, but cannot ...
>
> Please extend warm greetings to all your colleagues. And have a great Christmas. I heard that L. had to go to R., It made me feel so sad.
>
> For today warmest Holiday greetings,
>
> Yours, Leni and children

Leipzig, 1946, Maria, Mother, Gerhard, Klaus, and Herbert.

Please look at our faces. My mother's expression of grief and hardship, sadness, and her effort to remain a family and hold on to us without the presence of our father. Look at Gerhard's fancy west, Klaus knitted it with some wool that was sent to us. What a great job to keep him warm. There are smiles on faces. I was told that I wiggled and had a hard time sitting still and therefore my eyes needed to be photo shopped...

The following Christmas postcard pictures a vase with greenery, flowering Christmas roses, a candle, more greens, wrapped present and an apple in the foreground. The print is in black and white with no color, just as drab as the time of the year and the feeling among so many people at the time. When I see the postcard, I see the symbols of Christmas, the greens of Christmas, the red apple, a pinecone, and the burning flame of one candle. We held on to these symbols and remembered in our hearts the true meaning of the Season by singing hymns, reading the stories, and being assured of a Holy Night to come in peace.

I remember that my mother read to us a special story on Christmas Eve after all the packages had been opened, the tree shimmered with flickering lights,

CHAPTER SEVEN

and silvery lametta was moving gently from the Christmas tree branches. Yes, it was magical and so is the story written by Selma Lagerlöf, *The Holy Night*.[24] Here is a shortened version.

A long time ago, a man went out on a dark night to borrow coal to kindle a fire for his wife who had just given birth to a child. He walked and walked until he saw a gleam of fire far away. An old, grumpy shepherd was watching his sheep by night. The man approached and the shepherd's dogs did not bite him, their jaws did not clinch, the sheep did not mind when the man walked on their backs toward the fire, The shepherd's spear did not hit him. When he collected the burning coal, it did not burn him. The old shepherd heard of the man's demise and said,

"What kind of night is this, when dogs do not bite, sheep aren't waking, the staff does not kill, nor hot coal burns?" He called the stranger back and asked, "What kind of night is this? Why does everything show you compassion?'"

You know by now the shepherd followed the man and found the mother and the newborn child in a mountain cave. Worried that the child may freeze, he opened his bag and took out a white sheep skin to keep the child warm. At that moment, his eyes were opened, and he saw angels fluttering all around, singing everywhere, inside the cave and outside in the mountains. They sang joyfully of the Saviors birth, "We need eyes like the shepherd's so that we can see God's glory."

Mother would end the reading and we sat in silence with thoughts of the joyful magic of this Christmas night, full of kindness and compassion while the burned down tree candles painted shadows of branches and stars on the walls. We also saw the magic of Christmas…

* * *

> Leipzig, January 2, 1947
>
> My dear sister, Hilde,
>
> My letter is not getting to you in time for your birthday, I know. I just ran out of time and energy to write you any earlier. And that despite the many wonderful packages we received so that I became almost dizzy with

---

[24] Selma Lagerlöf, Christ Legends, 1904, in English by T. Werner Laurie, London, 1937, pp.7–10

so much kindness and care. I could not stop looking at everything. My warmest thank you for everything! I was speechless.

According to your instructions, it looks like all the packages have arrived on time and brought such happiness to all of us. I was deeply moved by your kindness and felt your love. I was just like when our mother cared for us. The sweets, especially the cocoa and chocolate brought big smiles to the children's faces. They had so much wished for such goodies. The undershirt for Maria was just what she needed. She immediately put it on. The other package with the blue fabric and the sweets arrived here on New Year's Eve. Everything looked so special. Also, my dear Hilde and Inge, my warmest thanks for the ? and the picture, the sewing material and the nightgown and the other items, and most of all, for the coffee, etc. Oh, you are doing so much good for me, you have no idea how much your kindness touches me. Most of all, for your love and care you have expressed to us all.

Foremost, I am sending my heartfelt wishes for your birthday, my dear Hilde. May God guide you in the New Year as he has done so often before! We are seeing God's guidance in all the signs of kindness that come our way, and we believe that God wants us to live. Otherwise, our hope for the future would be dismal—and we would feel such despair.

Hilde, if we do not get any help here in the Eastern section of Germany, we will all perish soon. Everything is so hopeless. The only thing that sustains us is the "help" from above, and we surely have not been abandoned.

I send you my best wishes for every day together with your daughter, Inge. May you experience joy and happiness!

Despite all the darkness in our lives, we had a very nice Christmas. The children were so happy and grateful. We sang and played together, and we had many presents among us. Even our food situation was not that bad as expected. We had a special food rationing of one extra pound of flour and one-half pound of sugar. Thank God, we had a few other food items!

I gave myself from Herbert a very nice, enlarged picture of him as a Christmas present. Unfortunately, there is no trace of him to be found anywhere. Therefore, I am faced with a series of problems. The city wants to hire me back, offered me a job on four different occasions even in my old childcare facility. Shall I accept it or not? If I would know for sure that Herbert will not come back, I would accept it. In order to offer the children a good education, I must earn some money. With my singing, I have earned about $1000 marks, which I really need because Gerhard's treatment in the sanatorium was very expensive, although the church helped me with the expenses. He is now healthy although he seems fragile. Even there, God was wonderful! All four are lively and there is a lot of life in this small flat. All will resolve with God's help!

We are receiving lots of mail from family, even Friedrich wrote us. My warmest greetings to you and your daughter, Inge, and again, best wishes on your birthday!

Gratefully, Your sister Leni, and children.

Please extent my greetings to your colleagues.

Leipzig, February 5, 1947

My dear Hilde,

You are such a sweet sister thinking of me with such love and endurance. During the last few days, several packages arrived. Four packages arrived with goodies and one with a beautiful velvet jacket in it. What great joy! Everything arrived intact. We just had run out of everything by now. I was thinking how God will help us through this tough time and then came help. Sometimes it is so hard, but it also difficult for me to see you sacrifice your own food items for us. We gladly opened your packages and have already opened the goody bags, of course, not all of them. Yesterday I received something[25] and I am relieved. God is helping us in wonderful ways. Even the cigarettes are so welcome and today they are invaluable. Maybe I will be able to buy some furniture with them. It looks like we will be staying here in Leipzig as a time of transition until Herbert comes home and we will be assigned to a new congregation.

---

[25] She does not spell out what it is here—usually some money from the Western section of Germany, which she could use on the black market. Mail was still censured, and she was careful to write any information to lead the police her way.

RETURN TO LEIPZIG

Her writing with an ink pen becomes unreadable, as the pages may have gotten wet and the ink runny, and I can only make out a few sentences. She indicates that Mr. Georgi, my father's church superintendent received a message from a soldier who may have known something about our father's where about and possible death. Maybe the letter represented her tears.

> I am waiting desperately for mail every day and can only say: God help us all! It would be devastating. I will call you as soon as I have more news. Despite of all I know, God does not make any mistakes. I still have hope that it will not be so.
>
> I received a package from the protestant Young Men's Organization, and I am grateful. I will send you packing material in the coming days.
>
> Enough for today. Warm greetings to you and Inge, and please pray for us.
>
> Yours, Leni and children
>
> PS. This February 13/14th marks already two years since we lost our dear ones. We think of them in love and miss them terribly, but they are in a better place. We want to shave off father's tombstone and add their names to it. Let me know what your thoughts are.
>
> Your, Leni

* * *

Chapter Eight

My dear Readers,

Let's get back to grandfather's diary and hear about his voice of sadness and grief.

> Leipzig, April 11, 1947
>
> "Only recently did we receive the painful news that our Herbert had to lay down his life on April 16, 1945. A comrade who was commander with him brought the news to my daughter-in-law. He apparently was immediately killed, "shot in the heart," during the fighting with the partisans. The news was horrible for us all especially for Leni. But God does not give us more to bear than we are able to, and he will for sure keep his promise to take care of the widows and orphans in need.
>
> Leni and children are still living with me. I arranged for her to have the larger living room and bedroom in my flat so that there is more space for all five of them. The smaller rooms are sufficient for me. The Methodist Church will provide her with an appropriate pension, so that she worries no longer about her daily existence. She is receiving support from many people. I was able to hand her a savings account of 4.600.00 Marks, I had saved in Herbert's name. She was able to immediately withdraw 400.00 Marks. I hope the rest will be available to her as needed."

In February 1947, in Leipzig, did we learn from a comrade that our father had died two years ago, on April 16, 1945, around Ossiek, Croatia, when his group was ambushed by Tito's guerrilla troops two to three weeks before Germany capitulated. The German Red Cross had no information on body count or burials. There is no cemetery, no grave to bring flowers to.

I am enclosing one of the saddest letters I found in my collection written by Mr. Karl Kirchner, a comrade of your grandfather Herbert Schnädelbach on January 27, 1947, after his return from a prisoner-of-war camp in Yugoslavia.

Rather than trying to describe his last days, the letter by Herr Kirchner sent to church officials will speak with painful details and empathic resignation.

Karl Kirchner   January 27, 1947
Merseburg
Klobikauerstr 62

Dear Mr. Superintendent,

Thank you very much for your letter dated January 17th. I actually knew that relatives of Mr. Schnädelbach were living in Leipzig, but I did not have their address. I had already considered putting an ad in a Leipzig paper in case my letter would not reach them. That is now no longer necessary.

You must have realized from my previous letter that fortunately, however superficially, I was familiar with Mr. Schnädelbach circumstances. I knew he was the pastor of the Friedenskirche in Breslau and that his wife and their four children had fled from Silesia via Dresden to the Erzgebirge. He still had been notified of this shortly before our retreat.

I was working as a secretary with Mr. Schnädelbach in the Security Battalion office 808—Feld post Nr. 44056A—and thanks to our daily companionship, I knew about his personal circumstances. This is also the reason why I had and have a special interest that his wife would find out for certain what happened in the end.

Since I was a POW in Yugoslavia until a month ago and since as a former civil servant, I have had significant professional difficulties, I could not write any sooner. Also, as a POW, I could not furnish any news; it was not until last September that I had any responses from my relatives. It was therefore impossible to trace anything.

Shortly before the collapse, our unit was stationed in Daly near Essegg and from there we started our retreat on April 12, 1945. Delayed

CHAPTER EIGHT

communication caused our way to be blocked by the Partisan[26] division, and we were cut off from our own division. With continued fighting and heavy losses we tried to gain a path towards home. On April 15, a number of those still alive were caught as prisoners. In the morning of April 16, those remaining (including me and Mr. Schnädelbach) found us near an unfamiliar village Nasice in Croatia. The village had to be taken to make any progress. During the attack, which was launched from a narrow pass in the road, I was climbing up a slope with Mr. Schnädelbach. However, I could not climb up easily because the day before and empty horse cart had run over both of my legs, and they were swollen; I climbed down again to climb up on the other side which was not quite that steep. From this moment on I have not seen Mr. Schnädelbach again. I was taken prisoner a few hours later and inquired about Mr. Schnädelbach whereabouts in the prisoner camp. There, the former colonel) merchant Robert Guenther from Niederpritschen, Fraustadt County/Silesia told me that Mr. Schnädelbach was killed in the early hours of April 16, 1945. He had observed how Mr. Schnädelbach was caught in the firefight with partisans and that after repeated exchanges seemed to have been fatally wounded, and, after moving for a short period, remained there motionless. In his opinion he was dead instantly. The possibility that he might have only been wounded and later could have been taken prisoner is highly impossible in my opinion, since the partisans shot all our disabled comrades. According to the witness's account, one cannot assume that Mr. Schnädelbach was still alive after being wounded; unfortunately, his death has to be accepted. The witness, Guenther, was also taken prisoner. I do not know his where about; I do not know if he is still a prisoner and where he might have moved later as a Silesian.

Unfortunately, I must give Mrs. Schnädelbach this very sad news, and I ask you to express my deepest sympathy to her. I feel obligated to bring her a truthful report, not to conceal the truth to relieve her painful uncertainty.

---

[26] He is referring to Josip Broz Tito (1892–1980) who was Secretary- General, later President of the League of communists of Yugoslavia (1939–80) and went on to lead the World War II Yugoslav guerrilla movement, the Yugoslav Partisans (1941–45). He was a popular public figure both in Yugoslavia and abroad, viewed as a unifying symbol for the nations of the Yugoslav federation.

> Please confirm the receipt of my letter, so I can be assured that you received it given the current postal difficulties.
>
> With best regards,
> Sincerely yours, Karl Kirchner

* * *

> Leipzig, February 23, 1947
>
> My dear Hilde,
>
> I am sure you are waiting to hear from me after you must have received my prosaic postcard with the shocking news of Herbert's death. Unfortunately, it is the truth, although I do not want to accept it in addition to all the other hardships. I believe that I will never overcome this loss although I know it all and believe it. But it is incomprehensible since we did not really expect this to happen. I have not been able to speak personally to the returned comrade yet, but I hope to do so to get some answers to my many questions. For sure, Herbert fell in the battle with the partisans and mostly likely, was instantly killed. Whoever was wounded was shot and killed so that there is no possibility of a mistake as to his whereabouts. It is

CHAPTER EIGHT

> unbelievable that Herbert is the only active pastor of the Middle-German conference who did not return home. I find myself in a totally new situation and everything that was 'temporary' will now be our 'home.' I have no idea how this all will be, but I do not think I have the energy to go back to my work. Mariechen came to see me for a few days and that was helpful.
>
> Your package has arrived and contained exactly what we needed to keep us afloat and not sink. Thank you for the coffee and the cigarettes and everything else, the flour. Everything arrived here intact. You are caring for us so lovingly; hopefully, you are not depriving yourself too much.
>
> With all my love to you both,
>
> Gratefully, Leni and children

* * *

Leipzig, June 3, 1947

Grandfather writes in his diary:

"Today was my last day of work at the firm Krock & Pohling after 47 years of service. I could not work much longer after I turned 75. I worked the last two years part time with part salary. By boss, Herr Kölblin, wants to pay me a monthly pension of 100.00 Mark to boost my monthly income to 190.00 Mark.

My termination came quite suddenly. How wonderful did the Lord guide me as he had promised: I will bear and carry you to your old age and to your gray hairs (Isaiah 44:4). The Lord may give me a quiet

Herbert Schnädelbach (1925)

Herbert Schnädelbach, 1925

> reflective way and a gentle, quiet spirit, so that these days will turn into an inner benefit and a blessing for me."

How wise are his words in this time of ending and grief! May I also hold on to his trust in God's grace and grow in inner reflection with a gentle quiet spirit. But no gray hair!

With more tears..........

Chapter Nine: 2014

My dear Readers,

On this Independence weekend, I find myself musing how your dad, your grandfather Winfried Ritter and I dared to come to the US in 1966 to serve the German Methodist Church in Los Angeles on Pershing Square "for two years!" (You can read more later in the chapter to come, *The Voyage*). Well, those two years stretched to over fifty plus years by now. Both of us are glad and grateful to live in this country far away from memories of bombs, and the images of frightening soldiers we both have from our childhood. To see you and your brother, you grandchildren and all family members grow up in a relatively peaceful world is our reward. To experience the grandchildren is a gift in addition to all our beloved pets. To think without fear, to feel without guilt, and to speak freely are the gifts and privileges of freedom. Nevertheless, a part of me is back home in Germany wherever it happened to be, in Dresden, or Leipzig, Bad Bergzabern, or in Heidelberg.

Not to forget while not give in to despair and resignation is the art of survival. Gratitude is the lifeline—kindness is the mandate.

I did not mean to get preachy, but a word of comfort might help as I began to tell you about the months before and after the end of the war in 1945. Rather than repeating my own memories I have written down in my book, *Return to Dresden* (2004), I found fully accurate and moving descriptions of the world we lived in by reading some more in my paternal grandfather, your great-grandfather, Paul Schnädelbach's diary. His narrative writing will lead us to the time the first CARE packages arrived in Leipzig and mother's letters of gratitude to

RETURN TO LEIPZIG

the members of the Sunday School Class in 1946. So, let's get back to grandfather's diary in 1948:

> Leipzig, June 30, 1948
>
> "I have been retired already for one year without my occupation. I am not quite happy about it; I sure would prefer if I had some professional activities. My health is relatively good even my gait, while walking on the street, is always steady.
>
> Sometime last year our nutrition improved somewhat because we received several packages from Switzerland and even from America; we are so deeply grateful to God and the donors. We also received some charitable gifts from America through our church congregation so that we are no longer suffering.
>
> Suddenly, on June 24, a currency reform was ordered which meant that our money was devalued 10 to 1. In early 1945, because of the lost war, all savings, banks, and post office accounts were annulled. As a result, I lost about 10.000.00 Marks I had saved up during the last ten years mainly by putting my pension aside. We now experience another financial loss. I must wait if my old firm, Krock & Pohling, will still be able to pay my monthly 100.00 Mark pension. Yet with all our losses, we are not losing.[27]
>
> The Lord, who provided for us during the war and during the even more difficult years after the war, will not leave or neglect us in the years ahead. Amen.
>
> The chapel at the bombed-out Johannes cemetery will be finally rebuilt so that funerals can be conducted again by this fall. After Mama died in October 1941, I had bought a double plot with the intention to be buried there with her. However, the bombings on March 12, 1943, destroyed the cemetery so badly that no further funerals could be conducted. I could have only been buried there with her if I would have been cremated at the South cemetery with the urn placed near her. The thought of being burnt, which is unnatural to me, made me so uncomfortable. Now, the faithful God has made it possible for me to be buried there, and I am so grateful.

---

[27] This line is freely translated from Martin Luther's hymn, "A Mighty Fortress."

CHAPTER NINE: 2014

> Although I did not pray to God for this favor, the faithful Lord took this worry away from me. His name shall be praised!"

What a stubborn yet gentle and kind man! Had he arrived at this time in his life as a broken man or as a resigned sage?

Two of his sons had died during WWII, one of them, my father, without a grave. He gladly shared his flat with my mother and us four children. My grandmother had died in 1941. At the end of the war, my grandfather's church stood bombed out, his fatherland shamefully defeated, the Fuehrer had killed himself in the bunkers of Berlin. Grandfather's other surviving adult children struggled, and he was hungry with the rest of us war survivors. Mother later said that he lost 80 pounds during the Hungersnot (famine). In his diary he was mostly silent about his inner thoughts and feelings except for the few comments he made after the defeat of the German nation and the punishment it deserved. How did he grieve? Was he suffering in silence? Was he so shamed by the events of the political fiasco that he sought solace in his church and atoned? Although he must have known of the Nuremberg Trial against the WWII Nazi leaders in 1945–1946. He did not mention it in his diary. I remember some hushed talk in the house, which frightened me even more of what was to come for all of us? None of his entries mention the atrocities committed by the Nazis by name and the 6 million Jews and other unwanted people murdered. What about the disappearance of his Jewish neighbors? Did he not know what happened to them? Was God punishing all of us survivors, the once that knew and did not know, or did not want to know due to political arrogance, grandiosity, murder, blind faith, violence, or insanity?

After the bitter collapse of the Nazi regime, Grandfather was exhausted and broken for sure, but not in his faith. I remember his unending trust in God when he sang hymns in his bedroom every evening before he went to sleep. I cannot remember the songs he sang, but my brother, Herbert, says that he sat at his desk for his nightly devotion, read, prayed, and sang. Those hymns for hope and God's forgiveness seeped through the walls all the way to us as a reminder for a better world to come in heaven, and a reassurance of God's enduring love on earth.

Grandfather was a faithful, yet stubborn man, more like an insistent, nagging petitioner, reminding God of his promise to all of us, losers and winners alike, and he better not betray us.

On Sundays, he always wore his suit to church. His gait was steady as he walked down the street to catch the streetcar and join the men's chorus rehearsal to sing the old familiar hymns of God's reign despite disaster and death and the promise of salvation.

We children spent much time outside Grandfather's flat in the courtyard. The boys played war games, Russia vs. Germany and caught and locked up the "prisoners" in a cellar of one of the bombed-out buildings. I worried about my brothers being caught by some bullies of a street gang nearby and wondered what would happen to them. Herr Ottrich, the neighbor a few houses away in the courtyard, screamed at us children when we came too close to his front yard and quickly held his water hose pointed at us and chased us away with cold water. We little ones drew grids with numbers on the sidewalk and threw pebbles on squares after we agreed on the exact jumping rules. The big boys at a distance shouted victory rhymes and laughed:

> *"Herr Churchill came a-riding*
> *on a can of gasoline.*
> *The Frenchmen, they were thinking*
> *it was the Zeppelin.*
> *They aimed their canon quickly*
> *and shot high in the air,*
> *and blasted Mr. Churchill,*
> *and all his underwear."*

One summer night, the neighborhood women organized a Summerfest with moon-faced, candle-lit lampions swinging from the trees in the warm evening breeze and folk music blaring from a radio. I was allowed to participate.

The boys stood at the side and laughed at us for swaying with the music as we formed a circle dancing around a tree. Gerhard did not like my participation in this dancing activity at all and said to me later on the way upstairs, "Du alte Tanze!" (You silly, old dance girl!) meaning that dancing was a stupid thing to do for anybody, especially for us Methodists.

CHAPTER NINE: 2014

After our arrival in Leipzig, at a time of strange and scary outdoor games, of little food and living in tight quarters, and of frightening events around us, Grandfather had time for me. He held my hand when we walked to a small, dusty park in the neighborhood with no cooling breeze on a hot and steamy summer day. While he sat on a cracked wooden bench, I skipped along the dirt path from one foot to the other, holding on to my new bride doll as tight as I could that was sent to me in one of the CARE packages from America.

Grandfather Paul Schnädelbach and Maria with doll, Leipzig, 1948

Chapter Ten

Dear Lisa, Peter, dear grandchildren, and all you brave readers,

Please hold on to me. The stories of our lives and our memories are sometimes dark and painful but thank you for reading along and allowing for shared emotions. Talking, listening and compassion are the tools for resilience and healing. Then, the journey can continue free of the heavy weight of the burden. The burden is shared with you all. Thank you!

So far in my letters, I have stayed close to personal recollections of our family's history. However, as a family, we belonged to a larger world in transition from war to a relative and fragile peace. Now that the folder of mother's letters is in front of me, I want to tell you about some of the political developments at the time, which I, as a girl, only partially understood. I do remember the adults talking and listened to news on the radio, picking up bits and pieces of information … "Russians raping women," … "Siberia labor camps, Walter Ulbricht, refugees, …electricity rationed from 8 o'clock on in the morning" … "No more Hackenkreuze (swastikas) on anything, not even on photos!" People took knives and scratched them out on family pictures and portraits of their sons and fathers. The German flag was banned. I understood the emotions, a mixture of fear, silent resentment, and shame. As if the holes on the family photos, the crude cut-outs of the swastikas on our father's or uncle's pictures, would do away with a horrific history of following a beguiling devil in disguise over the edge. The empty spaces stood for a lost and empty identity as people followed orders to remove all and every swastika from every household. Those were the orders of the Allied forces and the old, retrained Nazi party official functioned now as a denazification police. Silence fell over us like a thick fog.

RETURN TO LEIPZIG

The Yalta Conference, held in 1945 by the United States, the United Kingdom, and the Soviet Union, agreed on a division of Germany into occupational zones with demarcation lines and except for Berlin to be divided among the four powers. While there was an Allied Control Council assuming governmental control, various economic demilitarizing and de-Nazification programs as part of the overall reparation demand on Germany were decided upon by each occupying force. Since we lived in the Eastern part of Germany, we fell under the Russian occupation to be modeled after the Communist, Marxism-Leninism model of class struggle and socialist economy. The Stasi, the secret police, soon controlled daily life. There were *Spitzel* (spies) around, and a critical comment of the new regime or a nostalgic Nazi statement could send you to a Siberia labor camp. My brother Gerhard and I were afraid of the dark outside the house, even of the dark in our bedroom. Electricity was still rationed daily, and candle flickering painted strange shadows along the walls and the door frames. We were afraid of someone knocking on our door and arrest a family member for saying something hateful about the new political regime of idealized worker power, of the hard-working farmer in the new collective farming plans, and their rewards for productivity. Most of all, I worried someone could snatch and arrest our mother and take her to a labor camp in Siberia.

In 1944, 12.4 million Germans lived in territories that after the defeat of Germany became part of Poland and the Soviet Union. About six million fled or were evacuated before the Red Army occupied the area, us included. Of the remainders, up to 1.1 million died, 3.3 million were expelled from Poland, one million declared themselves Polish, and 300.000 remained in Poland as Germans. I understand that they could not speak German any longer. It is well known that thousands died, starved, or froze to death while being expelled on the road or in ill-equipped trains. Thousands died in forced labor camps; others were shipped off by the Soviets to Siberia. We were part of this exodus in January 1945, on our way from Silesia to Dresden.

In the East Germany/Russian occupied section, later called the DDR, the Soviets began to dismantle the East German war industry and extracted about $10bn worth of equipment, factory products, metals, natural resources, and agricultural produce. Military industries and those owned by Nazi activists or war criminals were confiscated. Industrial property was nationalized, leaving 40% of total industrial production in private enterprise. I remember that personal properties were taken away, people lost their land. The *Bodenreform*, (Agrarian reform) was put in place. Private estates were converted to collective people's farms and land was distributed among 500.000 peasant farmers, agricultural laborers, and refugees. State farms were called, *Volkseigenes Gut* (State owned Property). At the time of harvest, many young people were sent during their summer vacation to these farms to work in the fields.

Political tension between the USA and the Soviet Union manifested itself in 1947 with the SMAD (Soviet Military-administration in Germany) in their refusal to take part in plans by Joint Chief of Staff, and General Clay and Marshall to rebuild the German economy. In 1948, the Soviet Union, in response to US, Britain and France's agreement to create a West German Republic and a new currency, created an East German State with its own currency. Political tension arose which led to the eleven months Russian blockade of Berlin. In defiance, the Americans flew airlifts directly into the city of Berlin with food and supplies for all those Allied Forces and German people stranded in need. I thought the war would never end with new conflicts emerging between the occupying forces and their struggle for power in the region.

Grandfather, my aunts and my mother sat in front of the radio, listening to the news with serious faces and anxious thoughts. I listened to their comments without much understanding. It seemed that there would not be anything else but a world in shambles. They talked about the new currency and the loss of savings for many people they knew. We were waiting for something, maybe for a peaceful time, a new day with enough food and fewer worries written on my mother's face. Our Methodist church had opened its doors again soon after the bombings were over. We sang the old familiar songs as I huddled next to my mother during the church services and the lengthy sermons. I did like listening to the men's choir best, not only because my grandfather was a part of it and sang with a sincere heart and a full voice, but because the melodies followed a smooth and haunting line to speak of God's assurance and hope for our salvation. He believed in God's mercy before and after the war. I did question it. Why war?

It was hard for me to believe in God's mercy when I listened to him and his prayers. I learned that sometimes others hold on to the trust in God despite the harsh traumata we all had already seen and experienced. Maybe that is the message when they talked in church about the "cloud of witnesses..."[28] I still asked myself why would a merciful God send us all such evil, fear, and suffering? Was our survival a message of God's mercy to become a witness? Maybe we were not alone after all in the ruins and the darkness. We had candles in the home that streamed a flickering and warm light especially during the Christmas season. Mother told us that our loved ones and angels would watch over us—what comforting thoughts!

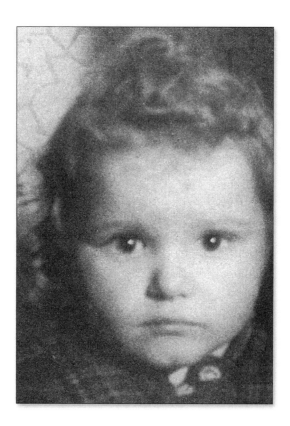

---

[28] Hebrews 12:1. "Therefore, since we are surrounded by so great a cloud of witnesses, let us also lay aside every weight, and sin which clings so closely, and let us run with perseverance the race that is set before us."

Chapter Eleven

Dear Lisa, Peter, and all you brave readers,

Back to the letters of grace. I hope you readers do not mind going forth and back with me in time and history. Memories just came back to me as if it were yesterday when I looked at the top page of the red folder Marcia had handed me, which contained my mother's letters to the Artaban Sunday School Class. I saw in midst the papers a printed brochure of the CARE program. It read, *Help sow the seeds of peace,* and it reads on, CARE's new seed package, 'Help Europe grow its own food.'

The picture shows an urban SoHo Garden in NYC, in the center of a city street, watered by a woman as a streetcar passes by. The Vegetable Seed Packages contained a variety of 28 different vegetables available for $4.00, CARE also offered a New Standard Food Package for $10.00. CARE would send these packages to the following countries: Austria, Belgium, Czechoslovakia, Finland, France, the Netherlands, Poland, and the American, French and British Zones of Germany. "Because of the blockade, CARE packages are being flown into Berlin. Air-freight brings the price up to $12.50 for Berlin only."

CARE stood for 'Cooperative for American Remittances to Europe' as an organization made up of 26 reliefs, religious, cooperative, and labor organizations. CARE had been approved by the US Government and Europeans governments with the idea of distributing free food packages to needy people. The organization was based on 50 Broad Street, New York 4, N.Y.

A Standard Food Package contained the following items:

- 1 lb. Beef in Beef Broth
- 1 lb. Honey
- 1 lb. Steak and Kidney
- 1 lb. Raisins
- ½ lb. Liver Loaf
- 1 lb. Chocolate
- ½ lb. Corned Beef
- 2 lb. Sugar
- ¾ lb. Prem (Luncheon Meat)
- ½ lb. Egg Powder (equals 18 eggs)
- ½ lb. Bacon
- 2 lbs. Whole Milk Powder (equals 2 gallons)
- 2 lbs. Margarine
- 2 lbs. Coffee
- 1 lb. Swift'ning (Lard)
- 2 lbs. Rice
- 1 lb. Apricot Preserves
- 2 lbs. Flour
- 12 oz. Soap

"These 22 pounds with nutritious food will supplement the sparse, monotonous diet of a hungry European family for weeks."

Other CARE packages for special needs were also available for $10.00, such as The British Food—newly designed to supplement the drab rations in Britain. Other packages offered these options: Kosher Food, Oriental Food, Italian and Greek Food, Wool, Knitting Wool, Layette, Infant Food, Baby Food, Household linen, Lard, and Blankets.

The CARE organization obtained permission from the US government to send US Army surplus "10-in-1" food parcels to Europe as a relief for large numbers of people starving in the wake of the war. Americans were given the opportunity to purchase such packages for $10.00 and guaranteed their arrival within four months. CARE would even try to find persons using their last address. This became a way of identifying 'missing persons' following the chaos of WWII. The first 20,000 packages reached the port of Le Havre on May 11, 1946. Over the next two decades 100 million more packages were delivered, first to Europe then to Asia and other developing countries. In June of 1946, the prohibition against sending CARE packages to occupied Germany was rescinded with General Lucius D. Clay signing the CARE treaty to allow packages into the US occupied section of Germany; soon thereafter, the British and the French followed pursuit.

The Russian occupying forces had not joined into this humanitarian effort and we were left to fend for ourselves. It was even worse in Raschau, Erzgebirge, where we had fled to after the Dresden bombing in February of 1945. Raschau

CHAPTER ELEVEN

was part of an area considered 'No-man's-land' for some months without occupying forces in place, and therefore was left without any rationing and governing directives. When our living situation in Raschau with my mother's cousin, Mariechen Körner, became utterly crowded and mother did no longer receive any further food rationing cards, my grandfather, Paul Schnädelbach, as you know, urged us in June of 1945 to move to Leipzig. His flat had two bedrooms, a kitchen with a small balcony, a living room, and a long, always cold bathroom. While sitting on the toilet, you could see the inner courtyard of the apartment complex with the trees when the window was open. Quite often, I sang there my 'Hallelujahs' to fill the room and enjoy the acoustics. When I had to pull the chain of the water tank to flush the toilet, I often ran out in a hurry. This place was especially scary when the electricity was out, and it was dark in there. Candlelight made it even spookier with the long shadows gliding and flickering on the walls. Klaus und Herbert slept next door, at Frau Lehman's flat since she had an empty bedroom.

Some persons in America saw us hungry, cold, and homeless and planned an organization to send us food, clothes, and blankets. How could they move through their own hate toward Germany and the Nazi destruction worldwide and look at us as suffering children in need? What changed their hearts to reach out while they still buried their sons and daughters?

And then there is the human capacity for compassion despite our own suffering. Maybe one own's suffering is soothed by identifying with other's suffering and by sharing with others in empathy and compassion. Maybe the following quote will say it all much better.

> *"A human being is a part of the whole called by us universe, a part limited in time and space. He experiences himself, his thoughts and feeling as something separated from the rest, a kind of optical delusion of his consciousness. This delusion is a kind of prison for us, restricting us to our personal desires and to affection for a few persons nearest to us. Our task must be to free ourselves from this prison by widening our circle of compassion to embrace all living creatures and the whole of nature in its beauty."* —Albert Einstein

RETURN TO LEIPZIG

Aunt Hilde, mother's older sister far away in the Western section of Germany, had long started to share her meager food rations with us and sent us packages in the mail containing food and clothing. You have read the letters written by her and my mother. Grandfather opened his home to give us shelter in Leipzig. It was our new home from now on and we were welcomed in his flat on Lössnigerstrasse 47.

Our Artaban story became very real all around us. "Truly I say to you, all that you ever did for your needy brothers and sisters, you did for me."

Chapter Twelve: 2011

My dear Lisa, Peter, and all my dear readers,

This year's summer came to an end with fond memories of our family gathering on the MS Queen Mary in Long Beach to celebrate my 70th birthday in 2011. What a nice evening we had with a festive table, plenty of food, and all of us gathered in one festive room, laughing, and chatting, hugging, and enjoying each other's company. Luke sang the table grace with a clear voice, and everyone joined in. The grandchildren busied themselves with a fun activity book, "Queen Mary Birthday Quiz-Oma" to keep them sitting, coloring pictures, and finding answers to various questions about the aging ship and their aging grandmother. I saw them giggling, smiling, and talking to each other like old friends. Cousin Horst, dressed in his formal attire, brought a copy of a Wunderlich family picture of my grandmother on her 70th birthday, most likely taken

MY 70th Birthday Party at the Queen Mary, Long Beach, California, September 2011

1934 in Dresden. Grandmother looks really like an old woman, slightly hunched over, dressed in a black dress with a white-collar bow, and her stern expression holds pride, aging resignation, and life fatigue. I hope, in my vanity, I looked less haggard and dressed more stylish at my own 70th birthday party.

Garndmother Lydia Wunderlich's 70th Birthday Party. Back row: Mariechen and Kurt Lange, Hilde Alrutz, Helene, and Herbert Schnädelbach, Paulus Wunderlich, Friedrich Wunderlich, Lydia Wunderlich or Liddy. Front row: Gudrun Lange, Inge Alrutz, Friedrich Wunderlich, Oma Lydia Wunderlich, Waltraud Lange, Erhard Wunderlich, Maria Wunderlich, Gertraud Wunderlich.

Looking at the Wunderlich family picture above, I see my parents standing in the middle of the second row, your grandparents, looking at the squiggly kids as they expected their first child that year. Their whole world was still in order despite the rumblings of the Third Reich and the beginning of the end. On the right side in the second row, you see Aunt Liddy, my mother's oldest sister, who lived with grandmother Wunderlich in Dresden until she also perished in the bombing in 1945. You might remember her name edged into the tombstone in her memory on my grandfather's grave, Engelbert Wunderlich

CHAPTER TWELVE: 2011

in Dresden, Tolkewitzer cemetery. We have a nice picture of you, Lisa and me standing by the graveside and honoring them all with our presence.

My brother, Herbert, had made an extra trip from Germany for my festive 70th's birthday celebration. He sat next to me at the head table and looked at all of you with surprised pleasure and astonishment; both of us siblings aware how time had passed since we grew up together. How differently we had experienced our life way back in Leipzig right after the war.

"I had a pretty good childhood," he said. "We were so busy," he chuckled. "I had violin and piano lessons and we played a lot outside." He did not say much more but did remember the early food rationing in 1947.

"At that time, we received portions of the Army meal supplies, their daily food rationing the "Marschverpflegung".[29] There was Komissbrot, a dense dark bread and cheese in it and other items such as cigarettes." He began to snicker, "and the packages also contained a condom!"

I asked him what he and his friends did with it. "Oh, we tried to blow it up." We both laughed out loud. He may not have remembered much of the worries I observed and lived with, but he did remember the condom.

I just shook my head. Doesn't he remember the hot summer of 1947, walking with our grandfather and my mother to the Voelkerschlachtdenkmal to collect sorrel? Mother and my aunts would later soak and rinsed the picked greens in the bathtub and cooked them like spinach—it tasted so awful. To this day, I avoid cooked or raw spinach. The bread was rationed weekly, and I heard my mother worrying about the stores having nothing to sell. People stood in long lines to get cucumber before they ran out of their meager supply.

The adults whispered about the black market near the main train station where you could buy food if you had cigarettes or coffee or traded in any treasures like special china and jewelry. The police were on the lookout and the trading was dangerous. I guess Herbert was busy learning an instrument or two, going to school, attending church, and playing with other boys on the block. He also had time to memorize large sections of our Opa's book, *Das Grosse Wilhelm Busch Album in Farbe*[30], a collection of stories and satirical as well as biting

---

[29] Daily military food rationing

[30] Wilhelm Busch, a large collection with colored illustrations. Current edition, 2004, Otus Verlag, Zurich, Switzerland.

poetic stories about ordinary and unusual people or children and their calamities, such as *"The Pious Helene," "The Bad Boys in Korinth," "Max und Moritz"*, and many more such stories with quotations he would later use at opportune times to entertain us, or use for a teaching moments. What was he to do anyway with a little, worried sister?

At night, we played cards and board games, Halma, Pick-up-Sticks, and Elfer Raus. Traditional playing cards were not allowed—"too worldly"—they said, and were associated with poker, sinning, or gambling. I tried so hard, but as the youngest, I did not ever win at playing games. On many evenings, we read the Bible out loud, prayed for our father in heaven, and spent "quiet time" to consider our daily sins, confess them to God and ask for forgiveness. Much later on did I learn that Klaus and Herbert arranged our Bible reading sequence around the table in such a way so Gerhard and I would have to read the verses with the most difficult words to pronounce, such as the names of geographic regions from where the ancient Jews traveled to Jerusalem for Pentecost: … "Parthians, Medes, Elamites, and residents of Mesopotamia, Phrygia …."[31] I stumbled and freelanced with "Hallelujahs" and "Amen" and consequently created much snickering from the rest of the pious listeners.

On Sunday afternoon, we also conducted our own church services in the living room. My dolls and Gerhard's Teddy Bear represented the congregation, all placed on the chairs from the dining table and a stool from the kitchen. Nobody noticed the empty seats. Sometimes friends from Sunday school or the neighborhood joined in. The preachers, my brothers, Herbert, and Gerhard, needed an audience. They took turn preaching, with Herbert already displaying extraordinary oratory skills rarely seen for someone his age. They read the scripture and interpreted the text standing up front at a makeshift pulpit, addressing all of us and the few who could understand. Klaus played familiar hymns on the piano. I learned to listen early on in life.

On other Sunday afternoons, we stood around the piano, sang chorales and choruses from J.S. Bach's Oratorios such as the *Christmas Oratorio* and the *St. Matthew Passion*, excerpts from the Messiah, all depending on the seasons of the year. At first, my mother would play on the piano the choral parts following the leading melodies, but soon, my brother, Klaus, took over the accompaniments

---

[31] Acts 2: 9–11. New Revised Standard Version

and we would manage to sing various choir pieces. I sang soprano lines and sometimes, I could not read the notes fast enough and either made up the melodies, or just followed along. Klaus began to accompany my mother singing Lieder, composed by Schubert, Schumann, Wolf and Brahms. I sat on the sofa listening and began to memorize and recognize their longing and melancholic melodies for beauty of nature, unending love, and the deep sounds of bitter loss.

During the winter of 1947, I had whooping cough and spit into the kitchen sink until I felt dizzy. I had to stay in bed during the day with warm, moist compresses on my chest and some awful tasting cough syrup or cod liver oil taste in my mouth. The idea was, if you are sick, you stay in bed—no playtime!

My mother, my brother, Gerhard, and I shared one bedroom. Gerhard slept in one bed, Mother and I shared the other twin-size bed. She would tuck me in at night, only later to gently ask me to move toward the wall, so she could lie down. She always complimented me how I could listen to her in my sleep. We kept each other warm, and I learned to sleep very quietly so not to disturb her. Gerhard and I chatted quietly about this and that before we fell asleep. We called it "pűhing."

Our household in Leipzig consisted of us five and my grandfather with his two daughters, Johanna and Lottel. Grandmother, Helene Schnädelbach, had passed away in 1941, just about two weeks after I was born. Somehow, each day mother placed something to eat on the table, for which we all said Grace and thanked God. On occasions, special guests like the ministers, Pastor Bierwirt, Pastor Witzel, or the choir director, Hans Buchholz, of the church joined us for dinner. As we gathered around the table, mother said in the kitchen to us children, "Familie hält zurück!" or just "FHZ" (family holds back), meaning that the guests would have first choice of the amount of food on the table, and we were not to ask for seconds.

One time, a special guest from the Western section of Germany came to visit us. Herr Schiele was a lay Conference leader in the Methodist church and came on business to the annual Leipzig Trade Show and visited us one night for dinner. Never in my life had I seen a round, so well-fed person, someone who apparently could have as much food as he wanted all the time and did not have to share every special bite. I was amazed and looked at his round belly hanging over his trousers, held up by suspenders. To my amazement, he presented us with two yellow lemons, fruit I had never seen or tasted before. For days, I kept squeezing out one more drop into a cup, the intriguing taste of sour and tangy sticking to my mouth. Where did this strange fruit come from? Only later did I learn that he also visited my mother to see about a job possibility for her in the Western part of Germany. All these conversations had to be held in secrecy given the fears of the local police and their strict control to prevent people from escaping the Eastern section of Germany. Since he was a business owner, he was allowed to visit Leipzig and could travel forth and back once a year. That seemed like a dream to us.

On Sundays, I wore a special dress to our Methodist church[32] and mother put a white ribbon in my braided hair. We often walked to church and played games in the bombed-out church grounds before our Sunday school lesson. Church services were held in a temporary building, which looked more like a barrack.

---

[32] Today the Methodist Church, Kreuzkirche, is still located on Paul-Gruner Str., Leipzig. It used to be an old Villa that burned down during the bombing of Leipzig. During our time in Leipzig 1945–49, a barrack-style building on the property served as a sanctuary. Later on, the church was rebuilt to its present view.

CHAPTER TWELVE: 2011

Sunday School Fest, 1948, in the ruins of the Methodist Church in Leipzig

After the war was finally over in May of 1945, the women, also called, 'Trümmerfrauen', (women of the ruins) all over the country picked up boulders, broke bricks apart, and collected loose metal scraps from the bombed-out buildings to pile them up high by the side of the road so the men could start building a new foundation for homes or stores. Our Methodist church building was also in ruins with bare brick walls and hollow windows, but the community had survived and now became our new home. We belonged there as a family, even without our father present. Grandfather was an elder in the church and even then, I understood that people argued in churches about the correct program, their minister, and the quality of his sermons every Sunday mornings. Most of all, people debated how to rebuild the church and where the money would come from. Not much has changed since then. Life had been so hard, but not all was so serious and pious. Humor and, at times, biting sarcasm rose to the surface of long suppressed fears of speaking out. My brothers brought home some jokes they had heard from their friends on the street. One went like this.

"Do you know how stupid the Russian soldiers were? They wanted to wash their potatoes one day, put them into the toilet and pulled the flushing chain!"

The other joke went like this.

RETURN TO LEIPZIG

> *"How fast can Genosse Ulbricht ride his bike?"*
> *"Our new Genosse Ulbricht can ride his bicycle so fast that the back wheel passes the front wheel...."* We thought it was very funny to laugh at the ignorant Russian soldiers, who had never seen a toilet before, or at a ridiculously over-effective party official on a bicycle.

The under swelling rage against the occupying forces and the new controlling authorities broke open with biting gossip, shifting prejudice, and degrading laughter.

Our grandfather, Opa, was known as one of the 'Eisheiligen' (Ice Saints) in the Methodist congregation, a description of his outward sternness, his outspoken and dedicated nature while sincerely seeking a deeper faith and holiness in his spiritual life. He was a member of the church administrative council and close friends with two others, 'ice saints', Gotthard Mueller and Herr Fischer. All of them sang in the Men's Chorus. I remember the first Sunday morning in the Advent Season, when their deeply felt rendition of *"O Du, mein Trost, und süsses Hoffen,"* inspired all of us during the worship service. Of course, no one called grandfather *'Eisheiliger'* openly, but I heard my mother and others whisper and shaking their heads in amusement and wonder. [33]

Herr Fischer had a younger brother who worked in a heating supply store. Through his help, we received a full ration of coal and briquette dumped

---

[33] The Ice Saints is the name given to St. Mamertus, St. Pancras, and St. Servatius in Flemish, French, Dutch, Hungarian, German, Austrian, Polish, Swiss and Croatian folklore. They are so named because their feast days fall on the days of May 11, May 12, and May 13 respectively. In Flanders St. Boniface of Tarsus is counted amongst the Ice Saints as well; St. Boniface's feast day falling on May 14. The period from May 12 to May 15 was noted to bring a brief spell of colder weather in many years, including the last nightly frosts of the spring, in the Northern Hemisphere under the Julian Calendar. With the change to the Gregorian Calendar, however, the equivalent days would be May 23–May 26.

In Poland and the Czech Republic, the Ice Saints are St. Pancras, St. Servatus and St. Boniface of Tarsus (i.e, May 12 to May 14). To the Poles, the trio are known collectively as *zimni ogrodnicy* (cold gardeners), and are followed by *zimna Zośka* (cold Sophia's) on the feast day of St. Sophia which falls on May 15. In Czech, the three saints are collectively referred to as "ledoví muži" (ice-men or icy men), and Sophia is known as "Žofie, ledová žena" (Sophia, the ice-woman).

In Sweden, the German legend of the ice saints has resulted in the belief that there are special "iron nights", especially in the middle of June, which are susceptible to frost. The term "iron nights" (*järnnätter*) has probably arisen through a mistranslation of German sources, where the term "Eismänner" (ice men) was read as "Eisenmänner" (iron men) and their nights then termed "iron nights", which then became shifted from May to June.

through the cellar window, a special gift during the cold winter of 1947. In my memory, this man must be remembered as one of the true Saints, who provided warmth for all of us so our mother could cook our meals on the kitchen stove. On freezing, cold nights, she heated a red brick in the stove, then wrapped it in towels, placed it in my bed. At other times, she poured hot steaming water into a copper pan with a lid on it. If need be, and with electricity rationed to a few hours a day, mother placed a pot of prepared sweet rice next to the heating brick in my bed during the day. Another Advent of hope returned to all of us through a heap of black lumps of coal for heating, some meager food for sharing, and pleading singing of familiar hymns and prayerful insistence by several Saints around us.

* * *

What a surprise! I found in the folder of the records of the Caravaners (Artaban) Sunday School Class a program of a concert, dated Friday, October 10, 1947, 8:00pm. I remember now quite clearly. Mother included it into a letter to the Sunday School Class much later as a witness to profess her belief in church music and her effort to sing again with other musicians in town. It looked like a thank you concert knowing of the universal language of music.

Mother had several friends that were musicians who were just as hungry and lost in a destroyed city as the rest of us, Herr Wedel, a blind organist, Frau Zieschang, a violinist, Frau Kubel, Soprano soloist. My mother sang Alto. They planned a concert tour into the area of Magdeburg, to Schönebeck—Salzelmen to perform music in the St. Johannes church. Their pay would not be much money, but food to bring back in their suitcases. I clearly remember her preparation and my fear of being left in Leipzig. So, she decided to take me along. We traveled by train and arrived in this small town to stay with parishioners. It must have been already cold because I remember the bed was so cold and moist. We wore our clothes to bed, and I snuggled close to my mother to keep warm.

The next day, I joined the musicians at the church, an old brick stone building with two steeples and the organ console placed on the balcony. In this freezing cold church, Herr Wedel who was blind fumbled with the stops next to the organ console while I sat by his feet watching his feet move the pedal keys. How his hands and feet moved along the keyboards in different directions bringing the organ pipes to soar to a heavenly orchestra remained a mystery to me. I also sang along with my mother's solos. Mother performed arias by J.S. Bach and Joh. Phil. Krieger accompanied by violin and organ. Her alto voice echoed in the cold, empty stone churches and filled them with the warm breath from above until the melodies floated to the last crevasses of the chancel walls. The sung words spoke of God's comfort and help in times of need and the music brought back a sense of calmness and enduring faith into our post-war time of chaos and defeat. When the time came for the evening performance, mother said to me,

"You have to be very quiet now, you cannot sing along."

So, I remained sitting as quiet as I could at Herr Wedel's feet and watched his shoes move in opposite directions while his cold hands slid along the keyboard. He wore special gloves with half covered fingers. Once in a while, he blew his warm breath on them to keep them from stiffening up.

The next day, we returned to Leipzig with a suitcase full of potatoes, carrots and eggs.

With much gratitude for food and music ...

Chapter Thirteen: 1947

My dear, brave readers,

Back to 1947, in the following letters, mother wrote to her sister, Hilde, of the darkness that had fallen over all of us. Some of the details in the letters may not mean much to us now, but they speak of their desperate effort to stay connected and check up on old friends and their whereabouts. Mother could share with Hilde more openly the effects of our traumatic journey on her body with symptoms of pain and mental collapse. Tears were dried up forever.

Not only the lack of day light with the incoming winter affected all of us, but also the lack of electricity and warmth and the lack of direction and hope. Mother's gall bladder infections reoccurred from time to time. She would rest on the sofa in the living room with a warm water bottle on her side. I had to be quiet—much noise made her feel worse. She was in pain.

> Leipzig, November 6, 1947
>
> My dear Hilde,
>
> Thank you so much for your nice letter. I was so glad to hear that you had nice days in Hohenschwangau. It feels so good to get away from it all and I hope you feel some rest and relaxation. I, myself yearn for such a rest. The last few years did not pass me by without serious effects on my body. I have an infection of the gall bladder bothering me quite a bit with painful episodes. The doctor x-rayed everything right away. He said, it was not surprising after all the trauma and stress we lived through.

November 25, 1947. In the meantime, this month is almost over—oh, so fast!

My letter should have been with you by now and instead will bring you greetings for the Advent season. Oh, may the horrible darkness in our world be pierced by the light of Bethlehem. I yearn for it so much and can hardly live on in this terrible dark time. If God would have mercy on our people and our country!

What you wrote me about Lydia (?) made me so sad. She is really bad off and it made me cry. What is wrong with Hanna? It reminded me of Tante M, but maybe it will turn out differently.

I have not heard anything from our brother, Paulus, and his family in Neheim. I received a letter on November 22 from our sister, Mariechen Lange. I actually wanted to travel to Dresden to audition with a Cantor but was not able to do so. Oh yes, singing, my dear Hilde, was not my intent for a small ensemble group, but for solo work. One week ago, I sang at the Michaelis Church, the Cantor used to work at the Frauenkirche in Dresden before the bombing. He wanted me to sing again. It would be good if I could find my roots here in Leipzig, but it is exceedingly difficult because of fierce competition among the musicians.

I read that Inge cannot live in W. maybe that is for the best. That way she would have a little bit of free time and feel fewer obligations to work all the time. It would be less taxing on her. Try to accept this fact, it is not a reason to become bitter. What you told me about Ulm was very interesting to me. It is unfortunate that we do not know those relatives. I was recently thinking of them. How nice that you started a connection again.

The children prepared a wonderful birthday celebration for me. Unfortunately, it was so dark that we could not see much. It is only 4 o'clock in the afternoon, and the blackouts have been ongoing all day starting at 6:30am through 5:30pm.

My warmest greetings to you and Inge, and God bless you!

Yours, Leni and Children

If a package arrives from you soon, I will keep it for Christmas.

CHAPTER THIRTEEN: 1947

Mother wrote a Christmas postcard to her sister Hilde, dated

> Leipzig, December 10, 1947:
>
> My dear Hilde,
>
> Warmest Christmas greetings from all of us to you and your daughter, Inge! We wish you a wonderful Christmas in all the darkness of our world around us. May there be light to bring us joy! Our thoughts are with you! This is our 4th Christmas without our Vati. It is incomprehensible! But the children are full of joy. Your package for my birthday did arrive and I want to thank you for everything. I sent you a package back and hope it will arrive in time. Please extend warm greetings to all your colleagues.
>
> God bless you, Leni and children

I am recalling such personal memories, so you can understand our family life a bit better at the time when the Sunday school packages finally arrived and the worst of the Hungersnot (famine) would be over.

Yes, they did arrive ...

Chapter Fourteen: The Thank You Letters...

Dear readers,

Here, in the folder in front of me with all the documents and mothers thank you letters, saved by the Sunday School class's archives of the Temple City Methodist Church, I discovered two original orders for the CARE packages that eventually reached us with the help of the Rev. Ernst Scholz in Berlin, Schöneberg. The delivery receipts had been mailed to the Temple City Community Church in Temple City, California and addressed to their pastor, Rev. W.V. Dougherty. The Rev. E. Scholz in Berlin must have singled out our family in need given that our father, Pastor Herbert Schnädelbach, a Methodist minister, had been killed in the war.

The receipts designated two food packages, delivered on April 1, 1948, and April 23, 1948. Those were the first packages that reached us when there was not much food in the house. Maybe I learned to eat very little during that time and suppressed hunger and thirst. Asking for more food was not necessary since the food on our plate was it, no questioning if we liked it or not. To not clear your plate would be disrespectful and almost sinful. I remember one night in Leipzig, I asked at the dinner table for a second helping, stating, "I am still hungry." My brother, Klaus, responded, "If I am not hungry (he was 12 years old; I was 5), then you cannot be hungry either." He looked serious and spoke with authority and parental conviction. I never forgot it and did not ask again.

Now I know, he meant to teach me to be content with little and protect my mother in her efforts to manage our food rationing. I learned to suppress hunger.

Here is the first letter in the folder that Mother wrote after a Care package arrived from the Artaban/Caravaners Sunday School Class in Temple City, California,—a true human connection across the Atlantic and across the bitter divide. I have left my mother's letters in the "Ginglish" broken English to show her heartfelt effort to express her gratitude and her deep connection by faith.

The receipts of the delivery documentation on January 4, 1948, and April 23, 1948, of the CARE packages had been sent from America to a Rev. Ernst Scholz in Berlin Schöneberg with the intent of sending it on to our family, still addressed in my father's name, Pastor Herbert Schnädelbach. Mother had to pick up the packages at the post office and for all of us, it was like Christmas had finally come.

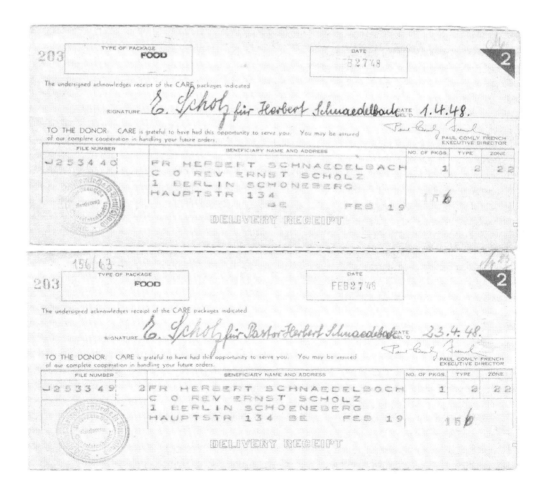

CHAPTER FOURTEEN: THE THANK YOU LETTERS...

Leipzig, January 4, 1948

Dear Mrs. Slosson,

Your letter from December 8, 1947, was coming to me some days ago. I was very surprised and very happy about it, and I shall try to answer your letter, but this is only my 2nd letter I have ever written in the English language. I please you to not see all the mistakes. Your children will be smiling about it, I am sure.

I feel that your greetings are coming from a warm heart and from the love of Jesus Christ.

You know, I have four children, three boys and a little girl, six years old. We have lost all belongings, our home—everything, everything; and now we know, our father went to God, three weeks before the end of the war. We have experienced so much sorrow and harm. But we have Christ's help and so it is easier to bear.

Our father was a preacher in the Methodist church in Breslau, the city belongs now to Poland. We had to flee from there and leave everything we had. We fled to our grandmother's home (my mother) in Dresden; she was 81 years old. After two weeks there, the city was demolished, and my dear old mother and my sister were killed. My four children and I survived. My little girl's, (age 3 ½ years old) clothes burned and she had horrible wounds, but our dear father in heaven helped her to recover. By now, we found a home at our dear grandfather in Leipzig. We are very glad that we can live here.

Your friend has written a very fine letter in very good German, I thank him so much. My English is not very good. I am glad to know that you are a mother of four children because you can understand all my worries.

Here are the answers to your inquiries about the children and my needs:
Klaus, age 13, 1,65 m
Herbert, age 11, 1,50 m
Gerhard, age 8, 1,30m
Maria, age 6, 1,25 m

For me: I need underwear and shoes, but not too narrow, size 7, the best would be sports shoes and stockings.

We also need clothing for the warmer times of the year, shorts, socks and cotton underwear, sweaters with long sleeves and casual clothing. I believe, we could use it all, even soap, linen, and thread for sewing. We have no night clothing like pajamas and nightgowns.

The boys are going to school, they love music and play instruments such as the piano, the violin, flute, and they all like to sing, especially Maria, all day long.

We need all kinds of food: butter, oil and fat, all nutritious food: milk, cacao, sugar, and noodles. I think you know what we need, the basics. We would be so grateful for it. If we receive a package, I will write back.

For now, many thanks to all the friends who help you in the Sunday School Class. May God bless you! Please give all friends my heartfelt thanks and greetings.

Your friend in Christ,
Leni Schnädelbach with Klaus, Herbert, Gerhard, and Maria

Leipzig, January 22, 1948

Dear Mrs. Slosson,

To our total surprise, your beautiful put together package arrived a few days ago.

This was like a special feast; the children and I were totally excited and happy. I wished you could have been here to see our excitement. You found the right items! Everything is beautiful and we can use it all. We are so deeply grateful! Please pass on our thanks to all the women of the Sunday school class that helped to put it all together. God bless you for your kindness and help. It would be nice to shake hands with each of you, although that is not possible because the ocean separates us. And still we are connected and feel your kindness and friendship. It is assuring that we are connected through our faith in Jesus Christ.

Little Maria tried on the little red suit right away; it is still too big on her, but I will fix it soon. She is sending special greetings to your little Margaret.

CHAPTER FOURTEEN: THE THANK YOU LETTERS...

> Luckily, this winter season is not as severe as the one last year. Therefore, we are not as cold. We are colder from the inside, due to lack of the right nutrition such as missing fat as in butter. Despite this hardship, the children are happy and content. They know that we have a strong faith in God who comforts us in all our needs. I am so deeply grateful for all your love; it is great comfort to us. I am not sure what is the greatest gift—I think it is your love! God bless you all.
>
> I hope that you received my English letter in the meantime; maybe Mr. Plank can translate my writing to you.
>
> For today, a heartfelt God be with you and God's blessings for the New Year, 1948!
>
> Yours, Leni Schnädelbach with Klaus, Herbert, Gerhard, and Maria
>
> PS. Special greetings to Mr. Plank.

According to this letter, mother must have written a previous letter to the members of the Sunday School Class either to introduce us or thank them for a previous package. As I go through the letters, I find small treasures and surprises. Beginning in 1947, the Caravaners, or also called, the members of the Artaban Sunday School Class, began to take us on as a mission project and started sending us packages through the organization of the Methodist church.

> Leipzig, January 31, 1948
>
> Dear Mrs. Slosson,
>
> Today came your package No. 2 and it arrived in perfect condition and we were happy over everything. We were so surprised over such rich gifts—we were happy over all the things- we can use them all. Especially Maria was totally excited about the skirt you sent. I was so happy to see the small items such as needles, wool, buttons and sewing yarn! How beautiful it is! May God bless you and your sisters in the Sunday school class for all your kindness. We would like to thank you personally with a warm handshake. I wished you could have been here when we opened this package and see our happiness.

Klaus must grow a bit more until the shoes will fit him, but we are so glad to have shoes for him. Everything comes at the right time if we put our trust in God. We have learned in these hard times to trust in God, and he will not forsake us!

Please give my regards to all the women of the Sunday school class who helped. It is wonderful to make other people happy. We know that you are making sacrifices in your lives, and we cannot pay you back. We pray that God will repay your kindness.

We are connected in love through God.

Gratefully, Leni Schnädelbach, Klaus, Herbert, Gerhard, and Maria

Leipzig, March 11, 1948

Dear Mrs. Slosson,

Yesterday another package arrived from you. I could not quite make out the date you sent it, maybe January? 1948! It arrived in good shape and contained besides a down comforter much needed clothing. Gerhard was so excited about the warm bathrobe and the pants, which fit him perfectly! He is sending a special thank you. Oh, this beautiful blanket! We will put it into a duvet cover, and it will be so helpful. Two days ago, a package arrived here, that you sent January 30, 1948. It arrived quickly. Our heartfelt thank you for everything! It is hard to name all the items we found in the package. I do not know how to express my gratitude to each one of you. Please pass on my joy and gratitude to all the members of the Sunday school class. I especially enjoyed receiving the soap you sent. We needed it so badly. And the detergent arrived especially well packed. And then, we found rubber bands for sewing; we needed it for mending.

It is amazing how we move forward with God's help; he has not forsaken us. Most important are the food articles: fat, margarine, butter, sugar, and flour (some coffee for me). These are the items we need most.

By now, we have received four packages in the mail. How gracious you all are and helpful! God bless all of you!

CHAPTER FOURTEEN: THE THANK YOU LETTERS...

> The children are happy despite the hardship. Maria is a small nightingale; she sings all day long the songs she hears in Sunday school—that is good!
>
> I hope, Mrs. Slosson, you can read my letter because my English is very poor.
>
> Maybe Mr. Plank can translate for you all. Greetings to him!
>
> Greetings to you and your husband, the children, and to all the friends.
>
> Yours, Leni Schnädelbach and children

The following letter written by mother on March 31, 1948, in Leipzig, is in response to a letter she had received from Mrs. Blanche Slosson in Temple City, California. Mother wrote back in English interspersed with German words and Grammar. I made a few minor changes in the letter so you can understand her writing. How grateful she is in her writing—her gratitude comes from the heart, and her broken English is her effort to breathe after having been rescued from drowning.

> Leipzig, March 31, 1948
>
> My dear friend,
>
> Your kind letter that came by airmail brought us great joy!
>
> You must have sent it on February 19th and arrived here on March 12th. I had just mailed a letter to you and hope you have received it in the meantime. The letter expressed our joy of the receipt of the four packages that arrived in good condition. Most of all, I enjoyed all the love expressed in your letter, it means so much to us. You do not know us personally, but you write with such warmth and love, it is hard for us to comprehend.
>
> Yesterday, a package with clothing arrived here, sent on February 21. Our heartfelt thanks!
>
> The clothing made me so very happy. The shoes are so beautiful. Klaus and I can wear them as needed. They are a bit too big for me, but it is fine. And this beautiful nightgown! The beautiful tablecloth, the hand towels and all the other items! Thank you so very much! The picture

books brought so much fun to the children. They are trying to spell the words and are astonished that Margaret can speak and read in English. Margaret's name is written in the book. Klaus is translating. He is studying English and Russian in school. I can translate a bit. The beautiful calendar is hanging above Maria's bed, so much to look at. You have been so kind. God bless you for all the goodness you brought to us.

The food packages through the CARE program have not yet arrived. It takes a long time. All the CARE packages are sent to Berlin. From there they are shipped to another city and then to the individual addresses. I am not sure if I will receive all the packages, maybe only one. Therefore, I ask you not to send packages through CARE, rather package them well and send them to us. In 4-6 weeks, they will arrive here. You can send the basics, flour, sugar, butter or margarine, cocoa, milk, (powder) the basics, maybe noodles. You have sent sweet cocoa and spam—great joy! Most of all, we need basic staples because the months before the harvest season are especially difficult. The children have no milk. Please send it to us. We would be so grateful for such items. I do not want to indicate that all the other items are not as important, however currently, we have so little food.

The children are learning to make music. Klaus plays Chopin, Beethoven, and Schumann. Herbert plays Grieg and Handel, both love to play Bach's music. I have a trained alto voice and sing church concerts. Music is our joy, all in praise of the Lord!

Enclosed please find some pictures. Klaus has grown quite a bit. He measures 1,63 m as tall as his mother. He is growing up. Maria is blinded from the sun; she laughs and likes to sing. I worry about Gerhard. He had tuberculosis of the lungs and he is coughing so much. He is such a happy guy. He misses milk and butter.

I am delighted that you were able to read my letter. I did not expect you to read my poor English writing, I had four years of English instruction, but so much time has passed since I have used it. I will try to write again at another time.

My dear Blanche, please write in English, it is good, I could understand it all. I am sure Mr. Plank can translate my writing.

CHAPTER FOURTEEN: THE THANK YOU LETTERS...

> My brother, Dr. Wunderlich, will be traveling to the General conference of the Methodist church in the US. Maybe your minister will be there also. They could exchange greetings there.
>
> Please extend our warm greetings to all the friends in the Sunday school class and report them of the joy you have brought us. God bless you all!
>
> As soon as the CARE packages arrive, I will write you again. Warm greetings to you, your dear family, and Herr Plank!
>
> Gratefully, Leni Schnädelbach, Klaus, Herbert, Gerhard, and Maria

* * *

I noticed that she addressed Mrs. Slosson now as a "dear friend". She is also addressing her in a less formal manner. Her letter was dated on March 31, 1948, but was received as late as April 26, 1948. It took a ship ride across the ocean and rode the train to the Los Angeles area. Hard to imagine now with email, telephone, and Facebook!

I marvel at her willingness to ask directly for what we needed the most. Her grateful begging came from a deep despair to feed us four children and prevent further deterioration of our health. With much pride she mentioned our music lessons to state our cultural roots and to keep the family history alive despite all the ruins around us. Music resurrected us out of the ashes.

She had enclosed a program of a church concert with musical selections of Handel, Bach, Mozart, and Mendelssohn. There is no date and no location printed on the simple program sheet. It is a true treasure I found in the Sunday school class folder. When I see, "Mein gläubiges Herze," J.S. Bach's joyful melodies begins playing in my head and I remember my mother's warm alto voice. Frau Kubel, the soprano soloist, gave her voice lessons and rescued her voice after the ashes of Dresden had darkened her voice register to an Alto. Mother would say, "Frau Kubel dug out my voice from the ashes!"

I am sure she received monetary compensation for the joint performances, and she brought food home in her suitcase, potatoes, eggs, apples, and flour. Familiar music of the old organ pipes, of soaring violin, and warm vocal melodies

RETURN TO LEIPZIG

brought comfort to the people who sat on those cold church benches and on dark evenings, hoping to have their torn bodies and souls restored.

Music comes into our lives sometimes with surprises, often bringing joy and familiar words of comfort. Playing music, learning an instrument, sharing old and new melodies nurture us, restore our history, and assure our legacy left by parents and grandparents.

I remember the below program and mother's singing during the concerts as she marked her contributions. If you look into our sheet music collection, you may find some of these arias.

Still singing from the heart and from her faith...

Musikalische Feierstunde

Gertrud Kubel, Sopran
Leni Schnädelbach, Alt
Dorothea Kiessig, Violine
Karl Zieschang, Orgel

Orgelvorspiel

1. Nun laßt uns gehn und treten, Duett für Sopran und Alt . . . . A. Mendelssohn
2. Adagio und Allegro für Violine . . . . C. Fiorelli
   oder: Adagio und Allegro . . . . G. F. Händel
3. Mein gläubiges Herze, frohlocke . . . . J. S. Bach
4. Air für Violine oder: Sarabande . . . . J. S. Bach
5. Benedictus, qui venit in nomine Domini, Arie für Sopran . . . . W. A. Mozart
   oder: Laßt uns singen von der Gnade des Herrn, aus dem Oratorium Paulus . . . . . F. Mendelssohn-Bartholdy
6. Adagio für Violine . . . . Fr. Schubert
7. a) Duett: Wunderbarer König . . . . A. Mendelssohn
   b) Choral: O liebe Seele, zieh die Sinnen . . . . . J. S. Bach
   c) Choral: Geh aus, mein Herz, und suche Freud . M. Wedel
8. Sonate für Violine . . . . Corelli

Orgelnachspiel

CHAPTER FOURTEEN: THE THANK YOU LETTERS...

Looking through the letters and collection of records and reports of the Sunday School project of sending CARE packages to us, some of mother's letters were translated by someone in the congregation who spoke and could read German, Herr Plank. Mother wrote to him in German, explaining the demise of our family at the time, and what we needed the most. He in turn would translate her writing into English and read it to the members of the class.

> Leipzig, April 9, 1948
>
> My dear Blanche Slosson,
>
> Your letter arrived today. I was so glad it arrived, and I am very grateful. I felt your love and it refreshed me.
>
> Yesterday, the first CARE package arrived yesterday in our home. O what a joy it was!
>
> All these wonderful items! I cannot believe they are all meant for us. I want to shake your hand in gratitude and thank all the members of the Sunday school class. I hope that the other announced packages will also arrive in the near future. I will let you know. The content of the package contains exactly what we need, although it took a very long time for them to arrive. But then came your letter and a list of all the items in the packages.
>
> My heart stood still with all that love and care in front of me. I still cannot believe it! You give us a new home! God bless you! My words cannot express my gratitude. God bless you all!
>
> I hope your daughter, Margaret, is healthy again. The picture of her is so sweet with her cute face. Maria liked her right away. It is very touching what you all are doing for us. I hope my letter from March 31 has arrived. Yes, the sporty shoes in package #5 fit me well. I am so happy with them. I have never owned a more beautiful pair of shoes. We recognize all your love as God's gift and thank him for his care.
>
> For now, many greetings from the children and myself,
>
> Leni Schnädelbach
>
> PS. I hope my brother, Dr. Wunderlich, took my letter along to the USA. He is traveling to the General Conference of the Methodist Church.

My measurement: Chest: 96 cm. Waist: 86cm. Height: 1,63 cm

The CARE packages will continue to help us in the future because the months before the local harvests are the most difficult ones. How lucky for us to look forward to other packages to arrive in the future.

Please give my best to the Rev. W. Vichery Dougherty.

O, how I remember these packages of solid, yellow cheese.
We called it 'eternity cheese' because they lasted so long.

Leipzig, April 26, 1948

My dear Blanche,

To our great joy your packages No.6 and 8 were coming to us. It was a great joy, I cannot tell you, my heart thanks you all the time and my thought are almost with you. And today, package No.8 arrived also.

Maria went with me to the post office and then we opened the great packages. I would be glad if you could look at us at this moment, and the box. My little girl! Such a sweet doll! We have not seen such a sweet, life like dolly! I could not wait to give this doll to her at Christmas, it was not possible. The little girl is so happy! The name of the doll is, Margaret—of

CHAPTER FOURTEEN: THE THANK YOU LETTERS...

course. And all day long this sweet Margaret is playing with Maria. I believe my English is very false, but I hope you can read my letter.

I hope package No. 7 will arrive these days too. I will write you soon. Now I have 2 CARE packages from you. I will talk {tell} you, this is our saving {you saved us}. I did not know what we would, should have eaten. Since the beginning of March, the children only got one time 50gr butter, no other fat, no milk, and your packages are our help. God bless you!

It is very difficult to cook for 4 children without anything, our potatoes are going out, and we have no fruit, no vegetables, no noodles, just a little bread, every day, 300 gr. I will not lament. I will only tell you that your help is great, and so we thank all day our Father in Heaven that he gives it in your heart to help us. I am sorry you cannot understand me too well. My heart is filled with thanks to you and our father in the heaven. He knows our need, but he also knows our trust. Since the days we left our home in Breslau until this very day, when we went through snow, freezing cold, fire, hunger, and illness. God was always with us. He has never forsaken us. All glory to him!

Please, my dear Blanche, give my thanks to all the friends in the Sunday School Class. I would like to thank everyone and say how grateful we are for everything and that we can use everything you sent. I am so happy about the bed linen, the beautiful tablecloth, and towels—all is so beautiful!

I have never owned anything like this—all was left in our home, or it burned. You have clothed us all. I have tears in my eyes, I cannot comprehend it. I have to think of the verses in the Bible: ... "and you have clothed me."

And there are other children around us who have nothing to wear. I am sure you are not angry with me if I pass on some items to help them.

The green wool blanket is wonderful! I had thought often how we need such a warm blanket, but I did not have the courage to write you and now ....it is in my hands. I am so happy. And the boys' suits, so much goodness you are doing. It was a great worry for me that Klaus is growing and now the help is there. All the things, the small items, such as the toothbrushes, the elastic band, and, and, and... The washcloths and shoes, and the can of fat and chocolate!!! Oh, the children! I can only say, God saves you!

I never believed that a watch would come to me. It is going very fine. The long trip did not harm it. Yes, you can give us a new home. I thank you always!

I hope my letter is coming to you. We hear many letters did not make to the USA. I wrote to you: Jan 22, Jan 5, March 11, March 31, April 4. I hope you received my letter from April 9. My brother, Dr. Wunderlich is going to the General Conference of the Methodist Church to Atlantic City, and I hope my letter is going with him.

We pray every day for little Margaret that her pain will be going out of her leg. Maria is also sick, she has a big cough, asthma, and bronchitis. Klaus is in danger of having TB, he must have milk and fat. Yes, and you are so kind to send it to us. God save you!

If you have some paper for writing letter it would be great, and Klaus would like an English Bible. We would be so happy. Also, we are missing a broom for the floor and for mother some stockings, please not the thin ones. What you might think if I express my need while you have done so much for us already.

My dear Blanche, A special thanks to you personally, you have a lot of work to help us out, I can never pay you back. My home has become so nice because of your help. Please give my warmest greetings to all the friends of the Sunday School Class and the Rev. Dougherty. I will write to him soon and tell him that two CARE packages arrived. I believe the other two will come soon. We are a great family, there is a grandfather and two sisters-in-law and so many dear ones who are hungry, but you know that!

I hope you can read this letter. Many greetings to you all, the best to you and the girls.

With love,

Yours, Leni Schnädelbach and Klaus, Herbert, Gerhard. and Maria

PS. Every day we read the Bible, everyone reads a verse, and we sing a song of Jesus Christ—it would be great if Klaus could read in an English Bible.

CHAPTER FOURTEEN: THE THANK YOU LETTERS...

Leipzig, 1948
Back row: Herbert, grandfather, Paul Schnädelbach, Mother, Klaus
Front row: Maria with favorite skirt and doll sent by Sunday School

Leipzig, May 1, 1948

Dear Mr. Plank,

How happy I was to receive the dear letter from Mrs. Slosson and my thanks to you for the trouble you took to write in German. Maybe it was a good practice to not forget your mother tongue. I have tried to respond in English, but I can imagine, that all of you especially the children will laugh out loud reading my funny writing. I wonder if you all could understand my writing at all. Somethings I could not express correctly, for example that the boys desperately need flannel shirts for the wintertime. We also need clothing for the summertime and night ware, towels and linen, or wool blankets to keep warm. We lost everything and have to start over. There is nothing to purchase here in the stores, maybe some items for outrageous prices.

We miss one item the worst since it was burned, a most important item in our life, a watch. A simple sports watch will do. We would be so grateful.

I hope you are not angry for the many wishes we have, but you wrote to us to let you know—that is what I am doing. Even shoe polish and shoelaces, all these things are missing in our households, sewing yarn, especially black and white mending yarn, so I can alter and fix socks.

We are including you all in our prayers and give thanks to God for touching human hearts to help us.

Our warmest greetings in gratitude,

Yours, Leni Schnädelbach

An original copy of a program that mother performed in with her colleagues. I can still hear her beautiful Alto voice, full of warmth and conviction for the music and the text.

Chapter Fifteen

Looking back now, I am amazed how long it took the mail to get to the USA or back to Germany. The following letter was written by mother on April 26, 1948, and arrived in Temple City, California on June 7. All mail went by ship and railroad. Even the mail to the Western part of Germany took days.

"They open up letters at the post office to see what we are thinking and planning to do," Mother would say. She feared of being spied on by the police as happened to other people she knew. The police used threats and instilled paranoia to keep order and enforce rules. No one was allowed to leave and travel anywhere without first registering with the local police station. Permissions were usually denied. Traveling to the Western part of Germany was strictly forbidden. Visitors from the West could come in for business matters. There was no wish for them to live in the Eastern section given the ongoing Russian occupation, the police control, and the famine. In addition, they brought in much wanted Western currency.

> May 13, 1948
>
> My dear sister Hilde,
>
> You have sent several packages, that all arrived here safely and brought us so much joy! I am really moved that we all are inheriting some nice items from Tante Caroline. I think in times past; we would not have valued it that much. But now, every piece is so welcome. Therefore, I am grateful for all your effort. I also enjoyed your long letter. I am so glad to know how everything turned out, also the information about our brother Friedrich. I hope you and Inge had a few nice days around Pentecost. This year, the weather looks very promising to have a good harvest later this summer.

> I have such good memories of your visit here with us. On May 16th our mother would have been 84 years old—she could still be alive …
>
> My heartfelt greetings and thank you,
>
> Your, Leni

This postcard written by my mother is a good example of how she used a cryptic way of writing to her sister and other family members. I remember their caution when writing anything in detail or giving any information about anybody's past or present activities given the fear of being accused of anti-political or anti-Communist statements or referring to anyone's past activities during the Third Reich. When mother referred to brother Friedrich such precaution was in place since he had been an officer of the Wehrmacht and served as a mayor of Verdun during the German occupation of France. After the war was over, he was later invited back and honored by the French government for having saved and hidden many Jews. Such actions could have cost him his life during the Hitler regime. He was a courageous man and later became the Bishop of the Methodist church even traveled to the Eastern part of Germany because he grew up there and the Government trusted him enough to let him visit the various congregations in East Germany.

* * *

> Leipzig, May 20, 1948
>
> Dear Mrs. Blanche, my dear friend,
>
> Your dear letter was coming to me some days ago. My joy was very great about it. I thank you very much.
>
> Now I can tell you that all your packages are in my hand now, also three of the Care packages, No.11 and 10 arrived yesterday and today. I cannot tell you what my heart would like to tell you to so much goodness of love and sacrifice. It is hard to tell you; my tears would like to come. I only hope that God will bless you all. I think in love of all the sisters of the Sunday School Class and would like to shake hands with each one of them. But it is not possible, so our prayers go to God that he will bless you.

CHAPTER FIFTEEN

My little boy, Herbert is going to the piano, and he plays the hymn, "Nun danket alle Gott" ... ("Now, thank we all our God") every time when the package arrives at our home. Yes, it is coming from our hearts!

I ask you not to worry so much about the butter for us. We are just as happy with the Crisco, which is helping us out just fine. Yes, I know, butter is very expensive, I know it and we are just as happy with Crisco or margarine. You have taken care of us so well, so that we by now are not in desperate need. I was able to help others because so many people are hungry. I am sure you are not upset about this.

I believe that your prayers came along with these packages. The one dated March 13 did not yet arrive. I was deeply sorry about it, and my children and I prayed to God. And now-last week ago—it arrived. Oh, our joy!

Klaus is also suspicious of TB (tuberculosis), but I know, God will help. Yes, milk! If I can tell you, send milk powder, because I can mix it myself as much as I need. This evening we had boiled cacao with milk! And my children! and bread with fat. God thank always.

You have given me a new home; I am very happy about all the fine blankets and towels and ...and...and. Yes, my home was in Breslau. The house is still there, but another family lives there. It was a fine city, our little church is still standing, and all our brothers and sisters of the church have lost everything. I have tried to find them for the last three years, but they are all somewhere in Germany. I have some correspondence with them. I know their needs. but as fast I wrote to them back, in all our needs—God was with us, we have a great Savior! They are all very sad that my husband did not come back from the war. We had a very fine congregation in Breslau, and we all would like to return there, but it is not possible. I hope you can read my letter; my English is not as exactly as I want to say it. My English words are not coming easily.

And to you, my dear Blanche, I want to thank you for all your effort and work you had with packaging the boxes. It is a lot of work that takes time and energy.

We are happy that Margaret is well again, her little picture is right in front of me. With the dolly, "Margaret", Maria is playing all day long.

God's blessing for Marilyn on her wedding, may she be very happy! Also, best wishes to the two persons who helped you.

And now, dear Blanche, I will close my letter with our thanks, our love and our prayers for you, your dear family, and to all the Sunday School Class members.

Always, yours gratefully,
Leni Schnädelbach, Klaus, Herbert, Gerhard, Maria

Leipzig, July 1, 1948

My dear friend,

Your letter came to me. I have received your letter of June 12. I hope you have received my letters. I wrote that all packages are in my hands, only not one of the CARE packages. I have written to my Superintendent, and I hope, I will get it soon. You are so kind to send packages again. I am very glad about it because it is so necessary to have them.

My little Gerhard is in a home for Tbc (tuberculosis). He wrote me today that he gained 3 pounds. I am so glad that he will return on July 31. His lungs are noticeable improved. He was so bad off, I did not believe he would make it. He contracted Tb from malnutrition and extreme stress. During the flight from Schlesien, we experienced extreme cold, hunger and blizzards, then this horrible bombing in Dresden and then the famine. If you, dear people, would not have helped us, Gerhard would not be better by now. It is the milk and the fat that is helping him and all the other children. Both, Klaus and Herbert are also at risk, and I am so grateful for all your help. You write, it is not much, but to us it is very much what you are doing. God may bless you.

It is the milk and the fat, and the fish oil supplements (Lebertran), Oleum jeuris aselli (?) and grape sugar (dextrose), the doctor said we need them; also, some raisins.

I am always embarrassed to ask you for certain items, but you have asked for me to tell you. I also ask for flour and sugar.

CHAPTER FIFTEEN

Today I went to the doctor. I have an inflammation of the gall bladder; it is very painful. The doctor did some X-rays, but I do not know the results yet. Next week, I will know more—I have much pain.

The doctor said, "You must weep three days." But I cannot weep, my tears have dried up since the Dresden night.

No further packages have arrived this week. The monetary reform stopped everything. We hope it will be settled soon.

We enjoyed the pictures of your daughters! We are so surprised and recognize little Margaret. Also, the program of the Sunday School Class party was very interesting. I thank you so very much for everything!

Maria looked at the beautiful daughters you have. Now I will close my letter for today.

Please accept my thanks and our love! Greetings to each of the Sunday School Class friends.

Warmly,

Yours, Leni Schnädelbach and the children

Leipzig, July 9, 1948

My dear friend,

You must think, I have forgotten you, but it is not so. But I was sick, and it is now possible to write you again. My gall bladder was sick—now it is better, and I am glad. My rheumatism in my knees and arms was and is very painful. I have taken some baths in mud treatment, and it is now better. I could not write, and I apologize.

Your packages No. 14 and 15 are in my hands now and our joy was great. Especially mother with the beautiful clothes! They fit me well with some alterations to be done. I am so grateful to you. The hairbrush was a special gift to us and the other household items we needed so much. Ah, and the food items! You know how we need them so desperately. I would like to shake hands with each one of you and thank you for all you have done for us. There are so many things in my home by now, which remind me of you all. God bless you!

Maybe, Blanche, you can read enough German that you are able to read this letter. I believe, if we would ever meet, you would not be able to understand my English. Before the war, we had an English friend of my husband in the home as a visitor. He was able to speak as little German as I speak English. We could not understand each other but laughed a lot.

My dear husband had to work one afternoon, and I wanted to show this friend our castle where a play was being performed. He could not understand what the actors were saying, and I wanted to explain the action to him in English. But he could not understand me, so we just laughed. In the evening, my husband returned, and we sang hymns and read the Gospel of Jesus Christ—we could understand each other! That is it! And it may be like this! We understand each other because we all believe in the same Jesus Christ. I am so happy that I know you also serve him with all your great sacrifices.

Maria started school yesterday and she is a real schoolgirl.

Gerhard was again in a treatment home because of his lung problems. He is much improved. We just must watch out that he does not get sick again. I am so grateful for all the wonderful milk and eggs you sent. Since the time you sent milk and food, the severe hunger is almost gone. It is milk that the children need. In Breslau, we had plenty for them. My heart almost stopped for joy when I saw the wonderful milk. Such a joy and help! We use it sparingly and still have some left. Herbert spent some time during summer vacation in Dresden with my sister-in-law. Klaus was working during the harvest on a farm. Now all four are back with me and I am so happy.

My brother, Friedrich, attended the Methodist General Conference and he told me very much about his voyage. He was very touched by all the love he received.

Now I will close my letter. I hope you are in good health, my dear Blanche and so are your girls, and all the Sunday school class members. God bless you all.

Greetings in love!

Gratefully, Leni Schnädelbach and children

(Received in Temple City on October 11, 1948)

CHAPTER FIFTEEN

* * *

A handwritten postcard, dated July 23, 1948, was written by mother to her sister, Hilde from a care home of the Methodist deaconesses in Kloster Lausnitz/Thűringen. I include it here since she mentioned her poor health and my presence with her during her stay.

> My dear sister Hilde,
>
> I have been here in Kloster Lausnitz for the last 10 days and the treatment is good for me, since my joints and my gall bladder have given me so much trouble. Unfortunately, it is so difficult to get water treatments even as they were authorized by my doctor. Maria is with me, Gerhard is in Pulsnitz. I wonder how you are doing. Many thanks for your letter, I hope you are doing better. Nothing has changed. The currency reform has not much affected us- we already have lost everything, so there was nothing else for us to lose. I have not heard anything form brother, Friedrich.
>
> Greetings, Yours, Leni and Maria

Chapter Sixteen: August 2012

My dear readers,

Thank you for following these detailed letters, mother's sister Hilde and Blanche and mother wrote, but maybe you can see by reading them how we lived during those dark years and her effort to find gratitude and God's assurance in all her grief and suffering.

I have noticed mother mailed her letters in envelopes framed by a black line. Such envelopes were used for death announcements and to be send out by mail. Since everything was so hard to come by including papers, I assume that mother used these envelopes for sending other letters including those to the United States.

Looking through the folder I found a little ring book, which contains the account for each item sent to us by the Sunday School Class documenting the contents of each package with the money value or purchase cost, starting with package No.15.

Package #15, sent the end of June 1948 or Package #16, sent September 2, 1948

- 3 pr. cotton stockings (new)
- 1 night gown (woman's)
- 1 brush   .29
- 2 pr. cotton hose (new) ladies
- 1 brush   .50
- 2 pr. cotton panties (new) ladies
- paper—envelopes + pad
- 2 pair undershirts (new) ladies
- 1 brush   .10
- 1 slip (new)
- 1 Bible   .10
- 1 muffler
- noodles   .28
- 1 can Libby's corn beef hash

- cake mix .25
- 1 can Leser (?) beef and gravy
- whole eggs 1.00
- 1 can Leser meat balls
- whole milk .52
- 1 pr. blue jeans (new) boys
- 1pr. women's shoes .10
- 4 pairs cotton socks (new) boys
- 1# sugar .10
- 1 can cocoa .35
- 1 bar ivory .10
- 1 can tooth powder & 1 toothbrush
- 1 dress .20
- 1 sweatshirt (new) boy
- 1 woman's suit .25
- 1 used sweater (boys) buttons
- 3 woman's dresses .10 @ .30
- 1 tinker toy
- 3 pr. socks .05
- spool thread—hooks + eyes
- 1pair of pants .10
- 1 pair boys pajamas
- 1 boy's shorts
- 3 slips .10
- 1 used suit
- a coin purse .29
- 1 comb, 1 belt—1B –V?
- 1 Crayola
- 1 paint book

Total value: $6.34

- 1 paint brush
- 1 child's scissors
- 1 blouse girl
- 1 bar soap, 1 toy car
- 1 child's purse

Total value: $8.19

The following letter was written by my Mother to her sister Hilde. The sheet is fragile and has holes in it, like the church mice had nibbled off the edges.

> Leipzig, September 14, 1948
>
> My dear Hilde,
>
> My warmest thank you for your letter and the package. The children were thrilled, and the noodles were delicious. I did not pay for the glasses, Mr. Schroeder asks you to send the money to Mr. Alfred Manig, Hamburg 39, Scheffelstrasse 26. I hope you have not bought too much because I have not been able to purchase anything... All is in short supply here, nothing has changed. Thank God we have been taken care off and are moving forward without too many worries.

CHAPTER SIXTEEN: AUGUST 2012

> The children are growing so much and are learning. Klaus is the top student in school and so is Herbert. Maria is now ready for school, and she is so excited. Herbert and Gerhard are saying thank you for all the gifts you have sent them. During the upcoming weeks, I will be busy with singing and performing. Please excuse if I cannot write on a regular basis. It is important for me to do so in order to earn some money.
>
> ...... With this short letter I send warm greetings....
>
> Yours, Leni

* * *

The following letter contains a Christmas card and the following writing send to Blanche of the Sunday School Class in Temple City, California.

> Leipzig, November 19, 1948
>
> My dear Blanche,
>
> A Merry Christmas and a Happy New Year to you, your family, and to all friends of the Sunday School Class! I think of many thanks to you all. You have helped us the past year more than we ever hoped for. I do not believe that we would have survived this year without you keeping us healthy. It is not possible to live without your helping love. God bless you all in your helping love. It is always need and hunger who stand by the door. But you have helped- we can say, "The Lord has done great things for us."
>
> It is a miracle that all the packages are in our hands now (No.16,17,18). There was not one that got lost, or unwrapped, also No.12 and 13. My letters must have gotten lost. They told you that they arrived. Yes, the five bottles of Vitamins! They are particularly good for Tuberculosis, and every day, the children take them. Everything the children need is in them. Many thanks!
>
> We are so deeply sorry for little Margaret. We pray all day for this good child with her many pains. Her little picture stands always on the table. We hope that the great friend of the children will make her healthy again.

The beautiful bride doll, you sent before, should be Maria's Christmas present again. Mother will make her another dress.

And now the Christmas season is here. The children have a great joy about it and my thoughts go back to the time our father was in our home. But God knows all things—he does not make mistakes.

We pray that God will give us blessings for the New Year, for you, and for us. We are God's children, and his love is in the USA and in Europe.

I hope you and your family and your church a wonderful Christmas Day. With many greetings you are always our friend,

Your friends, Leni and the children
(Dated November 19, 1948, and signed personally by us children)

PS. My dear Blanche,

I hope you understand me if I tell you what we need so desperately: soap for laundry, shoe buckles and shoelaces, and coffee. We cannot do our laundry well, our soap is so bad, the linen will turn out gray. It is very hard for me to tell you such things, but I know you are my friend, and you understand me always.

My gall bladder is better.

In love, Yours, Leni

PS2. My dear Blanche,

I thank you for the letter from Superintendent, Mr. Georgi. He is our Superintendent. He is like a father to us. He knows our family has suffered the worst needs and sorrows of all the minister's families in the Middle Conference of the Methodist Church. Our father is the only one of the ministers, who did not come back home from the war. Yes, and we lost our dear home in Breslau.

Dr. Georgi has a good heart, he thinks in love of us. I suppose, he gave you our name.

CHAPTER SIXTEEN: AUGUST 2012

Leipzig, December 14, 1948

My dear sister Hilde,

I am so sorry that you had to wait for a letter from us. Traudel was to tell you about our life and especially about my glasses. It looks like she never stayed with you as planned and you are not up to date. The package we sent came back and I assume you have not heard from us in a while. I am so sorry about that especially during this holiday season when we want to be close to our dear ones.

I am resting in bed again, fell down two days ago and must have some internal injury. The doctor will find out today what I need to do next, hopefully no treatment in the hospital. Most likely it is a bruised or broken rib.

Your Christmas letter with the hair ribbons and the elastics has arrived already and I thank you for all of it. I am so sorry that you must make such sacrifices for us, while I know you have very little yourself. Your kind birthday greetings for me and the warm water bottle arrived here recently. Since I have now two water bottles, I will send one to our sister, Maria. I am sure you won't mind. I am sure she will be glad to have it. The other package with apples and a ball for the children arrived already in addition to two long letters. Traudel was to tell you all about it especially about my glasses. I recently asked for a receipt, but since several offices are involved, it will make it all so complicated. The requested money must be West Mark currency.

We sent you and Inge a small smoky man[34] figure for Christmas to remind you of your old 'Heimat' and bring a sweet scent into your living room. However, it was returned by the local post office. Now we must exchange our love and caring thoughts under the Christmas tree. The children are happy and grateful, and we have enough food for the time being.

Heartfelt Christmas greetings to you and Inge,

Yours, Leni and children

PS. Greetings to Frau Oberin and Gertrud Meyer. Extend to them our thanks for their greetings to us.

---

[34] Incense burner made im Erzgebirge.

* * *

The letter she wrote to Hilde was handwritten on two yellow papers, her handwriting in larger font and much more uneven than her other letters. Maybe she wrote lying down or being uncomfortable. I do remember the time mother had fallen. She fell on the street and was in bitter pain. To see her resting on the sofa in the living room scared me so much, I worried about her leaving for the hospital or even dying. The aunts made her a warm water bottle to put on her chest in order to keep her warm and comfortable. I did not know what to do with a sick mother sleeping on the couch. And it was so close to Christmas! So, I tried to be quiet and watch her sleep.

December 31, 1948

My dear Hilde,

The year is coming to a quiet end and a few hours are left before we move into the New Year. Therefore, we are greeting you warmly since you are the first of us birthday children. We are thinking of you with much love and wish you comfort and joy and confide in our Lord as you move into the future. One of the best experiences of the last year was our reunion although a number of months have passed since then. Time is passing by so fast, but those horrible years have not. In the meantime, I received your letter which I enjoyed so much and arrived quite in time.

CHAPTER SIXTEEN: AUGUST 2012

We had a wonderful Christmas celebration full of joy for the children and happiness. The table was full of goodies, and we did not suffer any hunger. This was so important because Klaus has developed such an appetite, he could eat a whole 3pds loaf of bread in one sitting. So far, the Lord kept helping us, it is impossible to live from the food stamps rationing. You could just starve, although we have now 'free department stores where you can purchase anything for fantasy prices. For example: one piece of cake for 6.00 Mark, white bread 11.00 Mark, heating briquettes 16.00 Mark!!! And so on. We cannot find any words for this and of course, we cannot purchase anything there. It does not bother me that much, it is however very, very sad! That is how it is here!

My injured ribs are slowly healing. I could be up and around at Christmas, even prepared this and that with much effort besides repeated dizziness episodes which gives me the feeling of riding on a merry-go-round. I hope this will pass soon. Therefore, I am careful to leave the house and I am glad that I can be at home. Unfortunately, I missed several opportunities to perform in concerts and I miss the income. Fortunately, Klaus received a half stipend for his school which made me very happy. He is in the meantime half a head taller than I.

Two days before Christmas we received a package from the U.S.A. with a wonderful suit for him for his confirmation at church. It is dark blue and fits perfectly! We also received some more clothing. You know best what that means for us and the four children. I have a warm wool jacket sent from a friend in the US who remembers us from time to time. I found his address in one of the donated jackets and then wrote back to thank him. In that way, we have made a connection. Minna Sanns also has written me so kindly.

It might not be impossible, dear Hilde, that we may see each other next year. Of course, you are invited to Klaus's confirmation although you may not be able to travel here. There is a preliminary plan, I might direct a children's home in the Black Forest. I would be able to resettle there with the children. The other day, the newspaper announced that we "Umsiedler" (resettling refugees) may move to the West with 200kg of luggage per person. All with God's will!

> God bless you, dear Hilde. Maybe you can celebrate your birthday with your daughter, Inge, together.
>
> With warm greetings,
>
> Yours, Leni and the children
>
> Our sister, Mariechen and husband, Karl, were all alone over the Christmas Holiday. Gudrun was in the hospital. I felt so sad for them.

* * *

> Leipzig, January 19, 1949
>
> Dear Mr. Dougherty,
>
> With great joy, No.19 of the packages arrived. I did not expect you sent packages again, because No.16, 17, and18 were such a help to us during the Christmas time. The children were very happy with their gifts, and we had no hunger during this time. The package No. 19 was so special with such fine food and the items we needed so much. I thank you so very much, Mr. Dougherty and all the dear members of your church who helped us so generously. We were very, very happy!
>
> Now the Holiday Season is over, the children are back in school. It was a happy time, we sang all the dear Christmas songs, and our hearts were thankful to God, who has helped us so much during the last year. But we know with your help the children would not be healthy. My little Gerhard with his Tuberculosis of the lung, and now the doctor tells me, "He is better, healthy, but you must be careful!" Yes, the milk, the eggs from you, the Vitamins, this was so wonderful.
>
> I wrote to you before that our church had been burned down on December 1943. Till this day it is not possible to rebuild the church. We hope with the help of God, we will have a church in the future. It is very difficult. The youth and all the people able to help arranged the boulders of the ruins. But we have no nails, no screws, and no glue. These are items we cannot buy. The wood for a roof is here and we would like to build a church next year, but how???

CHAPTER SIXTEEN: AUGUST 2012

We have a new, young minister, and we have faith with him. Our small barrack building is a small substitute church. But we are glad to hear the Gospel of Jesus Christ there.

I hope you had a blissful Christmas time with your family and in your community. Our prayers go to God every day that he will bless you all. I cannot express in writing how grateful I am for your love. I believe you can feel it.

Now, I will stop my letter. My English is so poor, though I hope you can understand me.

With many greetings to all!

Yours, Leni Schnädelbach, Klaus, Herbert, Gerhard, Maria

In a great hurry!

Leipzig, March 18, 1949

My dear sister Hilde,

A warm thank you for your dear letter that arrived today with the 20.00 Marks per your request from Arnstadt! Also, my warmest thanks for that. I will give it to Klaus on his day of confirmation. I feel guilty that you share your small funds with us, well knowing that you have so little yourself. I ask you not to send us any further funds until you are feeling better. Still trouble with my glasses. I cannot tell you how often I have tried to get a receipt. Since I do not know the people and it has gone through different merchants, I have been unable to get a receipt. It is not that I am not trying. I thought back then I could do you a favor in ordering my glasses to help you, because even now we cannot get any new lenses for our glasses. I am embarrassed if the money has not arrived in Hamburg by now, and I will pay you back immediately when I will be near you. Even if it means no use of health insurance coverage. I have tried again for the last few days to request a receipt, but after that I will not try any longer. It is useless.

Our journey will most likely change this May. It is a huge decision, and all the details are not clear yet. But in God's help we will trust. Right now, I

> do not know much more, but it sounds quite good. It is a Children's Home and Sanatorium in Bergzabern/Pfalz for 30 children as well as a retreat home. I have not seen a picture yet, but the area must be beautiful. A small house for the director, the cook, etc. will be build, it is under construction. Schools are located about 10km away in Landau. I have no further information. It is a partnership project with the Swiss Methodist church. That is all I know by now. I wonder what the salaries for children's home directors this time are. How much is there to add for cost of living, laundry etc.? After bitter inner conflicts and struggle I am resolved and look forward to it.
>
> For today greetings to you and Inge!
>
> Your sister Leni and children

This is the first mentioning of the town of Bergzabern in the Western section of Germany, in the Palatinate area, south of Landau and close to the border to Alsace. It turned out to be our new Heimat, but I do not want to jump ahead.

> Leipzig, March 21, 1949
>
> My dear sister Hilde,
>
> Our best Easter greetings from all of us to you and Inge! How good it is to know of the risen Christ who continues to give us strength. I wanted to write you sooner and know you have waited for a letter from me. I had a bad conscience for not writing sooner because I still have your belated birthday present here, a silver pin (800). Maybe I can give it to you in person soon. I still hope that you can come to Maya's silver wedding anniversary. I would be so very happy to see you again. However, the travel would be so arduous given the crowded trains. Of course, you could stay with us. Since March 1, I have been able to rent another room where the two older boys can sleep. This is a great help. My small home is slowly taking shape with a few personal items. Two weeks ago, I purchased for an incredibly high price a desk. After Easter I will receive a combination credenza piece of furniture for the living room. In time, I am more organized and settled. I would be so happy if you could see it all in person.

CHAPTER SIXTEEN: AUGUST 2012

The children are growing up so fast and you do not know them. Klaus is taller than I, Herbert is just a bit behind in size. Gerhard is still quite fragile and restless. Maria has grown quite tall and still not in school, but a very sweet and tender little mother. This little girl is like a ray of sunshine, a small songbird. Today the little ones are in bed with a bad cough. It is Palm Sunday. Next year (Sunday?), Klaus will be confirmed. He looks like a young man, so tall and slender. I am so grateful that God continues to give us food, I would not know how to feed the children without it. It is a blessing. We never had any relatives in the USA and still helps comes from there. Also, friends of Herbert in Switzerland have cared for us and remembered us. All of this has been a sign of God's grace because we have not earned it. At other times, we have to feel the deep suffering and experience the need. But then, we move forward with God's help. We even have clothing for all of us—I am so surprised. We used to have absolutely nothing left. Now we all have underwear and clothing. A few weeks ago, I received a wonderful winter coat from our minister's wife, Frau Bierwirth, (born Rohr) with a real fur collar! Even our superintendent is doing what he can. All by the grace of God!

I loved your last letter, so interesting to hear from you and Inge. I was glad to hear that Lydia is doing better. Can she write openly how everything is going? We also are tense about the coming weeks. Everything is up in the air and let us hope!!! We received a newsletter from Paulus and family. They were able to return to their home.

Kurt (Mariechen's husband) was here for the Annual Trade show, the Messe. He looked so gaunt like so many other men here. Mariechen has a round, swollen face, maybe water retention. She spent just two days here not so long ago and rested a bit and then looked better. She always works like a wild woman. I cannot do that anymore; my strength has decreased. I still have trouble with my gallbladder.

My dear Hilde, God be with you! Maybe we can see each other in the near future. Please do be mad with me. Please take greetings to your colleagues.

In love,

Yours, Leni and children

RETURN TO LEIPZIG

* * *

Leipzig, May 5, 1949

My dear Blanche,

You must have thought all packages got lost. But it is not so. Those packages came finally to us, but after a very long time through Poland. They did not arrive until March 22, but 6 weeks later. But it is good now, they are in our hands. At first came No.20, then No.22, then No. 21. The content was complete, and all items were in it. This was a great joy again. The milk is the best for the children, every day now, they receive a little milk. They always ask for milk—even the big boys. Klaus likes to scoop his milk powder with a spoon and then he likes to eat it ....! So, does Maria. Mother says, "Children, watch your stomachs!"

Yes, my dear Blanche, you have sent again what we need most. The detergent soap! You did not know what a bar of soap means to us ... and the coffee. The children did not drink it, but their mother likes it very much. And there are people who like to buy the coffee from me, and I can buy potatoes for one whole month for all of us. Potatoes for the children and for me! This is wonderful and I am sure you cannot believe this. But it is true!

The postmaster told me that packages arrived now that were sent from the USA last September. Today the radio announced that the blockade of Berlin is over. We hope that letters and packages can arrive here sooner.

You wrote about a young man who was in Berlin this summer. I believe everything he told you is true. It makes us weep and I believe, you weep too, if you hear what we all have experienced especially us women. We cannot write it down, but this is only one of millions. But we know: God is greater than all our sorrow, tears, and hunger. His help is so wonderful! How often we are missing something and before we have prayed about it, it is in our hands. We have a great father in heaven.

With much gratitude, we think of you, dear Blanche and all the dear sisters of the Sunday School Class. We feel your love and believe Jesus Christ told you first what we needed. The need is still great here, but you always send us what we need at the time: milk, butter, you know. It is wonderful and we are so glad.

CHAPTER SIXTEEN: AUGUST 2012

Last Palm Sunday, Klaus was confirmed. This was a beautiful day for our family. How special it would have been if our dear father could have blessed him. Now he must give his blessings from heaven. I hope that Klaus will give his heart to Jesus Christ, he is his child, I know.

Now the springtime is here, the winter was not as cold. We had only a little snow. This was very good for us. I do not believe we had a worse winter as in 1946/47. Many people died or starved quietly in their beds. With your help it was possible for us to live.

And now from our church life: We are helping, all the members of the church, old and young to rebuild our church. Some clean stones or transport the dirt. Now the roof is on the structure, we are so very glad. But now we need nails and screws for the windows and for the doors and glue.

We are very glad, that the church is growing. God bless our work.

You can send nails in a package by itself as much as 10 kg, or some with other items. If you just send the nails, please send them to:

Pastor Hans Witzel
Leipzig S3
Kant Strasse 12 III.

We cannot send letters by airmail, but the letter paper is fine. I am glad about it. It is such great help.

Klaus birthday: 2. October 1934
Herbert birthday: 6. August 1936
Gerhard birthday: 26. August 1939
Maria birthday: 30. September 1941
Mother birthday: 22. November 1903

Gerhard is much better, the Vitamins and the medicine from Mrs. Wheeler were very fine. Through the milk the children grow. I do not know if the children had survived, especially Gerhard was so very ill. And now he is a happy boy always cheerful.

It is time to stop my writing. The children are sleeping in their beds, and it is time for me to go to sleep. My health is not the best. I broke two ribs before Christmas and my back is painful. The doctors give me massage and light box treatment. I hope it is better in the near future.

> I was glad to hear that Margaret is doing better. Maria is sending greetings. The food situation has improved.
>
> With all good wishes for your family and all the dear members of the Sunday School Class, to Mr. and Mrs. Dougherty.
>
> In deep gratitude, Leni Schnädelbach, Klaus, Herbert, Gerhard, Maria

Leipzig, 1949, Klaus' Confirmation:
Back row: Grandfather: Paul Schnädelbach, Elfriede Schnädelbach, Kurt Lange, Mariechen Lange, Klaus, ?, Mother, Erich Zahn, Lottel Schnädelbach
Front row: Maria, Gerhard, Herbert, Liesel Zahn.

Klaus' confirmation began with a festive morning service in church with the confirmands reciting scriptures and hymn texts by heart, answering statement of faith articles, and speaking in front of the congregation. I was so proud

CHAPTER SIXTEEN: AUGUST 2012

of him. He wore a dark suit and a bow tie. Aunts and uncles came to visit. Three of my father's sisters came, so did Mother's sister, Mariechen and Kurt from Dresden, and aunt Elfriede, the widow of my uncle Karl Schnädelbach, who had been killed during the war. I am still wondering how my mother managed to serve food that day. I am sure she traded some of the care package items for fresh bread and coffee. For super that day, we each had a plate of two slices of bread next to a slice of blood sausage, cold cuts and liverwurst. It was a feast day indeed! Klaus received a number of presents, a stack of sheet music for piano and organ, books, and a wristwatch. Mother was so glad to have a family celebration together with loved ones, a desperate effort to claim our survival and repeat traditions of faith and milestones of growing up.

Klaus' Confirmation, Leipzig, 1949:
Back row: Klaus, Herbert
Front row: Maria, Mother, Gerhard

My brother, Herbert, tried to write a letter in English to the Sawyer family. He was 12 years old at the time and had some English lessons at school.

RETURN TO LEIPZIG

Leipzig, May 5, 1949

Dear Anne!

I thank you for your kindly letter. The picture of Margret is very fine. You are also in my age?

In our school class is it all right. In our English-course have we the colors learnet. We have also Russian. We have a very good Russian teacher.

I like to study music. The piano and violin play I.

I learn languages very willingly and with many pleasures.

I have the books very gladly. The books from Mark Twain, Freytag, Loens, and Karl May. Please write me, what for books you gladly read.

Many greets, from Herbert

* * *

Leipzig, June 28, 1949

My dear sister Hide,

Thank you for your nice letter. I should have answered it a long time ago. I can let you know that we all will leave Leipzig in August or September although I have no official papers to leave. I met our brother Friedrich and Mr. Schiele at the Annual Conference and was able to discuss more details. It is true, our little house is being built and after our arrival, the children's home will be under construction. All the details should be decided on when I get there. We cannot move there until our little house is completed, where else should we live? It makes no sense to hire someone yet for the children's home, so we must wait. Nobody knows how long all this will take. How we all should travel to the West is total mystery to me and I must trust in God to find a way. There are absolutely no transfer passes available between the occupational zones.

Otherwise, nothing here has changed. Some items are available without rationing stamps such as potatoes, but cheese and cottage cheese is not available. At this time, we ran out of potatoes and the cupboard is empty. I am supposed to get a knapsack full of potatoes today. The

CHAPTER SIXTEEN: AUGUST 2012

> situation regarding food and supplies is hopeless. Imagine, you can buy everything in certain Free stores without rationing stamps! But nobody is able to purchase there, it is too expensive. A piece of cake costs 2.80 Marks, shoes costs 240.00 Marks. If we would not have help from you and the USA, we would not be able to live. We are experiencing a really bad time. For today, please accept this short letter. We are sending greetings to you and Inge,
>
> Yours, Leni and children

These Free Department stores appeared in the city, filled with all available goods stocked from the West. With this, the political propaganda portrayed the economic recovery in the Russian occupied section of Germany as fully recovered while nobody, except party officials and government employees of high communist status, could afford to shop there. Political compliance and submission to the Communist ideals were rewarded with money, food supply and later, vacation resorts by the Baltic Sea while the rest of the people were starving and humiliated.

> Leipzig, July 8, 1949
>
> My dear sister Hilde,
>
> In order to alleviate your worries, I want to let you know of the arrival of your noodle package today. All was intact. We all were so excited since all of all like to eat noodles so very much. I am sure they will look white when cooked, something we do not have here.
>
> I am so sorry that I did not acknowledge your beautiful Christmas-Pentecost or Pentecost-Christmas package. The children were jubilant when we opened it. Especially Gerhard was fascinated with the pocketknife. The other children were so happy and especially Maria when she shared her goodies with all of us. Her package was marked "Schulspeisung."[35] Can that be true?

---

[35] 'Schulspeisung' was a program organized by the American Marshall Plan and the Quakers to feed German children a full meal in school. I remember it well: hot oatmeal with cinnamon sugar, noodle soup, stew, bread, sweet rice with peaches, hot chocolate milk, etc.

Ah, we were all so happy and thank you all so much. Everything looked so nice.

Since a few days ago, we can by vegetable without rationing cards and even fruit is available.

I bought the following items:

- 10 pds cabbage for 7.00 Marks
- 10 pds Rhubarb for 3.00 Marks
- 5 pds red currants for 8.00 Marks
- 2 pds cherries for 3.20 Marks
- 2 pds cottage cheese for 1.10 Marks
- Three bunches of carrots for 4.05 Marks

This adds up to a total of 26.35 Marks. To pay for all this leaves me nothing for the rest of the week. Unbelievable prices! We can try to purchase these items maybe one time, but never again. However, this is the whole idea to keep our living standard as low as possible. Luckily, we received some fat products we can use with so much else.

Our little house should be ready to move in at the end of August of September. I will plan all the details for the Children's Home when we get there. The news from Emmi and Walter are devastating. I am so deeply sad about it.

My very best wishes for your vacation. How much I would like to just rest without pressure. Greetings to Inge and again, many, many thanks for all you do for us.

Warmly,

Yours, Leni, and the children

Leipzig, July 30, 1949

My dear sister Hilde,

A warm thank you for your nice package—it arrived all intact. Please do not send any more packages. We will start our vacation trip[36] very soon.

---

[36] She wrote "vacation trip" in order to disguise our illegal leaving for the West

CHAPTER SIXTEEN: AUGUST 2012

The children can travel to Frankfurt with an inter-zone bus if we have a resident note is available. We will do this as soon as possible. The children will have to stay with different people until the little house will be finished. I already wrote to brothers Paulus and Friedrich, and to my friend, Mrs. Peiter. I will take Maria with me to Bergzabern where I have rented a furnished room until the house is finished. Everything is getting more complicated, but with God's help it will work out. I am seriously planning. In two days, Gerhard and Klaus will travel to Dresden for a vacation, the other start will be around August 20th. I am not clear how my journey will lead me.

Warmest greetings for today with many thank you for all your help.

Leni and the children

PS. If I leave illegally, I will try to come to you first. I will not be able to receive a passport, I tried all I could.

*　*　*

Leipzig, August 8, 1949

My dear friend Myrtle in Amerika,

Two letters from you are in my hands, a very nice congratulation for the birthday, August 6th, and a package. This all was a great joy for us, and I thank you very much for all the love you give us. I was very happy that you wrote to me about you, your family, your little girls. It is so nice that I know you, it is like sister to sister. Jesus Christ is a great Master, the brother for all people and we are sisters and brothers in Him. Now I can tell you that the package from June 13 we received. There was not a number on it, the paper was gone, only parts of it still there. The content was in it and all things were fine, milk, cacao, Dextropur, coffee, flower, corned beef and another can beef. So also, the soap, a pair of hoses and shoelaces. We were very very glad about all, and we thank you very much. The coffee I have sold, because I can buy anything—potatoes, flour. We can buy it all in Free department store hall, but it is so expensive that we cannot buy it. Now I can sell the coffee that is my help. It is always still, we cannot live without help, all of it is so very costly when we like to buy anything without the *Lebensmittel*/food rationing papers.

We are so glad that Maria receives every day one cup of milk. But I hope, all this hardship is going to end. Please do not send to me any more packages until I send you my new address. We shall go to another city, and I will write to you all the information when we are in the new city.

I hope the other packages you sent will arrive soon. I will write to you when they are in my hands. It is a wonderful to be led by our father in the Heaven. He will give us a new home, we cannot believe it, but it is so. We are very glad and happy about it.

On August 6th was Herbert's Birthday. I give him your congratulations and he was very happy and gives you many thanks. He is 13, Maria's Birthday is September 30th, but she will find your congratulations.

Klaus and Gerhard are in Dresden, visiting a sister of my husband, who likes the boys very much. I hope they return tomorrow, then Herbert will go to Dresden. It was a wonderful city, now—only stones and ruins are left. Only the suburbs are still standing.

My dear Myrtle, please give many greetings and thanks to all sisters of your Sunday School Class. I will write to Blanche when I am at the new place. I know you all, my dear friends, would have a great joy.

But I am so sorry you cannot read my letter. I cannot write so well in English as my heart would like to do it. But I hope you can understand it a little bit.

So, I will stop now. God bless you all and bless your good deeds. To Mr. Dougherty many greetings!

In love, Leni Schnädelbach
with Klaus, Herbert, Gerhard, and Maria

Chapter Seventeen

My dear patient and faithful readers,

You know about our illegal flight from Leipzig to the Western section of Germany during the summer of 1949. Our goodbye from Grandfather was painful, tearful, and forever. Even I knew that at age 7 when he stood with us on the platform of the train station in Leipzig at the end of September. We could not express our deep feelings of sadness and sorrow because some police guard may become suspicious of us leaving for good and call the authorities. It was a quiet and almost sacred good-bye. No loud promises to "come back soon", no long suggestions for where we would go and when we would be there. "God be with you, Leni!" he said and looked at me with tears in his eyes.

He wore his old dark suit for the occasion. It fit him too loosely now from all the times of hunger and sorrowful waiting and bearing the losses of more family members and a misguided nation. He had lost so much weight. Mother and I knew he was not totally left alone after our departure. He stood there next to his daughter, Lottel, waiving his handkerchief for a long time. I can still see him standing there on platform # 1 under the huge clock after the train had slowly left the train station. I waved back as much I could until the train turned, and the walls blocked my view. All I knew was that we would not be able to visit him in the future ever again. We were fleeing the Russian Zone for good, and my three brothers were already in the Western part of Germany and would be waiting for us at my uncle's house. What if we would never see them again? Get stuck at the border crossing or be caught before we even got there, following my goodbye to my school principal the day before, "We will be leaving for the

West…" My mother overheard my words when she picked me up at school that day and was terrified. She was so upset with me that she did not speak to me for a whole day, hurrying around the flat to stuff the last few items into her bag and our suitcase. We had to leave as fast as possible before the local police who were on the lookout for people leaving illegally and could arrest us. There was no going back now, and grandfather's blessings had to be his last gift for all of us.

While I have written before in my book, *Return to Dresden*, in more detail how my mother and I crossed the border through the night in late September 1949, many people have asked me how my brothers escaped the Russian occupied section of Germany. They traveled alone without an adult, and they told me of their memories. Klaus was 14 at the time, Gerhard was 11, Herbert was 13.

Klaus remembered, "Our exit from the Russian Zone was possible through a program that allowed children to visit their relatives in the West for a summer vacation.

"Gerhard and I took a bus to Hannover and then went on by train to Hamm. We had to wait at the train station all night before we could travel on to Neheim. I think we had five West Marks with us." He paused for a while. His voice quivered ever so slightly as he continued.

"Now looking at the experience, this must have been extremely stressful for our mother. Our family was torn apart, Gerhard and I were already in the Western section of Germany under Allied occupation while you and our mother were still in the Eastern Russian occupied section, in Leipzig, with no official permission to leave. She took a great risk by fleeing."

I could sense his emerging feelings of dread and relief but did not want to probe his thoughts any further. This was his story and he needed to tell it his way, brief and focused of our mother. I gladly respected his memory, well knowing that there was much more to be told like reading between the lines of a poem.

Brother Herbert told me not long ago the following details about his escape to the Western part of Germany. It was hard for him to talk about his memories given the experience and feelings he could not easily put into words.

In August 1949, following the Annual Trade Show in Leipzig, someone in the Methodist Church offered my mother an official one-way return ticket to Frankfurt to the Western Section of Germany. Herbert had just turned 13. He soon left in a hurry, alone, with a small suitcase, his violin, and a coat. He wore

CHAPTER SEVENTEEN

a Trade Show badge. His wallet contained 20 Pfennige, about one Mark. The train traveled through the night.

"When we got to the border, at midnight, the Russian soldiers entered our compartment.

"Let me see your violin," one of them ordered loudly in broken German. I opened my violin case and he continued, "Can you play something?" I refused and remained silent.

Finally, after staring at me, he mumbled. "How should I alone understand this?"

"I have never made any sense out of his comment but remember it just like that. Nothing further happened. After checking my papers and those of the other travelers, the soldiers left the compartment slamming the doors. When I arrived in Frankfurt the next morning, I took the streetcar No. 2 to Ginnheim and arrived at our Uncle Friedrich's house."

Nobody picked him up because no one was allowed to know about his exit time, the date, and the train ride.

He paused a while and continued.

"I never understood why they sent me away after one week to a farm with a mill, the Hardmühle, in Kandel. Maybe they did not have time or room for me. Cousin George had showed me his motorcycle and how to fill it with gasoline and make it go. Uncle Friedrich did give me 20.00 Marks when I left."

A bitter silence followed, and I waited for him to go on.

"I was expected to help on the farm but could hardly understand their dialect.

"Oh yes, they spoke a different dialect from Saxony where we came from." I commented.

"For sure, they made fun of me, 'You olde Saxen!' they said and laughed out loud."

"But they were kind to me and tried to help me."

Chapter Eighteen

My dear readers,

Now back to mother's account of our arrival in the Western part of Germany, Bergzabern. I know some of you have memories of that town when we visited my mother much later. It seemed to me a more peaceful place, much safer than the ruined apartment block in Leipzig where we had lived for four years. We could go outside, play on the street, and even take walks into the nearby forest.

She keeps writing to her sister, Hilde Alrutz.

> October 10, 1949
>
> My dear Hilde,
>
> I know you are waiting for a letter from me. We have arrived last Thursday here in Bergzabern. We had a nice visit with Traudel, spent last Wednesday through Saturday in Frankfurt and from October 1 through the 5th in Neheim with brother Paulus. What a wonderful reunion! I am so grateful to have the children all together again and well off. We arrived here on October 6th and found a warm welcome in our new quarters. We can relax finally although every beginning is very difficult.
>
> Bergzabern is located near the rolling hills. The air is clear, and the forest begins next to the construction site of the Children's Home. The view from there is just beautiful. Only the little house should be finished soon, so we can move in before the cold weather arrives. I will make arrangements with the schools tomorrow. The boys will be able to start school very soon and that will be so great. All this will resolve itself soon.

> I already received some of our packages with our household items. I cannot ever thank you enough for all your help during the last few years. The days with you were the most special ones and relaxing ones of my journey. Warm greetings to Inge! I am so glad to have met her again after all these years. If she cannot get an internship, she can come here. The Children's Home will be very nice. Greetings also to Frau Oberin and all those who still remember me.
>
> With much love,
>
> Yours, Leni and the children

* * *

Now back to the letters to the members of the Sunday School Class in Temple City, CA.

> October 26, 1949
>
> My dear Blanche in America,
>
> It has been a long time since you have heard from me. My dear, it was a slow and treacherous trip to come to this new city. We do not reside any longer in the Russian zone. Since the beginning of October, we now live in the French occupied zone. Our Father in Heaven is a wonderful father, our life is in his hands.
>
> The Hilfswerk (Social Services Division) of our church will build here a home for children, and I will take on the administration of it. The first children will come next spring and there is much to do to get it all organized. I must purchase beds, bed linen, and so on. It is a wonderful job for me.
>
> We are so very glad to be here. It is possible here for the children to go into a good school without the Russian indoctrination. They are very happy. I hope you are not angry at me that I could not write you of my plans from Leipzig. It had to be a secret and it was very difficult to get out.
>
> During the last week in Leipzig, I received a package from you, dated August 12.

CHAPTER EIGHTEEN

It was very special to receive it and a great joy for all of us. Please, my dear, give my heartfelt thanks to all the members of the Sunday school class. I did not find a name as a sender, just the Methodist Church. So, I will write you and you can pass on my gratitude. I am thinking of Mrs. Unfriend (?) I hope that God will help her in the next weeks.

I hope you are in good health. My boys must now learn French instead of Russian. Here are good schools.

Since 1944 it is the 5th city we have moved to, and I hope this will be our new home. Without your help we would not have survived, especially our Gerhard. He is very fragile, but his TB is now gone—with your help! I Leipzig we were always very hungry, but your packages were the way out of our deep need. I know, our Father in Heaven will reward you for your kindness.

I will stop my letter. We are confederates in Jesus Christ. In love and gratitude always yours,

Leni Schnädelbach

October 26, 1949

My dear Blanche,

I want to add a few comments in German because I cannot express myself that well in English and I hope you find someone to help you translate my writing.

Well, we are finally out of the Russian zone and have arrived in a city within the French zone. It was a treacherous and very difficult escape for all of us. Now, we have arrived here and are very happy. We must start all over again and want to establish a new home here. It is wonderful that we were able to bring many of the wonderful things you sent us. They help us to feel more at home. Everything is still very expensive, and we cannot purchase many items we would need. We need many items to furnish our place. But we trust God to help us as he has done so in the past. We are so glad to be here. The children are able to attend a good school without political propaganda. Oh, I am so relieved about it! This was my deepest worry.

> Gerhard will most likely be totally healthy here. The children's home I will be administering, will have children who need special care, for those that were undernourished and in poor health. We hope the home will be completed in the spring of 1950. It will be funded by our Methodist's Hilfswerk and your generosity. God may bless the construction of this home and help many children that need health and care. I hope to send you some picture soon.
>
> I hope you all are healthy. We can finally rest up from the hardship of the Eastern section of Germany.
>
> God bless you all for all your help you have given us.
>
> Your friend, Leni Schnädelbach

* * *

In October 1949, we all were finally reunited in our new 'Heimat,' a small town called Bergzabern. We were temporarily housed in Frl. Gerda Kitzmann's house on Gartenstrasse, because she owned a home with several floors and had been asked to take us refugees in.

Another family lived upstairs, the Maurer's, with Almut, Heidrun and their mother. All eight of us had invaded Frl. Kitzmann's home and she was not amused by so much commotion. Next to the house, she had tended a vegetable garden and told us right away not to run through and step on her plants. A small wooden shed to the right was filled with piles of firewood, and a white painted pagoda to the left was reserved for Sunday afternoon coffee time only.

"You can play on the street," she said.

I loved her striped cat, Biewele, who was allowed to sit on the kitchen table during dinner and ate from her plate. He licked lustily along the rim of her plate as Frl. Kitzmann, or 'Tante Gerda,' we were allowed to call her soon, put pieces of food there for him; sometimes she even pre-chewed them for him especially larger chunks of meat.

My mother bit her tongue in protest to such bad table manners and looked not amused. Gerhard and I giggled and tried not to look at each other. I found the cat's presence on the table quite alright and enjoyed her licking of the plate

CHAPTER EIGHTEEN

and her loud chewing of the morsels with her open mouth, something I would have never been allowed to do.

"We shared the kitchen and all mealtimes, but we were able to eat until we were full," mother said quietly later.

Fräulein Gerda Kitzmann's house on Gartenstrasse. In Bergzabern, 1949.

We settled in, started school, and made friends in the neighborhood. Frl. Kitzmann had a parlor room that was off limits for all of us kids, but when Christmas came, we celebrated Christmas Eve in Frl. Kitzmann's parlor with a decorated tree, candles and presents. I missed being back in Leipzig with grandfather and my aunts. I missed the church and my friends on the street. I knew they missed us too. But I was glad that we had a warm kitchen and food to eat, and grandfather would have wanted that for us too.

RETURN TO LEIPZIG

Bergzabern, Pfalz, October 28, 1949
Gartenstrasse 375 I

My dear sister, Hilde,

I am so grateful and happy for your last letter. Also grateful for all your wishes for our future here. We have slowly adjusted to our new life after four full weeks. The three boys passed the exams for secondary education, these problems have resolved already. They have to study French very hard to catch up. Thank God, they are all bright boys and study well. Herbert jumped one grade and is has not lost one school year in his placement. Slowly our problems find a solution with God's help. Our little house has now a roof and we can walk inside the house from one room to the next. I am still in shock to imagine that we will be moving into a home. It is like a dream come true, I had dreamt for my children for a long time. Now it will come true. The location is wonderful, the air so clean. The children are developing an enormous appetite and thank God, I can meet their hunger. Milk, butter, and sugar are still rationed, but everything else is not restricted for purchase. I cannot count the breads I have bought and gulped down. The days are passing by so fast we are busy with school and homework. Maria has two times weekly school in the afternoon, and she is not happy about it.

I am pleased to hear that Walter has found his way back after such a difficult time. I am sure a way will be found for Albert. Please extend my warm greetings to Inge. I am so pleased that I could reconnect with her in person. You must be so proud of her. How was the 'ball' in Hofgeismar? For today warmest greetings to you and all that remember me.

Greetings,

Leni and the children. Enclosed please find the 4.00 Mark, I owe you.

Bergzabern, December 12, 1949

My dear Hilde,

Warmest thanks for your nice package for my birthday and all the good wishes. I was so happy to hear from you and all the latest news. We are already in the middle of the Advent Season. Time has passed by so fast.

CHAPTER EIGHTEEN

> Hard to believe that we are already here for 9 weeks and we have to be patient before we can move into the little house. The water and electricity connection is very difficult. It will take several weeks before all this can be done.
>
> How are you? I am sure your Advent Season is wonderful, but you are always so busy. Is Frau Oberin back? How is she doing? I am sure all is so interesting and stressful. The children are so stressed with all their studies, but they are sending greetings. Maria is sending greetings to Inge.
>
> Warmest greetings, Leni

When looking at the postcard mother sent to her sister Hilde, I notice the regular 10 Pfennige stamps of the Rheinland-Pfalz region and an extra small blue stamp that reads: *Notopfer 2Pfennige, Berlin Steuermark,* a special stamp with a charge for the city of Berlin and its much-needed recovery from the war years following the devastating destruction in 1945.

Chapter Nineteen

Dear readers,

Just going over these letters to mother's sister, Hilde, to Blanche or Lillian stir up much anxiety and relief. While having left the Eastern section of Germany with all its terror, dark nights, worries about food or coal, and a government employee teaching us Russian songs and commanding us to copy sentences from the blackboard, the new 'Heimat' seemed like an idyllic place with forests, historic castles, a quiet street to play on, friends to talk to and a kind 2nd grade teacher, Frau Schaefer.

Again, we lived in tight quarters and in the same house with Fräulein Kitzmann, a grumpy lady we had never met before. People spoke a different dialect there and we sounded funny to them. We were the children of the "refugee woman." Mother did not care much about what people said about her. She was so busy and worried about the construction site, the building permissions, the workers, and their beer supply, and how soon the winter storms would put a stop to the whole project. She also worried about our schooling. It was difficult to be a family. But we tried. A small Methodist church in town offered a community for support and prayer on Sunday evenings. Pastor Mann, his wife and their helper, Elisabeth, had fled at the end of the war from Hungary, the Batchka, and supported us. They invited us for Sunday coffee hour, and I remember the delicious peach-crème Torte served on fine China. Evening services in a small hall were mandatory and brother Gerhard and I giggled and poked each other when Pastor Mann prayed with a loud monologue, shouting at God about sacrificing his son on the cross for our salvation—even on Christmas Eve! He was already way ahead into Lent and Holy week, and we were still waiting for the Christ child to bring us presents that night with "Stille Nacht, Heilige Nacht…," gifts wrapped in special paper, nutcrackers and sweet goodies, Christmas tree with glowing candles and happy songs ….

* * *

Grandfather wrote the following letter to my mother three months after our escape to the West of Germany.

> December 28, 1949
> Leipzig
>
> My dear Leni,
>
> …. Otherwise, we are doing fine. There were no extra food supplements for the Christmas season. However, Elfriede (his daughter-in-law) and Zahn's (his daughter and husband in Dresden) thought of me, especially on my birthday and so did my previous accountant, who brought me a jar of strawberries and cherries. These gifts made the Holidays somewhat special.
>
> For the last few months, I am unable to attend the worship services on a regular basis. I do not feel safe walking on the street. I wanted to attend an evening service on Sunday, December 4. I was already on Bayer and Arndt Strasse when I fell due to a strong windstorm. My good coat was drenched wet in a rain puddle and my hat flew off; I could not retrieve it.
>
> I had to stop singing in the two choirs at church, nor could I go and attend the Christmas Eve Vesper, or the Children's Fest. Otherwise, I have no complaints, I have a good appetite, and my sleep is good. I feel general weakness and dizziness when walking on the street and then I have tremors in my right arm, which make it hard for me to write.
>
> With many warm greetings and a heartfelt 'God bless you'!
>
> Your father and Opa,
> Paul Schnädelbach. I hope you can read my handwriting.

Christmas did pass and mother managed to give us all a warm and loving feeling despite Fräulein Kitzmann's grumpy attitude. A photo below says it all. Klaus experimented with a new camera and a flashlight which made us all look

CHAPTER NINETEEN

in shock. That special Christmas Eve, we were allowed to go into her parlor—just for once. She brought her cat, Biewele, and I was so pleased feeling some peace on earth which included the animals. She even smiled ... a Christmas miracle, indeed.

Christmas 1950, in Bergzabern.
Front row: Mother, Maria, and Gerhard.
Back row: Klaus, Frl. Kitzmann with Kitty Biewele and Herbert

Now read up on mother's update on our life and the progress of the Children's Home in Bergzabern, West Germany.

Bergzabern, January 4, 1950

My dear sister Hilde,

My very best wishes for your birthday with God's blessings. May the Lord be with you and give you strength for all your challenges in your life. Most of all, do not worry so much! Thank you for all your wishes for the New Year. May all those wishes would come true. Your wonderful package for Christmas brought all of us such joy; it was too much. Such a slip I used to war as a young thing! Thank you for all your love! We celebrated a very nice and harmonious Christmas. The children were so happy although not all wishes could be met. Nevertheless, our joy was great.

Finally, yesterday we celebrated Richtfest, completing the roof on the Children's Home. The city officials attended, and the celebration was very special. We celebrated in the local restaurant with brats and wine. We are so grateful that we have come that far. It will be so nice. They are working on putting in the heating system.

Enclosed please find a picture of our family celebration done with flashlight in Frl. Kitzmann's festive Christmas parlor. It looked so wonderful. I am sure you will celebrate when Inge arrives next Sunday. How special that Traudel can be with you. Please extend my warmest greetings to all your colleagues and Frau Oberin.

May God bless you and with warm greetings,

Yours Leni and children

Christmas, 1949, (Klaus said, "A real flashlight picture").

CHAPTER NINETEEN

Bergzabern/ Pfalz
Gartenstrasse 375 I
January 6, 1950

My dear friends in America,

What a great joy to receive your wonderful letter from Mrs. Boek even written in German.

It is always a great joy when I hear from all of you. We have never seen each other, but I feel we know each other and understand each other in love. Your love and care have sustained me during many difficult hours of the last few years. What would have happened to us without your love? We all would have been severely ill or would have perished. But you carried us through these difficult years. Many times, a package from you arrived just at the moment, when I asked God how he would help us today because there was nothing left in the pantry. Those experiences strengthened my faith.

Finally, package No. 27[37] arrived here and brought us great joy. The package was in one piece and the content was untouched. You thought so carefully about each item we need. Many, many thanks for your care and love. The packages arrive much faster now since we are in the Western part of Germany including the CARE packages. Package No. 26 arrived in August, and I wrote you a letter. Hopefully, it did not get lost.

I am so pleased that you continue to care for the Children's Home. We can only complete it with help of our friends in the USA. Several congregations are willing to help complete this home in order to care for the many malnutritioned children. We need urgently such a home for these children because they suffered so much during this insane war.

You can send money (Dollars) to the following address:

Mr. Director, Dr. F. Sigg, Zurich, Badenerstrasse 60, Switzerland with the designation: Kinderheim, Bergzabern.

---

[37] Package #27 contained these items: 2#powdered milk 1.20. 2# sugar .22. ½ # semi-sweet baker's chocolate .35. ½# can dried eggs 1.15. 1# Crisco .31. 1Package sweatshirts .28. 1package Hydro Pura .26. 2packages soap 30. 1 ½# prunes .43. 1bar Ivory soap .13. 1# dates .29. 2 pair used wool sox .20. 1 child's dress used 1.00. Total value: $6.12

You may want to designate your contribution for a special project such as a sewing machine, or ironing machine, or tableware or dishes. We would look at these items and remember where they came from. The money needs to be sent to Dr. Sigg in Zurich.

Maybe you will discuss this project with Rev. Dougherty. Or course, we also would enjoy blankets and linen, fabric for nightgowns, etc. We still need clothing because we have children who arrive with the most minimal of clothing items and we could help them. There is so much suffering and need. The children of the refugees and the homeless following the bombings are bad off. Everything is so expensive because so much is needed. I know how it feels. When you have lost everything, you start again from scratch. We are so grateful that we are able to build a home for us; it is furnished and the rest I have to bring along. We hope to move in March. The children's home should be finished in May or June. Please pray for us that everything will work out.

We had a very harmonious Christmas time and thought of you in love. Please accept our warmest greetings and blessings for the New Year. God bless you and your families and your congregation. How is Mrs. Unfried doing? Does she have her baby by now?

With a grateful heart and much gratitude for all your efforts, my dear Florence Boek!

Gratefully, Leni Schnädelbach and Klaus, Herbert, Gerhard, and Maria

Bergzabern, January 9, 1950

My dear Mrs. Boek,

Last Saturday, your big package arrived here—we were so exited! What a great joy! The content: wool blankets, towels, and delicious food items, in addition to this special chocolate. You all in the Artaban Class cannot imagine what excitement and joy you brought to us, especially to me. What a great help. During the last few weeks, I began to worry about how to provide warm bedding for the children especially when we move into our new home. I knew that I would not have been able to purchase these items, and then your package arrived filled with warm blankets. The

CHAPTER NINETEEN

blankets you sent are so big and warm, they will be very comfortable. We are so grateful to you for your kindness and care for us. I am also grateful that your love will continue as we move into the children's home project. I sent a letter last Friday and told you much about the children's home with suggestions on how you might be helpful in the future.

The towels and the fabric you sent are also so wonderful and useful as welcome as money. God bless you and all your kindness.

I will send this letter by airmail, so you know that the packages #27 and #28 have arrived here. Warm greetings to all of you! May God be with you in the coming year, and may he bless you and your families, the members of the Sunday School Class including your congregation, your pastor, all the children and all the members.

In grateful connection through Christ, I am sending greetings to Mr. and Mrs. Boek for all their efforts in organizing packing these packages.

Yours, Leni Schnädelbach with Klaus, Herbert, Gerhard and, Maria

Thank you for following me during these letters telling a history of kindness and love despite the challenges of unpredictable future and losses......

Chapter Twenty

My dear loyal readers,

Remember Grandfather Paul Schnädelbach had remained in Leipzig, East Germany, after we had fled across the border into the Western section of Germany in September of 1949. He kept writing letters and notes—he missed us, but his health was deteriorating. I missed him, his singing at night and holding his hand when walking outside.

Grandfather Paul Schnädelbach wrote these lines to us:

> January 14, 1950
>
> Dear Leni,
>
> After I was unable to attend church services for several weeks, I want to try to go to church tomorrow. Our student, Horst Martin, wants to bring me there and then Martin Leiboltz. will bring me back. So far, I will not be able to attend the evening service any longer.

Then in March this letter from grandfather arrived:

> March 27, 1950
>
> Dear Leni, dear children,
>
> .... Now, to your question about my wellbeing, dear Leni. I am feeling somewhat better, thank God. I dared to walk on the streets again, was even today in the city, which is quite a challenge. Due to my unstable gait, I tend to bump into people on the street or people run into me. It has been

quite a while since I have been at the cemetery. As soon as the weather improves, I plan on going there. (His wife, Helene, was buried there in 1941).

Occasionally, I attend church services. Sometimes, someone will accompany me back home. I can no longer attend the choir rehearsals, which pains me. I feel so useless and worn out, which pains me even more. As long as I am not bedridden, I am grateful to God.

* * *

Letters were the connection. Waiting for letters brought by the mail man was so special—we all wanted to know who wrote them, hear about the news and care for each other. See the following letter my mother wrote to her sister, Hilde.

Bergzabern, February 27, 1950

Dear Hilde,

Again, I opened your loving and long letter from you, however I have a bad conscience that you take so much of your personal time for us. I was truly happy to hear from you and thank you so much. It is always so interesting what you have to tell me. Right away I went to Social Services in town. There are no internships available, maybe Inge could check in Landau or Neustadt, and there is no pay for such positions. An offer of 70.00 Marks in Wiesbaden would be quite good.

.... We still have no idea when we can dedicate the Children's Home. We had 6 weeks delay because of the ice and snow. We should be able to continue in March. For weeks we had nothing but wet and cold weather, such a sticky mess! The construction is framed, the heating system is installed, but we have no idea when the home will be completed. I hope for May and June as a target date, but we have a delay of those six weeks. Does your friend, Christel, want to wait that long? We could offer her 15.00 Marks spending money and free room and board. What do you think?

Please let me know as soon as you have finished the exams how much pay we should plan for a cook, helpers, etc. how much vacation we should give them and how much free time. I would be so grateful to have this information. How much do you pay a property manager?

I am receiving a certain pension, but since I have no official declaration of Herbert's death, Herbert's official status is "missing in action." In this category the wife can only earn 75.00 Marks per month. If she earns more, she will not get anything. If the husband is declared "fallen in action," the widow may earn up to 350.00 marks. This is very unjust, and I will not receive anything. Hopefully, the children will receive something. All this is still pending.

The French tutoring for the boys is so expensive, maybe this will end soon. The big boys are so busy learning, they have made such improvements, only Gerhard is behind. I, for myself, had a hard time adjusting. I am so very tired and have my period every 14 days for six days. Since I have no health insurance, I cannot go to the doctor. We are all suffering from this crammed living arrangement which I had never planned for that long. Maybe this spring things will change. We are never for us as a family because we share the living room and the kitchen with Frl. Kitzmann. But that is nothing compared what we have gone through in the past. God will help us through.

You have so many worries, too and I feel sorry for you. Do you ever have some time to relax?

Please give Inge my warmest greetings and extend those to your colleagues,

Yours, Leni and children

The layout of the Children's Home: There are large doors in the dining room, with smaller group and playrooms on the right and left of it. Sleeping quarters and bathrooms are on the 1st floor. Bathrooms, showers, heating system, kitchen and pantries are currently closed, not yet dry walled. (She must have put a picture with the letter)

* * *

RETURN TO LEIPZIG

To: Florence Boek
418 N. Cloverly
Temple City, CA

Bergzabern, March 28, 1950

My dear Mrs. Boek,

Again, your package arrived, No. 28, filled with wonderful clothing and things that bring us joy and help us so much. My heartfelt thank you to all the sisters of the Sunday school class. I continue to see behind the gift you sent your great love and assistance.

We all have adjusted in our new home and the community. it is a very different lifestyle here compared to the Russian zone. much freer and without pressure. The French occupation is present, but we do not feel effected by it. There is no political pressure or party indoctrination here. We are so grateful for this fact compared with the terrible political propaganda and indoctrination the children had to endure in the Russian zone.

I am sure it will be alright with you if I will pass on any clothing that do not fit my children to the children of the children's home who will come for care and recreation.

Foremost, we will have children coming for 6–8 weeks whose have been refugees, or whose parents are not alive anymore.

We are planning to dedicate the home on June 15 and begin with youth camps, young people (age 14-25) to stay here for 14 days for recreation and Bible study, later women and mothers who also need some vacation and care. Is this not a great task? May God let us be a blessing to other people.

Our dear bishop, Dr. Sommer, assigned me to this task and with God's help all will work out. I am so grateful to you all for your continuous help. Please pray for us as well; we are praying for you also.

I am not sure if I wrote to you that you can send money for the "Children's Home Bergzabern" directly to Director, Dr. Sigg in Zurich, Badenerstrasse 60, Switzerland. We are still in the construction and furnishing phase. Our people are so impoverished that we are unable to reconstruct this home without outside help. God bless you for all your goodness!

CHAPTER TWENTY

> How are you all? Dear Mrs. Bock, my dear Blanche Slosson, your children, Mrs. Unfried and your children, Mrs. Wheeler, and the others?
>
> Please extend my greetings to all the members and especially Mr. and Mrs. Dougherty.
>
> With best regards and greetings,
>
> Yours, Leni Schnädelbach and the children

This package No. 28 contained the following items and was sent November 29, 1949 and arrived in March 1950.

- 1# coffee .73
- 1# chocolate Ghirardelli .43
- 1# dates .29
- 2 bars soap, laundry .30
- 5 combs, 1 large .75
- 2 sheet blankets, 72x99 4.38
- 4 large milk chocolate bars .76
- 4 spool thread #50 .70
- 1 double sheet blanket 72x84 4.79
- 5 yards white percale 1.95
- 1 child's dress 1.00
- 2 women's dresses 10.00

* * *

> Bergzabern, May 31, 1950
>
> My dear sister Hilde,
>
> You have not received any mail from me, and I know this is not nice of me. Although we have not made much progress on the Children's Home project, I am constantly running with errands. We should be able to sail ahead. I hope we will be able to move into the little house. The stucco workers are already inside, but the water pipes are not functioning well. O well, I need some patience. I would have never thought how long all this would take. Any construction today is associated with lots of problems.
>
> In the meantime, I had a visit of a youth director who brought greetings from you. She was the niece of a well-known Dame Drollig, correct?
>
> What plans do you have for your vacation? And when?
>
> It is a pity that we are still not living in the little house, it would be so nice to have you here. Most likely, our niece, Traudel, will join us here for spiritual guidance for the children and the retreats once the Children's

home is finished. She will then be finally working in her field. Our sister, Mariechen, would like to come and visit here, I would need to get her a visitor permission, but do not have the money to pay for her long trip from Dresden. As you know, she is not able to pay for all of this. Slowly all of us have adjusted, only my severe fatigue is still bothering me. Klaus leaves for Landau by train at 6:30 am in the morning so that we must get up at 5:30am. Tomorrow his vacations for Pentecost are over. I am wondering if Inge was able to be with you over the Holidays. How is she doing? I tried to inquire for her about an internship, but the district is much too small.

By the way, we have a small German shepherd puppy and a small 14 days old Mohrli—a kitten. I am sure you can image the joy the children have. We are living in the country site.

Please, Hilde, send me some ideas about the payment scale and salaries for a cook, helpers, a custodian, teachers, and substitute teachers. I would be so grateful for your help. How much do you propose for home and board, or salary without living arrangements?

Do you have a chance to relax a bit?

The children are happy and healthy. They love to go to the pool and ride their bikes.

My warmest greetings to you and Inge!

Yours, Leni and the children

Bergzabern, July 21, 1950

My dear Mrs. Boek in America,

Since I last wrote to Mrs. Potter about the sewing machine, two packages have arrived here including the one that was missing, No. 31, 32, 33. The content again was so wonderful! Besides the fine clothing you sent, which we also share with the children of the Children's Home, we thank you for the valuable food items, which help us tremendously. We can purchase food by now, but everything is extremely expensive, and I have few funds available for establishing a new home. Furniture and other household items are very expensive. I am so grateful to you for your

CHAPTER TWENTY

continuous support and help. You have given such special attention to each item you sent, and I am so grateful to all the members of the Artaban Sunday school class.

My brother, Dr. Wunderlich, who lives in Frankfurt, is currently visiting in California. He was invited by Bishop Raines to visit several congregations in California. I am wondering if he might stop by at your church. How wonderful would that be?

He is the Director of our Minister's Theological Seminary in Frankfurt. With our heartfelt greetings and gratitude.

Yours, Leni Schnädelbach and the children

PS. To Mrs. Boek a very special thank you for all her efforts and love for packing those packages.

I found the following letter in the folder:

July 30, 1950

Frau Leni Schnädelbach
Gartenstrasse 375 L
Bergzabern, Pfalz
Germany French Zone

Dear Friend,

We are enclosing the Bill of Landing for the shipment of a sewing machine to you. This is a gift from the Artaban Class of the Community Methodist Church of Temple City, California.

As there was not sufficient money in the Treasury to buy a new one at this time and we felt it quite important that you get one as soon as possible, we obtained this one through one of our local dealers who has renewed most of the parts and he feels it will serve you for many years. May you enjoy using it and may it prove a blessing to those who come under your care.

May I explain that the class has designated me to take care of mailing things to you and that I am rather a newcomer to this church, so any explanation of what your needs are and any details of what your mission work consists of would be very welcome to me. It must be wonderful to be of such help and comfort to your kinsman. May God bless you and your home and all who come to you for help.

Sincerely, ??

Chapter Twenty-One

Dear readers,

Looking through so many letters and pictures to narrate the story of the care packages, mothers thank you letters and included family updates, I discovered this very special letter written to me by grandfather, Opa Paul Schnädelbach. I cannot remember when it arrived in the mail, quite sure that mother showed and read it to me. Look at the old German Sütterlin font. We were able to still read it. What a special gift. Here you see the original letter in his handwriting followed by a translation. I have it framed, and it has hung for many years in my office to remind me of his kindness and inspiration.

Translation: Leipzig, July 31, 1950
My dear Maria!
Your kind offerings brought me such joy. Just as written in the Bible, in the letter to the Hebrews, chapter 13, verse 16, "Do not neglect to do good and to share what you have, for such sacrifices are pleasing to God." (Look it up in your Bible)

You made a big sacrifice when you turned down the ice cream and rather bought a roll of candy for your Opa. Also, my warmest thank you for the chocolate and the raisins—all tasted so good. Our dear Jesus may keep your generous mind.

I also enjoyed the wonderful photos especially the one of you. Greetings to Klaus, Herbert and Gerhard and special greetings to you from

Your
Opa Paul Schnädelbach

CHAPTER TWENTY-ONE

* * *

Bergzabern, August 22, 1950

My dear sister Hilde,

It has been such a long time since you have heard from me; you may assume I do not think of you. The opposite is true—all this food canning, mending clothes and worrying did not allow me time in addition to much other correspondence. We are almost one year here in Bergzabern, and time has passed so fast, however with no progress of the Children's Home project. The buildings are under construction, and we are waiting—waiting... The anniversary church building in Bremen drains the church budget in addition to the Lübeck housing project which leaves our project way behind in funds. This is too bad and depressing, but there is nothing we can do, and we have to be patient. If I would have known this before we arrived here, I would have thought twice. Although our standard of living is much better here and so are the schools and the overall excellent education. Klaus travels every day to Landau for his Oberschule/Obersecunda and Herbert and Gerhard attend the local secondary education school. There is not much music going on in our house, and since everything is so expensive, we cannot pay for any extra lessons right now.

Traudel will arrive here on August 25th for a vacation and maybe she might be working in the Children's Home at a later time. Her mother, Mariechen wants to come here for a vacation if she can get an interzone pass for a visit. I have no idea where I should house her and pay for her ticket back home. Well, she is not here yet and in time, things will work out. Most of all, we must cope with faith given all the difficulties, and hang on to a deep trust in God for the future. We thought of Inge on her birthday and are sending belated wishes and God's blessings. What a shame we are not yet in our little home where you could visit us. There is so much that we could share and talk about.

I had a visitor from Leipzig, Karl Schnädelbach's (he is deceased) wife, Elfriede. We had a very nice visit and feel very close to each other. I need to finish for today. Have you had a vacation yet and where did you travel to? Did you get some rest? May God protect you and Inge.

> Warmly, Leni and Children
>
> Herbert spent a few days with Traudel in Heppenheim and Klaus spent time at a camp in Bavaria.

* * *

Back to the Care packages and the letter exchange with the members of the Artaban Sunday School Class. The following letter was written by the Artaban Sunday school class secretary, Wilma Vogt, to Lillian and Edward (Sawyer), who spearheaded the sewing machine project.

> Temple City, California
September 12, 1950
>
> Dear Lillian and Edward,
>
> The members of the Artaban class wish to thank you for your work in connection with the sewing machine sent to our German Family—and for the ten-dollar donation you made towards it purchase.
>
> We know the entire procedure entailed quite a bit of time and effort on your part, and we wish to let you know that we appreciate all that you did.
>
> We missed you at our "Back to School" party and hope you will be able to attend our meeting in October.
>
> Sincerely,
>
> Wilma Vogt
> Secretary, Artaban Class

* * *

CHAPTER TWENTY-ONE

Bergzabern, Pfalz
October 10, 1950

Dear Mrs. Sawyer,

Today I received your letter from October 4—many thanks. You were wondering why I did not write you if the sewing machine had arrived. However, the sewing machine is not here yet. Every day I am hoping it will arrive. Your last letter, written on July 22 arrived with $1.00 in it, and we were very happy to hear that the Sunday school class will send us the sewing machine. Now I am waiting every day. I went to a schoolteacher who speaks the English language perfectly. She read your letter and looked at all the papers you sent to me about the sewing machine. I thought it was possible to send a return note, but it was not so. Now I have to wait every day. I hope very much that we will find the machine. We are so excited that you will send it to us.

The dollar I received in the letter. You can put it in a letter, and I can exchange it here in Germany, or you can put money in a Bank in Temple City, and I receive it in German money.

I am so glad to hear that you finished the fine Sunday School building. We could not finish our Children's Home in the summer. We had no money to build it, but we hope that God will give us the money we need.

My four children are healthy and happy, they must study very hard in school. And now, please give my greetings to all the friends of the Artaban Sunday School class. Our prayers are our bond between us in Jesus Christ. I will send you some pictures from the children in my next letter.

With love,

Yours, Leni Schnädelbach

Chapter Twenty-Two

My dear readers,

You can hear my mother's agony in her letter waiting for the children's home to be finished and her worries about money. We were still living in cramped quarters with Frl. Kitzmann and waited for our new home to be finished next to the children's home. Patience ran short on every level. We were going to school, and I learned how to ride a bike out on the street. We made friends in the neighborhood and in the house. Heidrun and Almut lived upstairs and Dorle lived next door. Dorle's mother invited us into her garden when the cherries were ripe and we climbed up the tree, sat on its branches and spit the pits out of the darkest and sweetest cherries I had ever tasted. Dorle and I are still friends up to this day. She sends greetings every Christmas and around my birthday, always written on a special card of Bad Bergzabern.

Across the street lived the Wirt family. Herr Wirt was my music teacher in school and not treated well by the students. They made fun of him and interrupted his reflections on the great German composers such as Beethoven and Bach. He brought records to class and played them on his old record player to no avail. The music was familiar to me, and I sat there transfixed into a different world of art and language I understood.

Herr Wirt's daughters, Gerlinde and Reinhilde were fun to hang around with, especially the youngest one, Irmchen. She was always dirty and wild, running through their garden and chasing some creatures. One Christmas season, the Wirts invited us to the traditional St. Nikolaus evening. To our great surprise, St. Nikolaus actually knocked on the door and came into the house, carrying a heavy sac and a whip. I was stunned by his brown heavy coat, his beard and his dark, serious voice to ask us if we had done well in school or practiced our instruments. He read complaints from his golden open book and looked at each of us with a stern face. We did listen and nodded. I was scared until he opened his sac and poured goodies on the dining table, apples, nuts, chocolate, and oranges.

A German shepherd dog, Ria, joined our family at that time and several kittens. My love for animals never stopped since those days. One year, my mother did relent and allowed me to celebrate Mardi Gras with the other children since they were of Catholic faith. We Methodists were not allowed to party and dress up for fun like that, but my mother graciously chose a fancy hat for me, and I was able to join in the festivities outside. The best part of the day came when we begged for Fasnachtskűchle, (also called Carnival fritters, a round sugar coated fried doughnut treat filled with jam), at the local Catholic bakery.

Fasching (1950)

Frl. Kitzmann allowed us to take in Ria and the cats, and she needs to be remembered for her kind gesture. Our cats, however, were not allowed to sit on the kitchen table and lick from our plates like her cat, Biewele!

CHAPTER TWENTY-TWO

Klaus, Maria, with Ria, 1950

One summer day, my brother, Gerhard, baptized the kitten in a festive ceremony in the garden with guests all dressed up. We named her Mohrli.

A few times, Rheinhild took me to their Catholic church. I was so afraid that the priest would chase me out of the church, so I stayed way in the back in order not to be seen, but how I loved all the pictures of the Saints painted on walls, the colorful glass windows and the kind Madonna with child in the front, surrounded by flowers and candles. Our Methodist church did not even have a statue of angles or of a Madonna—just a vase full of meaningless flowers and the collection basket. Now back to the letters…

> Temple City, California
> October 26, 1950
>
> Dear Mrs. Schnädelbach,
>
> Your letter of October 10th was received, and I regret to hear that you do not have the sewing machine.
>
> With my letter of July 22nd, you received the Bill of Landing covering this shipment. You will note that the boat docked at either Amsterdam or Rotterdam, and no doubt the sewing machine is being held in storage at

either one of the ports. The steamship company was to send you a notice of the arrival so that you could arrange for the custom clearance and transportation to your home. May I suggest that you write the nearest office of the steamship company, as shown on the Bill of Lading, and request them to arrange for the forwarding. The transportation charges were paid as far as the port of import, but we were unable to determine the cost beyond. If you can pay these charges and will advise us of the amount, we will see that you are reimbursed. If you are unable to make the arrangements for the delivery of this shipment, you may contact the nearest office of the American Express Co., and by turning the Bill of Landing over to them, they will take care of the whole thing for you.

Recently, Rev. Weisberger from Stuttgart, Germany, who is visiting the United States, gave a talk at our church. He was interesting and brought us a good sermon on having faith in our God. There is no doubt the experiences you good people encountered made me thankful for the powerful and guiding hand of God. We were indeed pleased to hear from this man and feel we know you better because of talking to him first-hand.

We are always glad to hear that you and your family are well and getting along so nicely. The members of the Artaban Class are sending their greetings.

If you have difficulties in receiving delivery of the sewing machine, or are unable to locate it, do not hesitate to advise us so that further tracing may be made.

Sincerely,
Lillian Sawyer

P.S. I mailed package #34 on October 14th; Package #35 on October 18, 1950; and package #36 on October 24th. We hope these boxes of clothing, food and gifts arrive before the Christmas Holidays. Various members of the Artaban class contributed things and you will note, some of their names will be on packages.

RETURN TO LEIPZIG

Mrs. E.P. Sawyer
Temple City, California
750 No. Oak Ave

October 30, 1950

Dear Mrs. Sawyer,

I have a letter that the sewing machine is in Hamburg. I hope that it will be coming in the next week. Then I will write to you again.

With best wishes,
Yours, Leni Schnädelbach

Klaus, Herbert, Gerhard, and Maria Schnädelbach still
living with Frl. Kitzmann on Gartenstrasse

CHAPTER TWENTY-TWO

Children's Home under construction, 1950 with our dog, Ria

We received the following letter from our Grandfather Paul Schnädelbach back in Leipzig:

> November 11, 1950
>
> Dear Leni,
>
> Lottel brought me home yesterday from my stay in Plauen where I was taken care of for the last four weeks in our Methodist Hospital Bethanien. I had to be referred there by my doctor because of my bladder problems. I was hopeful to receive treatment by a specialist, Dr. Tymprien, a fine surgeon, to treat my prostate problems. Dr. Tymprien tried a medical procedure but could not operate fully due to my age of 78 and my body is too weak (I weigh only 100 pounds). The 4 weeks stay there made me feel better, with Sister Ursula's fine care day and night.
>
> I must be patient with my problems. It is so painful to urinate, by the way, an illness for many old men.
>
> My bladder problems started on September 3, the day we consecrated our church. I had to leave our worship service due to severe pain. But where should I go? The doctors' offices are closed on Sundays. Lottel took me to the Catholic Hospital and there they used a catheter to relieve my pain. That procedure helped only for a brief time. Dr. Zillgen who could not help me further, sent me to Dr. Neffe, a specialist on Albert Street

and from then on, Lottel has to take me two times a day to his office for a catheter procedure—what a torture! Since my stay in Plauen, I feel better, the urine is slowly coming out. I hope it stays this way because the pain is excruciating.

Now, God does not give us more than we can bear! Please pray for me and God's help.

Paul Schnädelbach

* * *

Bergzabern, December 20 (?), 1950

My dear sister Hilde,

Our very best wishes to you and Inge for a wonderful Christmas time. May God bless you at this special time of the Season and provide for days of rest and inspiration. We will be thinking of you when we gather around the Christmas tree. May the Babe in the manger warm your hearts and bring you joy, gifts we need so desperately during this hard time

Your special package has arrived already, but we will not open it before Christmas Eve. We already thank you for your kindness. We received a special Christmas gift of a permission to continue our construction project. Foremost, the completion of the little house as soon as the weather improves. I hope for all of us to be there when Herbert is celebrating his confirmation this spring. May God help us!

This past year was unendingly difficult. I thought of you so many times and your struggles in Műnden, often so alone with all these difficulties and troubles. You did not get much support and you had to manage through it all. Those were difficult years, and nothing was spared. Thank God, now we have peace here in the house and I am so grateful for that. May it be so in the future. The children are ready for a vacation, but our living arrangement is so tight etc., but the children are excited, all filled with expectation for Christmas. They all have their secret preparation for

CHAPTER TWENTY-TWO

Christmas Eve. Their wish lists were so high! The list began to shrink the closer we get to Christmas.

Klaus is playing tonight at a Christmas concert. He also has an organist job in the neighborhood, which does not interfere with our church services. He is earning some money—wonderful! Herbert has been asked to play violin. How nice that they can play and use what they have studied. Gerhard and Maria are busy planning for Christmas presents. Maria is crocheting something mysterious.

Opa Schnädelbach in Leipzig is very ill, spent four weeks in a clinic, but was recently released. He is 78 years old. You may know that Hanni is in a mental hospital. She has acute paranoia. They hope that electroshock therapy might help her. She seems improved, but it is so sad.

Have a wonderful celebration at Christmas and extend my warmest greetings to your colleagues.

With much love,
Leni, Klaus, Herbert, Gerhard, and Maria

* * *

December 15, 1950

Christmas will be lonely for me this year. How special it was two years ago on Christmas Eve with you all! I am sure you will have much joy and excitement this year.

Yes, be joyful all you Christians!

Opa Schnädelbach

* * *

Now back to the letters from America.

December 18, 1950

My dear Mrs. Sawyer,

> **The sewing machine is here!!**
>
> You can imagine, we are very, very happy! Several packages arrived here last week. I opened them up a little bit but decided to not open them until Christmas. We have received your love! Please, my dear, give my thanks to all the members of the Artaban class. We thank you from our hearts and think of you in love and gratitude. God bless you.
>
> After the Christmas Season is over, I will write you more in detail. I hope you will receive this letter before Christmas because our joy is so great.
>
> Now, a Merry Christmas, and the best wishes for 1951!
>
> In love, Klaus, Herbert, Gerhard, and Maria and
>
> Leni Schnädelbach
>
> (The letter contained two Christmas greetings cards)

Donated sewing machine, presented to mother with a 'birthday cake'

CHAPTER TWENTY-TWO

Grandfather wrote:

> January 7, 1951
>
> Dear Leni,
>
> Your dear letter and the beautiful pictures arrived here yesterday. Your report on your Christmas program had already arrived earlier.
>
> I am sorry to tell you that during the night last Friday I suffered another small stroke, and this time it affected my right side. There is a paralysis on the right side of my face. I cannot close my eyes, which results in a painful infection of the cornea. The right side of my mouth is drooping, and I am not able to chew and have difficulties talking.
>
> Maybe the Lord will come soon to take me home, I would prefer that, but whatever the Lord's will, I will be waiting patiently (Phil1, 23)[38].
>
> ... I have such difficulty writing and send you my heartfelt greetings and ask for your prayers.
>
> Yours,
> Opa Schnädelbach

* * *

> Bergzabern, Pfalz
> Gartenstrasse
>
> January 9, 1951
>
> Dear Mrs. Sawyer,
>
> It is time to write a letter to you, I know it! I hope you received my card that we received the sewing machine. It is now here, and we are very,

---

[38] For to me, living is Christ and dying is gain. If I am to live in the flesh, that means fruitful labor for me; and I do not know which I prefer. 23. I am hard pressed between the two: my desire is to depart and be with Christ, for that is far better; but to remain in the flesh is more necessary for you. Since I am convinced of this, I know that I will remain and continue with all of you for your progress and joy in faith, so that I may share abundantly in your boasting in Christ Jesus when I come to you again.
Phil, 1, 21–26. New Revised Standard Version. Holy Bible, 1989.

very happy about it. This was such an effort! The customs did not want to give it to me without a customs declaration, but after a long time they released it without a customs fee. The boys helped me with the electricity (voltage) adjustment, and it is wonderful to sew with it. It is not possible for me to express my joy in words. I would like to shake hands and thank every member of the Artaban class. (I should write in German in order to properly express my gratitude and all my thoughts, but I hope you can see and feel my joy and my gratitude.)

And now I wish you could have seen our joy when we opened the three parcels with the little gift packages. We opened them at Christmas. This was such a great joy. The nice paper, the beautiful cards, and all the good wishes and the little songs. We all went: "Ah!—Oooh! wonderful! Also, the mother was very surprised about the nice things for me. It is not possible to tell you what the greatest joy is when we feel your love and your friendship. Our thoughts went to you in gratitude and joy.

The Christmas days were beautiful and in peace. Our thoughts were going back to our dear home in Breslau with our dear father. In such days it is very difficult, and I must be brave. But God will help me in those days to stay brave and happy.

We hope that we can open the children's home in the springtime. It is very difficult, but God will help us. Every day our prayers are going to him. I know you will help us to pray.

Klaus, Herbert, Gerhard, and Maria are healthy. They are going to school; they can learn without the Russian indoctrination. It is very good so.

My dear Mrs. Sawyer, please read this letter to all the members. I know I have written many mistakes; I beg your pardon. I hope you have understood me with all my mistakes.

To all my warmest greetings. I think of you in love!

Yours,

Klaus, Herbert, Gerhard, Maria and Leni Schnädelbach

PS. Next Easter, my second son will be confirmed. We would need our dear father on this day to give his blessings to his son. He must give it from heaven.

CHAPTER TWENTY-TWO

Grandfather wrote:

January 19, 1951

Dear Leni,

...My condition has not improved. Dr. Zillgen has ordered me to rest in bed, therefore I had to let go of making coffee and turning on the stove each morning; Hanni had to take over for me. She likes to do so, and her care taking of me has given her a new meaning in life and new energy. The infection in my eyes is so painful with my whole face totally numb that I am unable to eat and feed myself. Your prayers sustain me, and I am so grateful to you all. I also keep you lifted up in my prayers.

Warm greetings,
Opa

Postcard

March 6, 1951

Dear Leni, dear Children!

Today we buried our dear father. We feel very connected to you all and know that you were here in spirit. It was a very wonderful celebration with many persons present. Our dear father looked so peaceful as if he were sleeping. Vater did not have to suffer much longer and passed away in peace on Wednesday, 9:10 am. During the last few weeks, he prepared for his passing and sang a lot. Pastor Witzel, Hans Buchhold, Karl und Walter Steinborn visited him in the hospital; he enjoyed their visits so much.

Greetings to you all,
Liesel

The official announcement of his death reads:

> Paul Schnädelbach
>
> born December 20, 1872, +++ died February 28, 1951
>
> God our Lord, called our dear Father to his heavenly kingdom after a rich and blessed life.
>
> Funeral Services will be held on Monday, March 5, 1951, at 11:30 am at the Südfriedhof, to start at the main chapel and lay him to his heavenly rest.
>
> In quiet mourning:
>
> Johanna Schnädelbach
>
> Charlotte Schnädelbach
>
> Adam Hecker and wife, Margaret (Schnädelbach)
>
> Erick Zahn and wife (Elisabeth Schnädelbach
>
> Friedrich Schnädelbach and wife (Hilde, born Mehner)
>
> Leni Schnädelbach, born Wunderlich
>
> Elfriede Schnädelbach born Naumann
>
> and 10 grandchildren.

I think of him often and know that he is resting in peace. He was so kind to us. He had invited us to seek refuge in his flat in Leipzig in 1945, and he had time for me. He sang in his bedroom at night and played table games. He did not mind having four children in his home ... and he kept his faith.

* * *

Chapter Twenty-Three

Bergzabern, April 8, 1951

My dear sister Hilde,

Thank you so much for your postcard. It was so good that you were here with me. It gave me courage and gave me strength. I wished you could have had a more relaxing time. Since you left a few changes have happened. The following Friday we met in Neustadt and last Monday and Friday during a business meeting, a decision was made to complete the little house. Friedrich is donating the money and has transferred it. This was a great relief.

The management of the construction site will be managed by Rev. Quiring in Pirmasens and will be different. Some freedom of choice I had enjoyed will be removed. I will have to wait and see. Somehow it will work out.

There is much to plan and organize. We can only purchase the absolute minimum of equipment to get the Home going. That will include our little house with only the minimum of furniture.

I wondered If you could send me a budget template maybe from your orphanage.

How many children are there? What are the expenses for each child per day? I would be so glad if you could send me the templates you use. I know it is more work for you and I am sorry.

We are still living in the boy's room, but otherwise it is peaceful here in the house.

I am so grateful for your love and help. It was what I needed so much.

Warm greetings, Leni and the children

Bergzabern, May 3, 1951

My dear Hilde,

Thank you so much for your kind letter and the professional categories. All this was very helpful. So was all the other interesting information. Our brother Friedrich transferred the needed money about four weeks ago, but there is one excuse after the other to delay the project. We also are approved for 50.000 Marks from the McCloy Funds, according to the newspaper, but nothing has come through so far. The only bright spot is our little garden which shows our effort. All the jobs for the Children's Home are posted, but nothing has been decided on and we are waiting from one week to the next. You will hear from me as soon as we move forward.

Mr. Schiele has no more responsibility for this project, everything is being managed by Rev. Kurt Quiring in Pirmasens. How this will work is still a mystery to me.

For today, just this brief note. Enclosed please find 2.00 Mark for Mrs. Oberin's typewriter. Many, many thanks for the wonderful package. You always think of us with such affection. The robe is already in use and the sweets are shared by all.

Loving greetings,
Leni and the children

June 26, 1951

Kinder- and Judgendheim-Erholungsheim
Am Wonneberg
Luftkurort Bergzabern/ Pfalz

My dear Hilde,

I know you have not heard much from me lately, but I hope that Inge wrote you more in detail from her visit with us. We would have liked to have her here a bit longer. The boys got along with her so well. It was a great visit.

CHAPTER TWENTY-THREE

I am sure she told you about all our difficulties during these wonderful summer months. As of July 1, 1951, we will be finally starting our Children's Home, Thank God! There was so much demand for the summertime that I had to write 50 denials. We must be known for what we are doing first. Recently, the Youth Services in Zweibrücken asked for the care of eight children in September. Even the Refugee Service Administration wants to send children for one year. I am missing one childcare teacher. I am not sure to hire someone permanently but would hire someone for a few months. Do you know someone? I had two offers, but they moved on due to the long waiting time here.

Otherwise, we are doing well. With Miss Stier here, my work is much easier. Klaus is so busy with school. Yesterday I received a letter from Inge telling me about your upcoming vacation plans. Best wishes for a wonderful and relaxing time.

With love,
Leni and the children

THIS IS THE END OF MOTHER'S LETTERS TO HER SISTER HILDE.

Back to the Care packages and their kind organizers. They continued to be concerned to rebuild homes for children and care for their health. See the following letter.

October 17, 1951

Director Dr. Sigg
60 Badenerstrasse
Zurich, Switzerland

Dear Dr. Sigg,

We are enclosing a Foreign Money Order No. 60280 for $25.00, payable to you, which we ask that you give to Frau Leni Schnädelbach, Bergzabern, Germany, to be used for the Orphanage there.

Sometime ago, Frau Schnädelbach informed us that we were to send money to you for this purpose. At that time, we were unable to send money, but have been sending her packages of clothing and some food. However, several our Methodist church people have just recently returned from Bergzabern, and we learned that the Orphanage is nearly completed, but that funds were needed. These people are trying to raise the needed funds and are speaking to many churches in and around Pasadena. Our Artaban Class of the Temple City Community Church decided to send $25.00 immediately.

Kindly advise us if this is the correct procedure to send funds to Bergzabern Orphanage. We would appreciate any other information that might guide us to most effectively help Frau Schnädelbach, as we do have every confidence in her sincerity and well-doing.

Sincerely,
Mrs. Edw. P. Sawyer
6319 No. Oak Avenue,
Temple City, California
Artaban Class, Temple City. Community Methodist Church
Golden West & Woodruff
Temple City, California

Chapter Twenty-Four

The letters from America kept coming, the connection continued even after the war had ended six years earlier. The following letters were placed into the Artaban folder documenting their mission project and the ongoing concern and commitment to the re-building of the children's home in Bergzabern and the care for our family.

November 6, 1951

6319 North. Oak Avenue
Temple City, Calif., USA

Dear Mrs. Schnädelbach,

We were so pleased to learn a little more about you, your family, and the wonderful work that is being done through the Orphanage. Dr. Frank Williams, of the Holliston Methodist Church of Pasadena, spoke to us Sunday night and showed us some movie pictures that were taken while he and his group of young people visited with you this summer.

We had been rather at a loss as to just what means we should use to help you and whether conditions were such that you no longer needed clothes, etc. that we were mailing. Dr. Williams mentioned that warm clothes would still be acceptable, he thought, but the need was great for immediate funds with which to equip the Orphanage. Consequently, our Artaban Class designated $25.00 to be sent immediately, and as you wrote that Dr. Sigg at Zurich should handle the funds, a Foreign Money Order for $25.00 was Air Mailed to him October 17th. Has the money come to your hands yet? We expect to send some more money shortly, but it will be handled through the fund Dr. Williams is raising for the Orphanage.

However, several people had already donated some clothing, so we boxed up several boxes and did mailbox #40 to you on November 6th. I hope to get the other boxes on the way as soon as I get over my "flu'" which came so suddenly but does not leave me that way. Will you let us know whether you have too many clothes or not; whether you still would like to send us some now and then? How is the food supply and does sending of coffee and shortening help? We pay about 89 cents for 1lb. of coffee and 89 cents for 3 lbs. of shortening.

Dr. Williams gave us such glowing accounts of you and your lovely family. It made us feel so much closer to you and your problems and the worthwhileness of helping whenever we can. God bless you and your family and those lives you touch.

Sincerely,
Lillian Sawyer

* * *

I kept the following letters and other documents in this collection of letters to see the effort of the church official to complete the Kinderheim project and to raise the funds.

Methodist Church in Switzerland
Headquarters: Methodist Publishing House
Badenerstrasse 69
Zurich

November 7, 1951

Mrs. Edw. P. Sawyer
6319 No. Oak Avenue
Temple City, Cal., USA

Dear Mrs. Sawyer:

CHAPTER TWENTY-FOUR

Very many thanks for your kind letter of October 17, 1951, with enclosed Money Order in the amount of $25.00. I will gladly forward the money to Mrs. Leni Schnädelbach at Bergzabern.

It is admirable how your people are trying to help the Bergzabern Orphanage. Mrs. Schnädelbach is doing a fine work and she deserves all help and confidence. It is my opinion that the most effective help can be rendered now in raising enough funds. The situation in Germany today has much improved materials at any kind are at hand, but there is a great lack of funds to buy anything. I am acting as Branch Treasurer of the Board of Missions in New York for whole Europe and am therefore also handling all money for Germany. Any check forwarded to me will be transferred to Germany. There is no other way. I hope you will {hear} form Mrs. Schnädelbach in due time. The transfer generally takes some time as it is not so easy even now to get them through to Germany.

With all good wishes to you and the Artaban Class,

I remain yours, very sincerely,
Bishop Rev. Ferdinand Sigg

November 16, 1951

Commission on World Service and Finance
Southern California–Arizona Annual Conference

The Methodist Church
125 East Sunset Boulevard
Los Angeles, 12 California
Telephone Madison 6-2355

J. Wesley Hole, Treasurer
Rev. Randall B. Scott
5956 N. Golden West Avenue
Temple City, California

Dear Randall:

I recently received a remittance in the amount of $50.00 from Mr. Vogt of the Artaban Class of your church designated for the Children's Home in Bergzabern, Germany. We are not forwarding this money immediately because we are still trying to get Advance credit for the designations. I am pretty sure we will authority for Advance credit. Just as soon as that matter has been cleared, all the funds collected will be forwarded to the Division of Foreign Missions at New York. In the meantime, please express to the class our sincere appreciation for their interest in this project.

Yours very truly,
Wesley Hole, Treasurer

December 12, 1951

22 b Bergzabern/Pfalz
Wiesenstrasse Kinderheim

Dear Mrs. Sawyer,

It was a great joy to me to receive your last letter and to have news from you and the Artaban class. I am glad that you have heard Mr. Williams and that he has told about Bergzabern and has shown you the pictures. It was a wonderful time with him and the six young people. We were very glad to see them and live with them.

It is very fine that Mr. Williams work for our Kinderheim and that he raised funds. We thank you very much for your kindness. The $25.00 did not come to me directly, but I hope to receive it soon. I will write you again when it arrives.

The box #39 has arrived. I have written to you in August.

Yes, it is so. We need most of all warm clothes. I cannot buy warm, wool clothes, it is too expensive. I must buy my own furniture. As you know, I must establish my own household again. Therefore, I cannot buy warm winter clothes, too. If you want to send anything, please send coffee, but only one pound per month, not more because of customs regulations. We pay for coffee 18.00 Mark, so we cannot buy it. It is always a joy to have coffee. The food does not seem so expensive in pour country. But you can also just send money directly to me through the Bank. Then we can

CHAPTER TWENTY-FOUR

purchase some items here because your money stretches much farther here.

I think when the children's home is finished, I will write you again what clothes we need for the children. If you want to send items for my family, we would like warm clothes, or food, or money so we can buy things here.

Now the Christmas time in here. My children are so excited about it. We have a home, a little house, and we are very thankful. We have seen that the Lord is our father, who did not forget his children.

We wish you and all the dear friends at the Artaban Sunday school class a very merry Christmas and a happy New Year.

God bless you for all your love.

Sincerely yours,
Klaus, Herbert, Gerhard, Maria and Leni Schnädelbach

Bergzabern, Pfalz
February 12, 1952

My dear friends,

It is a great joy for us that we received from the secretariat of our dear Bishop Sommer the money, you had sent to Dr. Sigg (DM 114.00) We are so glad about it and we thank you very much. We use it very well and we will use it for furniture for our house. The three packages have also arrived, and we thank you so much. I was happy that Mr. Williams from Pasadena was in your church. I think he can tell you many things about Bergzabern. It is better when one of our friends was here and can see our home, our house, our work, my children and all the things that are here. I wished that a friend of the Artaban class would come and visit here. We would be so happy about that.

I had spoken with Marty Hessell[39] about my friends in Temple City. She was here with Mr. Williams. She was sewing on the sewing machine you had sent. I told her about you very much. She would like to come to you and tell you about here.

---

[39] Marty Hessel was one the students that participated in the work team in 1951.

Currently, we have much snow. But we hope that the springtime will come. In the middle of March, we will begin with our children's Home. We hope and we know that God will help us to do his work.

My children are healthy and very happy. It was a bad time the last few years, but I am so thankful for everything you have done for my family and me. It is best for now to send money, then we can purchase what we need the most.

God bless you all!

In love and always thankful,

Yours,

Klaus, Herbert, Gerhard, Maria and Leni Schnädelbach

Kinder and Jugendheim am Wonneberg
Kneipp Kurheim
Wiesenstrasse 20/22

CHAPTER TWENTY-FOUR

The brochure describes the services of the completed Children's Home and our "little house" to the left where we lived as a family, starting in 1951. The inside shows the dining room and me taking water treatment, and the deaconess, sister Hanna, from the Methodist congregation in Pirmasens, who came to help with the activities of the Kinderheim on several occasions. I liked her very much. She was warm and friendly and did not seem so worried so much about everything.

Leni Schnädelbach
Kinder—und Jugend -Erholungsheim am Wonneberg
Luftkurort Bergzabern/Pfalz

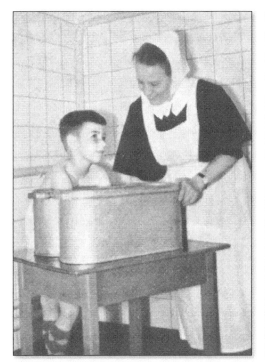 

I practiced cold and warm water treatment a la Kneipp to enhance circulation.

(22b) Bergzabern, December 14, 1954
Wiesenstrasse

Dear Mrs. Sawyer and all the friends of the Artaban Class,

We thank you very much for your fine letter, which came to us in the beginning of November. The bank draft was in it and we have received the money in a short time, it was not so late like last year, and we have had a great joy.

This at first, that you know that your letter and the joy you want to do to us, is in our hands just in the Christmas time. We are very enjoyed about it, and we want to give you our hands and our thanks for all your love and friendship.

It is so fine that we have friends who are children of Jesus Christ also. My heart is happy to know that in so many countries are people, who like Jesus Christ, and all these people are like a family. I believe, if one of us comes to you or one of you comes to us, we were brothers and sisters, who know the name of the other and had a heart for the others.

I am very unhappy that I cannot tell you the way I would like to, the words do not come. But I believe you know what I want to express. Just in the last time I have often thought of you and your work you have done for my family.

First in Leipzig you have saved our lives especially those of the children. I believe we would not have survived because there was so little food we could not live on. Gerhard was so ill, his lungs were very sick, and all your help had given us life. Just now I think it is not possible to understand that people can survive in such a time of need, but in all this suffering the Lord did not forsake us.

We are thankful for this time, now we know that the Lord never comes too late.

So often I hope we can see one of you. It was so fine that Mr. Williams was here, and he can tell you about our work and our family.

My children are now in good health. Only Herbert's heart is not that well. He wants to go to the University to study music and Germanistic. Klaus is studying in Karlsruhe (Technic) and Gerhard and Maria are going to school in Bergzabern. Gerhard wants to study Theology in Frankfurt at the Theological Seminary.

Our Kinderheim is at work, which gives us many joys, but also many worries. We have had many children here last year and we hope that the children get not only healthy, but that the name of the best friend of the children, Jesus, will remain in their hearts.

CHAPTER TWENTY-FOUR

We hope that we can have in the next year special children here who were ill with infantile paralysis (Kinderlähmung) and we can help such children through baths by using a new method. We have a fine medical doctor for our Home, and we hope that we can help many children.

We will have many children visiting again from the Eastern/Russian Zone; this work is very necessary. Last year we had children from Saxony, and it was a joy to see the eyes of these children light up. These children have no money to pay for their stay here, only our Bishop, Dr. Friedrich Wunderlich and the Methodist Treasury were able to pay for them with the help of our friends in the USA.

Last year we had a girl here who had not recovered from this illness, but after her treatment here with baths and massages, she greatly improved. We were so glad to see this, and the parents of the girl were very happy.

I am very unhappy that I cannot tell you better all that I want to tell you so I will write a brief paragraph in German.

My dear friends, (translated)

Allow me a brief greeting in German, I am so sorry that I cannot write you exactly what I want to tell you because I do not have the words available in your language. But I hope you can understand my stammering and my thoughts. Our heart is always filled with gratitude when we think of you especially at this time of Christmas when our thoughts turn to you as we walk to the Christ child in the manger.

It is such a great help to me that you are always thinking of us because wherever a father is missing so much more is missing and it is so hard to care for four children. Therefore, we thank you for all your love and your gifts.

Please extent heartfelt and grateful greetings of the Family Schnädelbach to all the members of the Sunday School class.

Especially yours,
Leni Schnädelbach

Mother sent the following Christmas greeting card in December 1955.

> Greetings for a Merry Christmas and for a happy New Year!
>
> We have received your fine card with all the names on it and the warm greetings. We thank you so very much for your love and for the money.
>
> We are so glad to know that we have the same Lord who gives us love into our hearts. Although we have never met, we feel we know you and you know us through Jesus Christ. God bless you all!
>
> My children are healthy, Klaus and Herbert are studying at the university. We are so glad to have the guidance of the Lord.
>
> We wish to meet some of you here like we were able to meet Mr. Williams in 1951. Our Children's Home had many visiting children in 1955 and we are so glad to see the blessings of His work. Only my heart does not function as I want, the last 10 years have been so very difficult and terrible.
>
> In love always,
> Yours, Leni Schnädelbach

> December 18, 1957
>
> Mr. and Mrs. Sawyer
> 6319 No. Oak Ave
> Temple City, Calif
> USA
>
> A Christmas card reads:
>
> A blessed Christmas and a peaceful New Year to you and all the Artabans!
>
> Yours,
>
> Schnädelbach family

Chapter Twenty-Five

My brother Klaus visited the United States sponsored by the Methodist church during the summer of 1957 together with a minister couple (Elfriede and Karl Beisiegel—Winfried's aunt and uncle) and a medical doctor. They also visited Southern California and churches in the Los Angeles area including the Temple City Methodist church. I found the following thank you note in the Artaban Sunday School class folder. When he returned from this special trip, he talked about all the sites he had seen including the Grand Canyon. His camera pictures were proof of a country I could not even imagine, desert land, large cities, churches with stain glass windows, friendly faces and most of all, a view of the Grand Canyon. Oh, I promised myself to travel there sometime during my lifetime and see the deep valleys, the rock layers and the riverbed, and the Indian tribe, the Navahos, and the Hopi people. I began to imagine when I would be there in the far future, but I hoped it would happen. And it did.

Klaus' visit to the US and the Artaban Sunday School Class, Temple City, 1957
Klaus' visit to the Artaban Sunday School Class in 1957, Temple City
Klaus Schnädelbach stands in the second row, middle

Lillian and William Sawyer with Estella, 1957, Temple City, CA

CHAPTER TWENTY-FIVE

> Bergzabern/Pfalz
> 1957

Dear Sawyer family,

Now I am at home for nearly two months and this great trip seems nearly to be a lovely dream. But all the signs of love and brotherhood we got over there keep the remembrances alive and deep. One of the nicest times I had was the afternoon in your family, your Sunday School Class and your congregation. I wish to say "thank you" to you all.

In the meantime, I have been adjusted to all our home condition. I had to pass my first part of exams for my Master's degree just after my arrival here and I had to feel at home immediately. But I left a part of my heart in your country and someday we will meet again.

I heard that your sanctuary is ready now—must be a very nice one. With much love, I remain,

Yours, Klaus

> December 12, 1958

Dear Friends,

We think of you and of all members of the Artaban Class with our best wishes for this Christmas Season and a Happy New Year!

The best of all when our Lord will bless you and us in our families, church and work we happy that Klaus could see you all and tell you of our life in Bergzabern.

It is now 10 years ago that your love helped us in our great need, at first in the Russian Zone. Maybe Klaus told you that we had often nothing to eat and then God gave us a package from the Artaban Class. Yes, we shall never forget it. He helped me to find the way with my children, and they give me much joy. Gerhard is studying to be a minister in our church just like his father.

We are happy to know you all and you pray for us, and we pray for you. This is the best friendship.

I have been sick for the last 6 weeks. My heart is acting up, but during the last few days I feel better, and I can get up. I believe much in my life was so difficult and the work at the Kinderheim is very hard. But I hope that in the New Year I will be able to work again.

Klaus brought to you many greetings. He works in Landau and in the evening, he returns to Bergzabern. He told me of his visit with Mr. and Mrs. Sawyer and he was very glad about it.

With many greetings Yours,
Leni Schnädelbach
Klaus, Herbert, Gerhard, Maria

This is the last letter in the Artaban Sunday School class folder.

Bergzabern, December 19, 1961

Merry Christmas and a Happy New Year!

We hope you are in good health. The picture from your family and Klaus is a joy.

God bless you in your family and all people of the Artaban class.

We think of you in love and now are fourteen years that you have helped us in our need.

Klaus is married with Elisabeth, his little son, Christian.

I was sick a long time, now it is better. I hope to work again this springtime.

Always yours,
Leni Schnädelbach and family

CHAPTER TWENTY-FIVE

SUMMARY SHEET
of the Schnädelbach Family—in the Artaban Sunday School Folder

- From Breslau to Leipzig
- Church burned December 4, 1943
- January 3, 1948, Package No.2 received and April 26, 1948, No. 6, 7
- August 8, 1949, Mrs. Slosson
- October 1949: Out of the Russian Zone Via French Zone to Bergzabern
- Started December 1947—Mrs. Slosson
- January 1, 1948: Klaus, 13 years, Herbert, 11, Gerhard, 8, Maria 6, piano, violin, flute + sing.
- Father, minister of Breslau (Poland), forced to give up church (burned December 4, 1943, dies 3 weeks before the end of war. Leni went to Dresden to be with grandmother, 81 years old. After 2 weeks, city was demolished, and Leni's mother and sister died.
- Leni lost everything, but children and clothes on their back.
- Maria was burned badly.
- Moved to Leipzig where grandfather lived (Russian Zone). Then in 1946 our packages were begun.
- Letter in January 1948 lists of gifts, red suit for Maria
- Packages were sent from 1946—November 1951
- Money for Kinderheim was sent $25.00 in October 1951, $50.00 November 1951, $25.00 in November 1954, 1955, 1956.
- September 15, 1957, Klaus visited us on Exchange program
- June 1966 at Conference, Maria and her husband, Rev. Winfried Ritter made themselves known. Rev. Winfried Ritter was assigned to German Methodist Church in Los Angeles.
- Maria and her husband visited the Caravaners class party, January 1967, and talked about the Schnädelbach family. She also attended the Christmas Party (1966) Circle Meeting with me at Mrs. Hart's home.
- In April 1967, Klaus Peter Ritter was born to Maria. In May 1967, Mrs. Leni Schnädelbach came here to be with Maria. She stayed until August 17, when she returned to Germany via airplane.

Los Angeles, 1967. Meeting members of the Artaban Sunday school Class in Los Angeles, Hepburn Ave. From left to right: Winfried, Maria, Mother, Lillian Sawyer?

Artaban Sunday School Members visited my mother in 1967 during her visit in Los Angeles. Mother and Lillian Sawyer sit next to each other in back row, five and six.

CHAPTER TWENTY-FIVE

Mother visited us in Los Angeles in 1967 shortly after our son Peter's birth and during her stay, we invited the members of the Artaban Sunday School Class in Temple City to our home on Hepburn Avenue. What had been a long friendship across the Atlantic through CARE packages, letters and pictures could now be solidified by an actual reunion. Mother could thank them all with handshakes, hugs, and smiles, recalling their life saving actions following the war. It was a testament to the importance of building human bridges of kindness and relationships despite the abyss of hate and violence. Giving and receiving had come full circle, since it is by receiving that we can give.

The following documents are official business papers that belong to the Artaban project and their ongoing effort to assist those in need.

Report of Commission on Christian Social Concerns

October 19, 1966

The Committee for sponsorship of a Cuban Refugee Family met prior to the scheduled meeting of the Commission. The main topic of discussion was on which of two alternative courses of action to take.

As outlined in the letter previously sent to Committee members, a copy of which is attached (end of text).

The little brown notebook containing the content of the packages sent to us reads on the last page:

October 1951 (written in pencil)

Maria, 11 years old
Klaus 18 years old
Herbert 16 years old
Gerhard 14 years old

Contributions started in 1946.

Name of Leni Schnädelbach received through Emanuel Methodist Church.

Dr. Frank A. Williams of Holliston Methodist, Pasadena, and a crew of six young people visited them and helped finish the construction of the Orphanage at Bergzabern in summer of 1951.

Note:

Blanche Slosson was born on January 12, 1903: died in October 1984.

Lillian Sawyer was born September 28, 1902: died May 1, 1972, at age 75.

Mother's sister, Hilde Alrutz (Wunderlich) was born June 1, 1890: died November 13, 1960, at age 70. Her kindness is never forgotten.

My Mother, Leni Schnädelbach was born November 22, 1903, in Berlin, Germany. She died peacefully September 6, 1983, at age 79 in Bad Bergzabern. The last words she uttered to me when I sat by her bedside were, "Herbert is coming today." Finally, her waiting for him to come back was over, and she is reunited with our Vati, Herbert Schnädelbach.

May all these Saintly women rest in Peace!

The following art song composed by Richard Strauss was one of my mother's favorite. May her souls also rest after the storms of her life. "Rest, My Soul!

Ruhe. meine Seele! ... Ruhe, Ruhe, Meine Seele, Und vergiss, Was Dich bedroht!

CHAPTER TWENTY-FIVE

Mother's grave site in Bad Bergzabern, September 1983. Notice that our father's name, Herbert Schnädelbach, is included here since he had no official grave somewhere in Croatia in April 1945.

Chapter Twenty-Six: 2020–21

My dear readers,

Much time has passed to contemplate these wonderful, lifesaving 64 care packages when kindness and compassion were offered and received during this difficult time of WWII and recovery despite war, losses, and resentment. Letters were written in English and returned in 'Ginglish' with words of gratitude and love. Remember, when a package arrived, Herbert went to the piano and played a hymn of gratitude, "Now praise we all our God …" It was like opening presents at Christmas all year long with gifts to sustain and surprise us.

But here we are in 2020 and even in December 2021 in the middle of another life-threatening crisis, the Corona virus pandemic or COVID-19. A new wave of a variant is upon us. The constant news reports full of dark, shockingly upsetting facts with human suffering and climbing numbers of deaths—each life a loss to a family and a community in grief. The numbers are staggering on the screen, cold and impersonal. The medical helpers are overwhelmed and unsupported by lack of equipment, relying on their own dedication and sacrifice. In December 2021, people are still resisting vaccines and insist on their personal freedom to make decisions. We are isolated and fearful again.

I never thought to have to face in my lifetime another war-like health crisis like this one with poor leadership, an incompetent, emotionally cold, cruel, and a narcissistic of a past president, unprepared professionals around him and fighting politicians. I am, though, familiar with people hoarding in supermarkets again, looking at half empty store shelves, finding no potatoes or meat and strict instructions to socially distance and avoid outings. I am familiar with not being allowed to go out at night or fearing the darkness in the home, especially in the bathroom. Even scared if there would be enough food later in the day. As you remember, my older brother, Klaus, did have an assuring answer when I said that I was hungry. He said, "If I am not hungry, then you cannot be hungry either."

When we get scared, we start obsessive behaviors. Hoarding toilet paper has been the number one in 2020 and laughing of the anal compulsion to make sure we have soft tissue to leave no dirty traces. Way back in Leipzig after the war, we used newspapers nicely cut into squares or old yellow telephone book sheets that were somewhat softer when used correctly.

And yet, kindness is still all around us. People are sharing resources and sending encouragements. With today's technology we are truly connected by television, emails and texts, pictures, and face time—not having to wait weeks for letters and packages to arrive. We just go to amazon, click, and receive our orders. Neighbors check in on us older folks and offer to shop for us. They leave the packages by the door. It does not matter where we all have come from or if we have arrived as immigrants from different countries or from different traditions. We are together and see each other's faces in the light of grace.

Another change has come as we have moved to Austin, TX in May 2020 to be close to Lisa and family and share time and love in person. Thank you for taking us in while the new house on Baldovino Skyway was being built by brave men during the brutal summer heat. Now we have a home again already decorated for Christmas. Thank you for your patience reading along and discovering part of your own history and challenges.

And now, it is December 2021. The pandemic had lifted gradually during the year after so much social isolation and human suffering. Six hundred thousand plus people have died. A silence fell over us all. We are here to remember and give thanks to all persons who provided care and security. Many people are fully vaccinated and dare to go outside. But waves of covid infections continue and people squabble over whom to believe, science or self-declared influencers, preachers or physicians, political party celebrities or Tik/Tok. Some people insist on freedom and pay the price of a stubborn death.

We did attend Luke Pickard's graduation from Highschool in person in May 2020 and spent some weeks in San Francisco with Peter's family. Another week in Santa Fe, NM for lectures and opera. And we are hopeful and look forward

CHAPTER TWENTY-SIX: 2020–21

to eventually traveling again, listening with others to live music, studying, and soon being together with more family and friends. Deep gratitude and relief follow so many worries and painful memories. We know that changes and challenges will be with us again in the future. How do we meet them?

Reading mother's letters again deepened my courage and trust in her faith. She was so determined and argued with God to bless and protect us—she insisted, she did not beg! She also reminded God of his protection for us in the past and assured herself of God's guidance now and in the future. This is an active faith, leaving her and us time to do and care for others just like the members of the Artaban Sunday School class did. Remember, Artaban heard these words at the end of his journey, "Truly, I say to you, all that you ever did for your needy brothers and sisters and all of God's creatures, you did for me."

Thank you for sharing my memories, the many letters, documents, heartfelt thoughts, and reflections of daily joys and worries, fears and grief. My journey is your history and will help you gain insight into times of adversity, turmoil, war, suffering, perseverance, and courage. Sigmund Freud said that power struggles, war and violence will never end but that we can stem the tide by building affective and supportive communities. Stemming the tide of hate and violence is possible and we have powerful tools to do so.

Maybe this current time of change in our lives is a good one to tell you how Winfried and I came to this country in May of 1966, our brave decision to leave behind a familiar yet painful, scarred world, and ventured with hope and faith to the New World. It is difficult to end the familiar, say goodbye and trust a new beginning. We never regretted it! Maybe this is our challenge during these dark months of 2020/21. We dare and renew human connections, embrace change, and seek purpose with compassion shining brightly among all of God's creatures.

THE VOYAGE: 1966

"How would you like to move to America?" Winfried asked me while running into our apartment in Hockenheim in late 1965. He was breathless from running up four flights of stairs. I looked at him stunned; a quick twinge of excitement made my heartbeat faster.

"What do you have in mind?"

"I just met Professor Knierim in front of the old Post Office in Heidelberg. He told me that the German Methodist church in Los Angeles is looking for a young German speaking minister to supply their pulpit for two years. He wants to find someone in Germany who would be interested in the job."

"What did you tell him?"

"I told him; I was interested. There is someone else qualified for the position, but that person has a family, and it might be too complicated for them. It would just be for two years."

"Just two years?"

We both had been hoping and praying for a sign to direct us into our personal and professional future. Winfried had finished his studies in Theology at the University of Heidelberg during the spring semester of 1965 and was waiting to complete his last examination. After that the Methodist church expected his entrance into its seminary in Frankfurt, to align with the Methodist theology, and train him to become a minister during an additional year. We would be separated, of course, since no seminary students were to be married and could not live together at their facility. We were not to be an exception. I still had one more year left of my studies in clinical psychology at Heidelberg. A separation

CHAPTER TWENTY-SIX: 2020–21

in the coming months seemed unimaginable since we had just married on May 15, 1965, and had moved into our first apartment in Hockenheim. Our belated honeymoon was planned for the first week of September, a flight to a Black Sea resort. It would be our first air plane ride!

We both struggled with the outlined path for Winfried to enter the Methodist church in Germany as an incoming clergy. Academic theology and actual parish life seemed miles apart, separated by a deep rift of theological views, a traditional, literal interpretation of the Bible on the Methodist side, and an academic, historical and contextual-research interpretation and application on the other side. The leaders in the Methodist church had tolerated the academic degrees of Methodist University students in preparation for the ministry, but really much preferred the Bible seminary education in Frankfurt, to provide tighter training objectives and denominational control; any candidates did not require a University degree. Suspicion and inattention toward the University students over the years had led to mutual alienation and a spiritual distance between the students and the Methodist church leaders.

Winfried and I were caught in the middle of these tense religious times. Mother's brother, Friedrich Wunderlich, was the current, presiding Bishop of the German Methodist church, and Winfried's uncle, Karl Beisiegel, was a teacher at the seminary in Frankfurt, the place where Winfried was to spend one year. Family obligation and a surge for expansion of our spiritual mind had come to a clashing stand still. It would be quite a scandal if Winfried would opt to join the large Protestant, Lutheran or Reformed denomination in Germany and start his ministry away from the Methodist church, we both grew up in. What would the family say? How much guilt would we have to feel?

My studies in psychology with an emphasis on Humanities and Philosophy at the University in Heidelberg had opened my mind toward human behavior and various therapeutic treatment methods and most of all, to ask questions and integrate history and current scientific discoveries. Diagnostic evaluations and the understanding of the human personality widened my horizon of human functioning beyond the religious guidelines of obedience and pure life style of my Methodist teachers and preachers. I had heard them say that all we needed was a loyal trust in God, blindly believe in his guidance, and accept what comes our way. In order to do this, we needed to be saved through a conscious act of total devotion, which included a giving up of all questions and doubting forever, it seemed. To be saved, meant to give your life over to Jesus Christ, our Savior, confess your sins and become a follower by answering an altar call during a revival meeting and kneel at the altar. Then "our God will take care of the rest." The leaders of the church would forge ahead and protect the way of faith for the rest of us. The Holy Spirit would lead them.

My trust was visibly shaken by this time. Our past political history of blind trust into a leader had led our nation into black disaster, forever to be retold and warned about to every generation. The focus of education had switched from repeating truths, slogans indoctrination, and censured literary treasures to a scientific, critical and often hyper-critical approach to life and self expression. The way of emotional and blind learning was over and done with. It had led to an abyss and unrepairable damage. Excellence and achievement were to be reached by competition and had lead to the selection of the brightest students on every level of education. Resources became available but dialogue developed slowly. Difficult questions were asked but no more clear answers were given. Nothing was for sure anymore. The best argument would win.

So here was the church as an institution clashing with the remnants of my faith. I held on to the respect for the history of faith throughout the centuries, the basic sayings of a man, Jesus,—who lived 2000 years ago who saw the true value in each human being, and lived a life of reaching out to others and giving a hand. This message was best exemplified in practical terms by simple sharing with the hungry and thirsty, the suffering and the stranger. This message seemed quite clear to me: a practical theology, inclusive to all, and a one person to person approach in the middle of a community that respects the tradition of sacraments and prayers. My psychological elaborations were quite in line with this thinking as it pursued healing and relief from suffering. Through the sounds and words of music though, faith was most directly communicated to me. I could hear, express, and understand God in meaning and melody. My family history had provided a long path of listening and interpreting sacred music. I understood its message. I heard the melody of devotion in the arts.

In contrast, much of the faith talk within the Methodist church I lived in had become stale and constraining. Maybe I did not want to try to understand it any longer. Family obligation and my marriage to a future clergy man compounded in me a sense of doubt and restlessness. Our future plans needed to include a place of free expression of thoughts and freedom to pose complicated

CHAPTER TWENTY-SIX: 2020–21

questions with no simple, pat answers prescribing as a total resolution. The thought of spending two years in the United States became more and more appealing. It also would buy us time to make a long-term decision as to Winfried's affiliation with the church in Germany. A glimmer of excitement joined our considerations. Yes, we would have to dig up our English language skills, somewhat forgotten and rusty after many years in school. I was able to translate texts forth and back between the two language given some time—and a dictionary, but had no experience in actually speaking English with another person, be understood, and have a dialogue. Would we be able to manage?

"Just for two years..."

What would our families say to such plans? Winfried's sister, Irmgard, with her family lived in Pasadena, California, and our possible stay in Los Angeles would give us an opportunity to be near her. She would be delighted. A reunion of brother and sister after years of separation seemed like a great idea. With her in the area, we would not be alone in a big city on the West coast that had filled the paper with shocking news of the Watts riot during the summer of 1965. We had heard of a racial breakdown of communities in the midst of fires, looters and senseless killings. A city had gone up in smoke.

"The German church is located right on Pershing Square, in the center of Los Angeles," Prof. Knierim had said. "It would be an opportunity for you."

"Don't tell my Mother," I said to Winfried. "She will be so worried. Her daughter so far away in another country!"

During the following days, Winfried wrote a letter of intent to a certain Rev. Richard Cain, the Methodist District Superintendent in Los Angeles, to inquire and explore the request. And then we waited for a reply.

My Mother took the news in her usual, calm, but thoughtful way, her head tilted slightly and saying,

"Hmm, do you think you will come back once you have left and worked there?"

"Of course, we will, it is a two year assignment. After that we'll return back home. And just think, you could come and visit us!"

She looked away and nothing else was said that day.

Within a few weeks, a letter arrived from Los Angeles with an official invitation to supply the Methodist church in Los Angeles. The pulpit needed to be filled as soon as possible given the current minister's retirement plans. Yes, there was a completely furnished parsonage to move into, a salary, and immigration papers could be arranged. A car was an absolute necessity in such a city, we had heard from Winfried's sister. The distances were too enormous. The American Bishop Kennedy was in agreement with our intent. We were told to make preparation for immigration as soon as possible. We looked at each other and realized that our vague, future plans and diffuse imaginations could materialize into an adventure which would involve geographical distance, and change of culture, language and customs.

A visit to Frankfurt and the American consulate provided us with a first window into the United States of America. The flag of stars and stripes greeted us at the entrance hall, a picture of President Lyndon Johnson proudly displayed on the wall. Passport preparation, stacks of paperwork, unending written questions in front of us which we had never thought of asking before. Had we ever been a communist? Did we plan to assassinate the president once in the country? Did we plan to organize a pimping business? Had we ever been a member of the Mafia? Did we have plans to assassinate the President of the United States? Where did we live during the last twenty years? Addresses, health, family, money?? Fingerprints, pictures, medical exams… I was surprised how friendly everyone was, German bureaucracy reversed by customer service. We returned to our flat in Hockenheim with thoughts of moving, packing and looking toward our future with enthusiasm and little doubts.

The summer semester at the University in Heidelberg came to an end at the last day in July 1965. One more year before graduation, I thought, two full semesters which would include my diploma project and a full, written psychological evaluation of a real 'case' study. Summer came as a welcome break. We were able to spend time together, and planned our honeymoon to the Black Sea in Bulgaria at the end of August.

One sleepy Monday morning with bright sun shine, lingering dreams, and bath robes came to a quick halt when we heard three knocks at our apartment door at about 9 o'clock on the fourth floor. Thinking it to be Winfried's cousins down at the grocery store, who always needed some quick help, I opened the door, only to look at four total strangers.

"Are you the Ritters?" they asked. I nodded silently.

CHAPTER TWENTY-SIX: 2020–21

"We are the Doehnels and the Lorenzs from the German church in Los Angeles. We are traveling in the area and thought to stop by and meet you, so we could tell our Pastor-Parish committee all about you!"

With that they smiled and huffed and puffed a bit more after their climb of four flights of stairs.

My heart sank. This was to be our first job interview! Here we stood with unwashed hair, in pajamas and night gown, our one-room apartment in full view with unmade beds, a total college students lived-in look. Our first day of vacation! Not a place to entertain strangers or future employers from Los Angeles. No extra goodies in the house.

"Could you give us twenty minutes, to get ready to receive you more formally?" we asked cautiously.

They laughed and nodded. So down the steps they trotted, hands on the railings, the women in tow, while Winfried and I flew into the shower which consisted of a swine troth, built in as a shower basin with a plastic curtain for privacy.

"Oh my God, look at us, what an impression we are already making. What if they don't even come back after what they saw? Maybe this was all they needed to see!" I carried on for a while.

Winfried did not say much as he hurried down the stairs to get some fresh pastry from the bakery for our visitors while I fixed some coffee. Maybe our new dishes would make up for our first bad impression.

The beds were made, the stuff had disappeared somewhere in the apartment when our visitors returned. This time, we led them in the apartment, offered them a seat, served coffee and pastry, and while chatting along, we tried to start this whole visitation over again.

"Many of our parishioners come from a village in Zschorlau, in East Germany, you know. Some family relations… business relations… Methodists for a long time … We need our young people involved; they don't speak German anymore.…"

"What about your call to be in the ministry, Bruder Ritter? Do you accept Jesus Christ as your Savior?"

"Good."

"When did this happen and how? We need Bible preaching, you know. Can you do youth work? Do you teach Bible classes because we have two house circles per week? And you should know that we have two services each Sunday with two different sermons."

"By the way, on Sunday morning, you must present a brief English summary of your German sermon."

"And what about you, Maria? What are you planning to do as a minister's wife?"

"Frau Weber, the retiring minister's wife, conducts the Women Society meetings and leads the prayers? You are not planning on working?"

"I will be supportive of Winfried" I said.

I was glad they did not ask me about my salvation.

"We hope you will sing in the choir!" Frau Lorenz chimed in.

Thank God, my Methodist pedigree impressed them somewhat.

"Yes, we know your uncle, the bishop here in Germany. He is a good man; we have known him for a long time when we all lived in Zschorlau in East Germany. He also visited us in Los Angeles once."

Their Saxon dialect began to sound amazingly comfortable. I had heard my family talk like that. I spoke like them way back in Leipzig and now, here it was again, the soft tone, the consonants, the drawn-out words ringing in my ears. Actually, a piece of home in Los Angeles?

"Nooo, nooo, es werd schon rechd werden mit Goddes Huelfe, Brooder Ridder!"[40] Herr Doehnel said. The others chimed in.

"Yao, Yao!"

And on they chatted about Los Angeles, a city close to the ocean and the mountains, with orange groves and warm weather all year round. They liked it there, but they enjoy visiting the Old Country, helping out the relatives in Zschorlau with packages of food and other goodies.

"It is still a harsh living over there, they have so very little," they commented.

"Life in East Germany is still difficult with no permission for the people to leave the country, legally. They can't repair their homes, nothing is available. The stores have no meat, no butter on a regular basis. The worst is not having freedom to go anywhere. The wall in Berlin is a terrible thing, people are being shot while fleeing."

We knew all about it.

---

[40] "Nooo, nooo, It will all work out fine with God's help, Brother Ritter!"

CHAPTER TWENTY-SIX: 2020–21

"How soon would you be able to come to Los Angeles?" Herr Lorenz asked.

"Maybe, I could come ahead, then Maria could join me when she has finished her studies at the University, next May," Winfried said.

"It probably will depend on the immigration papers."

They seemed to accept this explanation and stood up to leave.

"Bruder Ritter, can you say a prayer before we leave?"

I am sure they asked him to see if he could come up with a spontaneous prayer, a spiritual test of sorts to see about his ability to bless us all. That skill was definitely needed in Los Angeles. We all stood up and bowed our heads. I could see the dirty shoes of Mister Doehnel as I looked down, hoping that Winfried would find the right words in prayer. He prayed for their safe return and for spiritual guidance to make the right decision. They smiled as he said "Amen." Obviously, he passed this last hurdle much better than the first one of our stumbling, unwashed welcome. With that they shook our hands and left with the traditional courtesies of well wishes and complimentary niceties about our apartment.

"We hope, everything will work out, with God's help," someone muttered.

Down the stairs they went. Herr Döhnel and Herr Lorenz ahead, the women in tow holding on to the railing. Their high heels clapped along the stone steps, all four flights of stairs to the street. Off they drove with their rental car. What were they saying to each other? Were we too young, too inexperienced, too worldly?

Our baptism by fire had just begun.

It took me a few days to recover from their visit and our first experience with our future congregants, giving thought to what might be ahead of us. But then it would just be for two years in another country...

More letters arrived from Los Angeles, more papers were needed, many questions had to be clarified and answered correctly. All of it took so long, waiting with uncertainty became uncomfortable. As we made final plans for our honeymoon, we learned that the fall semester at the Methodist seminary in Frankfurt was to start in late August with a festive witness Sunday service for the incoming young students. Winfried had committed to attend the seminary until his travel plans to America would be fully clarified.

"No, you must be there for that first Sunday in September. No, we cannot make an exception." That was the official message from the church officials in

Frankfurt, delivered to him by his uncle, Karl Beisiegel, who also taught at the seminary. According to the church rules for clergy students, we were not to be married before his completion of the seminary year. We had broken this rule already. I felt some guilt about that, fearful of a reprimand from the church leaders.

They would not hear of starting his seminary year two days late, under no circumstances. It could not be done—no exceptions. Our honeymoon plans dissolved. We never saw the Black Sea, the resort by the beach, and never got a taste of Bulgaria. No airplane ride, no time away alone. Instead, I found myself alone in the apartment, a young bride with Winfried away in Frankfurt where he lived in a dormitory with other future ministers.

By the beginning of October, most of the immigration papers were ready, and the church assignment in Los Angeles became official. With that assurance and an accepted offer, Winfried left the seminary to come home so he could prepare his move to Los Angeles.

"I could not stand it there any longer. It was absolutely boring, it made no sense for me to be there any longer." I was glad to have him home.

Our financial situation became increasingly strained. My University tuition was still exempt with the standing condition that I was not allowed to earn any additional money through a part time job. Winfried had no income either. We lived on very little during the following weeks, waiting for the final papers and tickets to arrive from Los Angeles. Winfried's cousins offered him some work for food. The fresh rolls and the pretzels were always free.

On one of the following Sundays, Winfried's grandmother, her daughter and her husband, Elfriede and Karl Beisiegel, announced their visit. This time, I was prepared for the traditional Sunday afternoon coffee ritual with cake and other refreshments. The table was set for them.

They arrived at the announced time, their greeting was brief and cold. Not much was spoken at first as they helped themselves to the goodies on the table.

"We don't want to stay very long but we have to talk to you," Herr Beisiegel started as he looked at both of us.

"We are shocked about your plans to leave the country. You have not asked us about them. How can you do this to your family and the church, just to leave like that? The church needs you here. How can you do this to us?"

His voice became loud and shrill. He looked straight at Winfried.

CHAPTER TWENTY-SIX: 2020–21

"We think it would be a good idea to spend some time abroad." Winfried started his explanations.

"Besides, the church did not seem to care much for us university students anyway. You know it as a District Superintendent how the official church treated us at the last meeting, just ignoring us. We students were not attended to while we were studying at the various universities. Don't you know that most of my friends have left the Methodist church and entered the Protestant denomination, including Maria's brother, Gerhard?"

"Well, that's different. They have their reasons. But we waited for you to finish and enter the ministry here, not in some God-awful part of America!"

With that, he got out of his chair and started to pace up and down.

Winfried's grandmother started to cry. The aunt's face had turned red. She had tried to interrupt him several times but did not get a word in until now.

"You are forgetting what sacrifices your family has made for you. You were supposed to take over the roof tile business in Hoffenheim after your father did not return from the war. Then, you had your call into the ministry. How can you do this to us and your grandmother who brought you up after your mother died?" By now, she was screaming at us.

"Don't you feel any gratitude for all we have done for you? How can you just leave?"

Winfried and I both were stunned and silenced by now. I did not know what to say. Winfried was getting angry, his lips pressed together, preparing his next response to them. He tried to stay calm.

"Look, I will commit for the next two years, not the rest of our lives. They have offered me to attend their Methodist seminary in Claremont for additional graduate courses and a possible doctorate degree while I work at the church. You all know that my sister Irmgard and her family lives nearby in Pasadena, and we would be able to spend some time together. Why are you so against that?"

"It is not the right thing to do, this is not God's will for you!" Karl Beisiegel blurted out in a final effort. Winfried's aunt chimed right in,

"It cannot be, we need you here."

Grandmother who had been quiet for most of this discussion suddenly looked sternly at me and said,

"And it is you who wants him to learn English, isn't that right?"

I did not answer her and looked away. I felt her sting and intended accusation that I was behind the whole plan to run away with him to America. I was the one who would take him away from them. I kept silent.

I remembered all the instruction of English we both had in school. Year after year we reviewed grammar, vocabulary, translation skills, in addition to reading about people's life in England. We eagerly translated Shakespeare. For what?... Now we had an opportunity to master the language fluently—the thought sent shivers down my spine. My British pronunciation though would not do much good anyway in America. Maybe they would not understand me at all....

"And what is your uncle, the Bishop, saying to all this?"

"He has not said anything to us. Bishop Kennedy and him have been friends for a long time. I don't know ... they must have talked about it."

Nothing much else was said as they got up and walked toward the door. No warm goodbye followed. Their visit to our first home left a foul cloud of anger in the air mixed with waves of disapproval and coldness. While Winfried closed the door behind them I felt tears wallowing up my throat but wanted to be strong for both of us and bravely swallowed them down. I had to sit on the bench by the table because my knees were beginning to shake, their dirty dishes laid out in front of me. The cups were half empty, the pastry hardly touched. Winfried, in turn., took their visit with a whiff of nonchalance.

"That's how they are. They have done this before to other people in my family, when they did not agree with them and did not get their way. I can give you a few examples...."

He looked angry. I did not really want to hear more examples, but I remembered that some of his family members had not come to our wedding the year before, and I had wondered and worried about their approval of our relationship.

It was hard to plan our future with so much disapproval in the air and a nagging reminder of an unfulfilled will of God on our shoulders and in my hearts; but we went ahead anyway with our preparations to leave the country for two years.

The immigration process came to a screeching halt when the American Congress changed all immigration laws by December 1, 1965. Winfried's remaining letters validating full employment had not arrived in time. This meant that

CHAPTER TWENTY-SIX: 2020-21

we had to start all over again with the application and investigation process at the American Consulate in Frankfurt. From this new date on, a special document was needed to assure the American government that no American in The United States was available to perform a job before a foreigner from Europe was allowed to immigrate and be lawfully employed. Winfried's work in the church would require bilingual skills and a theological, professional level of expertise—not an easy combination. In addition, the quota for immigrants for Western European countries was drastically cut with the new law. Therefore, it took several more months before our final travel plans finalized.

March came around when all our immigration papers finally arrived. By that time, my graduation was in clear sight, my diploma thesis and my complete diagnostic case study completed. Winfried wrote to Los Angeles to request our joint departure for early May. Our trip would take us per train to Rotterdam, then per ocean liner to New York, and we would fly the last leg to Los Angeles. Maybe we would have a delayed honeymoon after all while crossing the Atlantic. The tickets arrived in our hands, the time to plan our departure had come.

On May 1, 1966, I finished my final oral exam with Professor de Boor at the University in Heidelberg. All the exams had been very formal in conduct including this last one. The atmosphere had been solemn and ceremonial. I had worn a black suit to these occasions. Some of my professors I had never personally met during my years of study until such a final exam. It consisted of an academic dialogue on any content matter they had taught in the last two years. I don't remember what we discussed but following this hour, the director of the psychological faculty shook my hand outside in the hallway with a formal "congratulations". That was it: five years of studying psychology had passed. I had completed my formal education, ready to work as a clinical psychologist. My plans had been to continue training in psychoanalysis at the Sigmund Freud Institute in Frankfurt while working with children and their families in a clinic setting. These plans however had to be shelved for the next two years. The University had no formal graduation ceremony. The formal diploma was to be mailed to me later.

My psychological department at the University of Heidelberg though had an informal graduation party planned up on the hills overlooking the valley and the river Neckar. There were about twelve psychology graduates that year and the celebration was boisterous and loud. We said goodbye to each other.

We shared our experiences and plans for the future. The heavy spring air was hanging in the vineyards and orchards. The stars were out in full illumination. We shared food and drank *Mai Bowle,* a sweet mixture of wine punch which contains *Waldmeister* or woodruff, a fragrant herb found in the woods, with strawberries floating on top. I don't know how late at night we got back on the bus to Hockenheim. The sweet wine and the academic relief had gotten the best of me. I slept on Winfried's shoulders all the way home.

The next few days passed in a blur with final packing and storing of our belongings in several locations. We had sold our new bedroom furniture and bought a small harpsichord instead which was to be shipped with the rest of our freight boxes.

We had already gone to Bad Bergzabern and said goodbye to my mother. Her eyes had been moist when we left her by the gate of her house. She did not want to show her emotions by crying. When she hugged Winfried, she said,

"Be good to her, take care of her!"

He nodded. She shed a few tears despite our assurance of our return in two years. I could not feel much inside, my thoughts were on the upcoming adventure. The future was too bright at the moment, the past too blurry. As we drove off, Mother stood by the garden gate. Her smile had vanished. I saw her standing by the curb, her arm raised, waving at us until we turned toward the main road in town. This moment froze in time.

Winfried's family had not said much more to us after that Sunday afternoon visit in Hockenheim. His goodbye to them was more a matter of fact. His grandmother's health was beginning to fail and she was going to miss his company. They had shared the same home for so many years. She had enjoyed his presence and his laughter. All her life, she had taken care of children, not only her own children, but also her stepchildren, her grandchildren, only to see them grow up and leave home. Mending socks, gardening and cooking seemed suddenly so useless to her. Food would be waiting for visitors only. The harvests in the garden would become more a burden than the annual victory. She could not express those feelings in words, but the deep folds in her face, her slight smile, and her slow gait spoke of a life full of hard work and heavy burden. Would we ever see her again? After all, she was the person that had taken Winfried and her sister in when their mother died in 1948.

CHAPTER TWENTY-SIX: 2020–21

On one of our visits to Frankfurt, we had stopped by my uncle's house, Bishop Wunderlich, and asked for his blessing on our lives and for our assignment at the church in Los Angeles. He smiled,

"I know, the Methodist church is much larger than our German denomination here. It is a global church; we all belong together in the spirit of God. Now you will be part of that larger connection in the faith."

Not a harsh word was said about our absence for the next two years. He understood it seemed. He knew of the internal tension within his church, the spiritual rigidity and harshness expressed in the name of Christ, the politics, and powers at work among his leaders. Year after year, he diligently worked with them, keeping the vision of an honest faith and a better world before them. He knew that common roots in faith could be expressed in different languages as well as in different places. For years, he had traveled extensively, spoke English fluently, and had befriended other church leaders around the globe, including Bishop Kennedy, Winfried's future bishop in California. He truly saw the world as one parish. I believe that he saw a wonderful opportunity for us in America where we could find a new spiritual freedom and a personal growth within the Methodist world community.

As we left his house, he hugged me, then dismissed us warmly with his blessing and best wishes for our voyage.

Our suitcases were packed, the apartment emptied, the coziness of the place had vanished into the dark of uncertainty. There was one last look over our shoulders as we walked down the stairs. No more time to say goodbye; but then, it was just for the next two years…

A few uncomfortable hours of sleep ended with a short car ride at 3:30 am in the morning of May 12th, 1966, to the train station in Mannheim where we were to catch the inter-city train heading North toward Rotterdam. The night was so dark, so empty and so quiet. Winfried's cousin, Horst, dropped us off at the train station with our suitcases, bags and coats. A hushed '*Auf Wiedersehen*' and a sleepy '*Danke Schön*' followed outside the train station. Then he was gone, and we stood alone on the train platform as the fast train moved swiftly toward us. Within minutes, the train began to move out of the station into the darkness of the night.

RETURN TO LEIPZIG

We scrambled for a place to put our luggage and found a seat in one of the dimly lit compartments. People sat quietly in their seats; their faces blurry in the gray shadows of the breaking day. I slumped down in one of the few empty seats and closed my eyes. Sleep and wake mixed in thought and faint images. This was an important moment in our life, I could feel it. The two of us were on our way, traveling to a place thousands of miles away to start a new life together. An adventure waited for us. A different language to adjust to, an unfamiliar climate to enter in, and most of all—we were leaving home. I could not think much about it now. Puzzling feelings of anticipation mixed with relief and numbness, joined by my light doze grounded in the rhythmic thrust of the fast moving train. We would be living in America, a land where 'milk and honey' flows. So many years had passed since the war and the much needed help we received from the people somewhere in California. We would be able to distance ourselves from the war torn history of Germany and live in a free country. Maybe even the church would be less rigid and restrictive. Maybe God had a different face there. I could not think about leaving my family behind. My brothers were busy with their lives, we really did not need each other anymore it seemed. My Mother had built finally her home and had settled in the small town. She still worked hard and could manage nicely for the next few years without me. As her only daughter, however, I pushed away feelings of guilt for leaving her alone. In my silence, I could not allow myself to feel more losses. Life had already brought too many changes which I could not reflect on at this moment. I was going one more time through the night into a new territory, an unknown future. So I looked into the flickering lights of the window and the shadows dancing on the compartment walls; only the silence carried the heaviness of the moment. I waited for an uneasy sleep.

The day broke slowly as we entered the Rhine valley. The river led the way along vineyards, past small villages, and pointed church steeples. Castles had been placed on strategic hill sides, ruins stood untouched for centuries—still there to tell tales of faded glory and fighting for power and access to the river. Short tunnels opened surprising views of the valley, bringing the first glare of the morning sun light. The darkness of the night with its shadows was forced to vanish quickly; a new day dawned ahead of us.

"Where are you going with all this luggage?" the man sitting across from Winfried asked him in perfect English.

CHAPTER TWENTY-SIX: 2020–21

Was this our first language test right here along the Rhine valley in the early morning?

"We are on our way to Los Angeles. We are traveling to Rotterdam today." Winfried answered.

"You are going to America? We live in Seattle, in the Northwest of the States along the same Pacific coastline. We really like it there. Are you visiting there? Your English is really good!"

"No, we are going to be there for about two years to work in a church."

The man nodded and smiled while he started to tell us all about Los Angeles: the great location, the center of Hollywood, the city of Pasadena, and the snow covered mountains in the winter with the orange trees in the valleys. The sandy beaches by the Pacific would be waiting for us. I got lost in the details of his descriptions.

"They make good Mexican food there, it's a bit hot, though."

"What is hot Mexican food?" Winfried asked.

"Yeah, I mean, it is really spicy." He laughed.

"You have to get used to it—we really like it a lot. You have to try it. Tamales are the best, so are the Margaritas."

By that time, my language skills had given out. Hot food and tamales at six o'clock in the morning was too confusing to think about. I was surprised to find these Amis so friendly, so talkative, so accepting of our plans. He did not seem at all surprised about our church assignment in Los Angeles. I felt so hesitant to talk to a stranger on the train about our plans, but Winfried kept chatting along in the new language, looking quite at ease.

The train pulled into Cologne, stopped long enough in the station to see the enormous cathedral nearby from our train window. The Amis left our compartment and told us that they wanted to see the city before returning to Seattle in a few days. They waved goodbye and wished us a good trip. We headed North toward the border to the Netherlands, arriving in Rotterdam in the early afternoon.

RETURN TO LEIPZIG

Our first look at the ocean liner 'New Amsterdam' of the Holland-America Line was truly stunning. I had never seen such an enormous ship topped by two huge yellow and green-white striped chimney stacks. Various decks were marked by many windows and walkways. I noticed the life saving rafts suspended on each top level. This boat would be our hotel on water for the next five days, a special time to make up for our missed honeymoon.

We checked into our room on board of the ship that afternoon with great anticipation. The long, carpeted hallways had been lined by handrails to assist the passengers during a storm. Our room had a round bull-eye window at water level which allowed for some day light and a view of the coast line. Two Pullman bunk beds had been made up with white linen. The small bathroom in our cabin was quite sufficient. A steward had been assigned to each section of a floor and was available for questions and extra service. While we explored the dining room and ate our first dinner on ship, he attended to our beds by opening the blankets and draping our night ware in a decorative way over each bed. My nightgown had never gotten such an elegant display before. A rose was placed next to it.

CHAPTER TWENTY-SIX: 2020–21

Winfried and I explored the boat with its unending, carpeted corridors, the various deck levels for viewing and parading, and the seating areas with resting chairs. There was an outdoor pool on the top deck. A newspaper announced the entertainment calendar for the next few days. Another level housed a full general store, a hairdresser, and full medical services. A small library and a sitting area open at all times. Mealtimes were scheduled at convenient hours. Food was always available, it seemed. People dressed up for their dinner time in the big dining room. We were not really prepared for much elegance and fancy. I did not own a dinner dress. The little we had was in crates on some freighter.

The weather was overcast, the winds calm as we pulled out of the harbor during the early evening hours. The captain had warned us over the loudspeaker of the deep upcoming horn signals which would announce our noisy departure. Several guide ships pulled ahead of us to assure a safe exit through the harbor canals toward the open channel. As night fell, the coast lined up in a string of lights with the dark space announcing the beginning distance to the Old Country.

What a strange night this was for us. Sleeping along with the deep hum of the roaring engines while floating on water. The rhythm of the waves added a rocking comfort to my uneasy feelings of an unknown future. We were on our way to the New World.

The next morning returned the brightness of light and mind with the clear blue sky and the open view of the ocean ahead of us. We headed toward the Irish coast, docked in the open waters and took on a number of passengers and some cargo. Although the liner could house up to 1300 passengers, the official count on our passage was more like 500 people. We enjoyed the comfort of the day, the colorful spectacle of nature including the traveling birds in tow. In the afternoon at 3 o'clock, a *Glockenspiel*, a carillon organ, was played at the tail end of the boat. The keyboard consisted of a row of wooden sticks to be hammered by hand and would cause the bells to ring. A string of melodies lifted into the wet and salty ocean air and vanished into the gray sky with a flair of mystery.

My bonnie flew over the ocean, my bonnie flew over the sea....

Every mealtime brought delightful surprises. We had met a young couple from Switzerland who actually was on their honeymoon to New York. With their help did we slowly decipher each printed Menu, handed to us by attentive waiters. The most confusing part included the breakfast menu. Who would eat potatoes, *Bratkartoffel,* early in the morning together with ham and eggs? I looked around—and they did! Scrambled eggs, small sausages, and something like 'sunny-side-up' eggs, they called it. I was used to a boiled egg on Sunday mornings, but these people around us ate this heavy combination of food every day. To my surprise, the pancakes looked so different compared to the crepes I knew. They heaped butter and sweet-sweet syrup on top of it—too much! The toast we ordered looked more like white, fluffy paper. They used it as a side dish to soak up the drips of the meal. Winfried discovered the waffles they offered and took a liking to them immediately. Water over ice cubes and juice was always available. All the passengers liked to drink at breakfast, lunch and dinner. It was so strange; why were they always thirsty? Even at 11 o'clock in the morning while lying on deck in one of the chairs, the steward offered a bowl

CHAPTER TWENTY-SIX: 2020–21

of broth in a white china dish with a white cloth linen napkin and drinks! So much food to choose from in just one day!

I had noticed that the tables were sturdy. The legs had been anchored in the floor and were equipped with a wooden rim in case the heavy sea would move dishes and glasses around. I thought nothing of it, the steady motion of the ship hardly conveyed any swells as we headed toward the Irish Sea. The story of the fateful Titanic colliding with icebergs somewhere remained a fantastic trauma a long time ago. A foolish adventure anyway, it seemed.

It was not long after we left Ireland that the captain's weather report included the announcement of a few stormy days ahead of us. The Irish Sea was known for its unpredictable weather and has a long history of sea lore and shanties. Stories commemorate the beauty of the ocean, the sea life, and the challenge that comes in the face of nature.

Within hours, the captain's predictions were verified by the choppy sea around us, the white crowns riding the waves, and the misty air whipping around us on the open decks. To walk straight forward became a task by itself. Suddenly there was a good reason for the hand railings everywhere. Fewer people walked the decks that day. The dining room was almost completely empty that night as the ship moved into the storm raging around us. The table rims came in handy too, catching the slipping cups and plates. Winfried and I walked down to the inside pool on one of the lower decks. Of course, it was closed, but we could see through the door what was happening to the water inside the pool. With each breaking ocean swell, the water content of the pool smashed against one wall only to crash into the opposite wall with the change of motion. It was a spectacle by itself to see the water move in such powerful motion.

Within a few hours, Winfried's stomach succumbed to the strong motions around us. The most comfortable place from now on was a horizontal one, the bed. I held up pretty well, keeping my eyes toward the water and taking in the breezy air whenever I could.

The motions around us changed from a rocking wave to a jammed, arrhythmic and suspenseful crashing. We could hear the ship propeller lifting out of the water, the screeching of the blades, and the sudden drop of the boat into the massive water like falling into a bottomless pit. The ship seemed to quiver and rumble before a new cycle of motion. The stomach understood these events exactly and responded accordingly… nausea set in. The solid ground was no more. Waves and flowing swells, surf and white caps, surge and flood announced a different path ahead of us.

I sat by the window looking at nature's rage outside, the wind hauling in between the ship engines' forced rest. Night had fallen. The lights of the ship were barely reflected in the wild sea. The darkness seemed endless. Only the rising moon between the dark clouds added a gray shimmer as if to illuminate the mystery of the storm.

I began to feel scared. Danger was so close and so enormous. There was nothing I could do but ride the waves in the middle of the Atlantic Ocean. The storm outside had stirred up my deeper, held down feelings as doubts slowly drifted to the surface. Was this storm a signal that we should have stayed at home in Germany? Were we on a shipwreck course just like the Titanic had been? Was God punishing us for leaving his church back home where we belonged? Maybe Winfried's family was right when they told us this whole idea about going to America was leading us into the wrong direction.

There was no use in lying down and sleeping, the emotions too strong, the questions so deep. I looked at Winfried lying on his bed. He was asleep, his regular breathing a soothing sound in the middle of the storm. The boat rocked him forth and back, carrying him like Jonah in the swimming whale. He had told me that as a boy he had lived next to the train station in Hoffenheim. Therefore, he was used to engine noises, to incoming and out-going trains, and the sounds of the steam and later diesel engines. To him the boat ride and engine's rattle blended in familiar sounds, a memory of comfort? I smiled. Here he was, the servant of the Lord asleep in midst of a raging storm with hurricane forces outside and rocked in the arms of God. My faith was more blown out of the window and floating in the waves of the water, hoping for the calming of the sea.

This was to be our honeymoon time, a restful journey to enjoy before we would enter the New World and the ministry in Los Angeles. I thought back to the time when we first met in 1961 at the University in Heidelberg. My brother, Gerhard, had introduced us at the *Mensa,* the commons, one day in May of 1961. We had sat across the table from each other eating *Eintopf,* some one dish meal, maybe lentil soup with wieners. We had looked at each other with interest. Winfried still commuted back and forth between Hoffenheim and Heidelberg, but soon became a regular visitor in my world. He would remember to bring strawberries from the family's garden and fresh flowers for my dark room. With his presence, the beautiful sites in Heidelberg took on a special shine. Our walks across the Old Bridge and along the Neckar filled many afternoons. One Saturday night, we watched the old castle illuminated by fireworks and orange flames as we sat by the banks of the river. That night, I did not get back until the wee hours.

My room became a special refuge to discover feelings of love and affection. Thank God for the warm down comforter I had in my room to keep us warm. We were able to share our histories and began to see our joint future ahead of us. Both of us were committed to completing our education at the University as soon as possible. I studied on a financial aid program that did not allow me to work during semester breaks. Instead, I was to use the extra time for further study. During the fall semester, Winfried and I attended the same lectures in the *Alte Aula* of the University; he usually would save me a seat. We also shared our interests in music. Sometimes, he would join me on a concert tour, and we both sang in the University choir under Professor Penzien who also gave Winfried some organ lessons.

Life seemed so much lighter with his presence in my life. It was clear to me that our lives would be joined as our commitment to each other became clearer. On a vacation trip to Switzerland together with my mother and my brother, Gerhard and his girlfriend, Sigrid, we secretly bought wedding bands in Davos at a local jeweler. Winfried put the little box with the rings in his pocket and nobody knew about them, not even the customs at the border. Winfried never formally proposed to me, he just kind of assumed that I had said yes to our marriage plans. I smiled about it but remembered that he had gone to speak to my mother about his plans to marry me first and had asked her for her blessings. She gladly had done so. We were engaged in 1963 at a small celebration when he put that gold band on my finger. At that time, I had met Winfried's sister, Irmgard, and her husband, Erich, for the first time, who lived in Pasadena and now awaited our arrival.

After our engagement in 1963, we had spent some time apart from each other. Winfried had studied a semester at the University of Mainz, then one semester at the University of Marburg before returning to Heidelberg to finish up his degree. Theological education was enriched by studying at different Universities, depending on the presence of a well-known professor. I stayed in

Heidelberg for the whole course of my studies. We wrote letters to each other and occasionally visited each other.

The day of our wedding in Bergzabern came in May of 1965. I had the jitters in the morning as I put on the white gown I had bought used from a friend. Winfried and I had already been legally married in a small civil ceremony the day before at the city hall in Bergzabern. The church wedding on May 15th in the *Bergkirche* was conducted by Winfried's uncle, Karl Beisiegel, and attended by most of our immediate family members. My brothers Klaus and Herbert provided the festive music performed from the balcony of the old church. Organ and flute music filled the beautiful chapel. I cannot remember much of what was said during the sermon....

That night after the festivities, we left for Hockenheim, for our own apartment that Winfried's cousin, Theophil, had fixed up for us....

I looked over to Winfried lying in his bunk bed. He still was deep asleep in the middle of the storm. I crawled in my bed and tried to close my eyes, my mind was floating on water, drifting on waves, in the storm and through the night....

The next day, the dining room seemed deserted. Nobody felt like eating much or could not even think of food. Our new friends at the table looked tired and shaken up,

"Guess what, they came to our door in the middle of the night, knocked, and told us that we needed to close the metal shutters of the windows. We thought it was time for the lifeboats!" They shook their heads with a chocked laughter.

Winfried smiled at them. He had spent a pretty restful night and his stomach was getting used to the surf. He bent over the pancakes in front of him topped them with butter and syrup and then requested special sunny side up eggs. His coffee cups was filled to the rim and swayed with the ride over the next wave. I did not report my dark rumination by the window during the night, nor my fears of knocks at the door to call us to the lifeboats.

"You should see the front area of the boat," the man said.

"The windows in the sitting rooms were smashed in last night. There is glass all over the place, actually the whole side of the ship is closed right now. They have boarded up the windows."

The dancing ocean had toyed with our boat, kicked it around a bit on top of the waves. The dining tables were still swaying with the tide, the cups sliding

CHAPTER TWENTY-SIX: 2020–21

ever so slightly. That morning, the captain announced that we had experienced a hurricane last night with wind strength ten. I had little idea what exactly the number meant, but I knew of the sounds and sights of a rough voyage. I quickly dismissed the notion of a dark omen for our future to a country we were about to enter.

"The storm should be subsiding soon, maybe tomorrow. Due to the general weather forecast, we will not be arriving in New York as planned. We'll be delayed a day or so," the captain casually announced.

We quickly realized that our connection to Los Angeles per plane out of New York would be lost.

The Atlantic storm traveled with us for the next three days though to a less violent degree but brought more rain, wind and fog banks. On the 15th of May, we received a telegram from Winfried's sister and family in Pasadena to wish us a happy first anniversary. We were so surprised to be remembered in the middle of the ocean.

There was time to write and start reporting home the experiences of our stormy voyage. I sat on one the lounge chairs and wrote:

In the middle of the ocean,

May 15, 1966

Dear Mutti!

You should receive some news from us, even if the letter will be sent off from New York. Please excuse the scribble here but I am lying in a deck chair and try to write on my lap. We are enjoying our voyage with the good and the bad. We have experienced so much during the last few days; we have not been bored.

The ocean liner is enormous. Since there are only about 500 passengers on board (and about 700 crew members), there is enough space to move around comfortably. We can even visit the captain, his control wheel, and the bridge. The service is outstanding, we have nothing to worry about but eat, sleep and look around! The first one is going well except for a few incidents. Each mealtime is announced by a printed menu with choices for each course. Sleeping is not that easy because for about three days, we had a bad storm. The captain talked about wind strength 10; it could have been more. The ship was aching and groaning, and we could hardly sleep with that noise. A huge wave smashed in some windows and shook the boat mightily. Nature was presenting us with a show; I had the feeling we were constantly riding in an elevator, up and down. Late last night, the storm subsided, and this morning we had dense fog that the sun will push aside. Yes, we lived through moving days! Winfried made offerings only once to the God of the ocean. That happened in the Irish Sea, famous for its tricky weather. I managed ok so far. We try to eat a lot and to stay in the fresh air. That's the best you can do.

Because of the storm, we will be delayed and will arrive one day later in New York than scheduled. This way, we can stay here a little longer and enjoy ourselves. The whole ship is like a small town. There are stores, a pool, and a ship newspaper with the latest announcements. Even a fashion designer is on board, maybe on his way to New York. On two different occasions did we see a fashion show with beautiful Dutch models. Then there was a hat parade. All the passengers were invited to make their own hats, the best ones won a prize. Every day brings something new.

It is so interesting to meet new people on board. We share our table with a Swiss couple on their honeymoon. We also have to start speaking English which we need to practice. Yesterday, we celebrated our first wedding anniversary. We received a radio telegram from Irmgard and Erich—what a surprise! Maybe you are interested in the route of crossing we took so far. We started in Rotterdam, then on to Southampton, on to Cob, Ireland, and then we headed across the Atlantic. Tonight, we should be close to Newfoundland, and by then the bad weather should be over with. Despite it all, we spent a lot of time on the open deck, wrapped up in blankets. The air is so clear, so salty and so cold. Even this letter got some sprinkles—that's what happens when you write on the open deck.

This short letter should be it for today. Just wanted to let you know how we are doing and that we are ok given the circumstances. I have been thinking about a line of a song, but can't remember the rest:

"Eine Seefahrt, die ist lustig, eine Seefahrt die ist schön, ... (A sea voyage is great; a sea voyage is so beautiful ...)

Greetings to all, I will write later from Los Angeles. Give my greetings to Klaus,

CHAPTER TWENTY-SIX: 2020–21

> Elizabeth and children, Gerhard, Sigrid, Karlchen, Herbert and Gerhild.
>
> Love,
> *Maria and Winfried*

We got our first glimpse of the New World early on May 18th, when the tugboats decorated with the American flag met us out in the foggy weather. In the far distance, a gray mountain emerged outlining the silhouette of buildings.

"It is New York, the skyline of Manhattan!" someone said on the front deck.

We had crowded on the top deck and watched the gray mist dissolve into clearer lines of towers. I had heard about the Empire State building to be the highest of all the skyscrapers. I never dreamt of seeing it for myself one day. We passed the Statue of Liberty on the left, the welcoming symbol for all immigrants. Today she was greetings us, too? We did not really feel like immigrants. Our plans included a two year stay in California, I reminded myself. We would be more like post-graduate visitors, having a chance to travel, to learn a language we only had practiced in a dark classroom many years ago. I did not want to think about how I felt leaving my family behind and arriving in a huge and dangerous city where millions of people lived. I tried very hard not to be scared and ignored my twinges of fear.

The excitement of arriving in the New World was written all over our faces. The stormy nights were forgotten including Winfried's peaceful slumber and my fretting at the window. People talked, laughed, and pointed to various directions. Everyone rushed to their cabin to fetch their luggage. Final goodbye was said. Finally, we pulled to the West side docks of town and got ready to disembark. One final blow of the horn and the mighty engines began to slow down to a soft hum.

"Be aware that New York is going through a bus and taxi strike. There may be no regular transportation available in town!" the captain had announced early that morning.

During our crossing, we had met several American students who were on their way back from an exchange year. They had taken this information with great ease and advised us to seek overnight stay at a student house similar to the European Youth Hostels, they had used in Europe. Since we had no accommodations waiting for us, we took them up on their advice and decided to spend a night or two there, explore New York, and then proceed to Los Angeles by plane.

"Just take the 1-0-5 Bus North," they had said and had given us the address, too.

The process of immigration went smoothly. We handed over all the required papers, and received our blue laminated card documenting the day of entrance, and our social security number. From this moment on, we were official, resident aliens, and stepped on land. Our first day in the United States, Manhattan in front of us—the New World!

We managed to drag our luggage to Central Station and stored it in one of the lockers. I felt quite uneasy about leaving our luggage in a locker somewhere in the middle of Manhattan, but Winfried was assured about it and did not notice my hesitation. After some effort, we were able to find a bus to take us into the area of the student house. At first, the bus drove along streets with busy shops and restaurants where people were walking. Everything looked so different: strange street signs, store windows stuffed with merchandise, and a new chatter of language in our ears. As the bus headed North, the neighborhood changed quickly. Fewer people were walking on the road, the houses were neglected, and trash everywhere: in the gutters, hanging from fences, flying in the air. We exited the bus and found ourselves walking in a quiet residential neighborhood carrying our suitcases, purse and camera hanging over our shoulders. We knocked at the open door of a brown-stone house matching the given address.

"Come on in!" someone yelled from upstairs.

We stepped inside. The house was dark and smelled moldy. Waves of sweet smoke lingered in the hallway.

A young man greeted us and sent us upstairs to the top floor, where we could stay in separate rooms and spend the night. One room for women, the other for men. The bathroom would be shared, he said. My bedroom had several beds in it, covered with some grayish-white linen. On the way upstairs, I had seen several people lying on the floor, actually in front of a fire place. They seemed sleepy but not really asleep. The dim light coming through the window shades gave them a green-dusty look. They appeared to stare into another world. A strange odor filled the hallway. They were smoking thin cigarettes.

CHAPTER TWENTY-SIX: 2020–21

After I had put down my luggage in the bedroom assigned to me, I stepped into the bathroom. In the middle of the bathtub crawled a large brown cockroach, moving toward the window—I jumped. I had never seen such a big bug in my life. The German, *Maikäfer* I knew, were a weak imitation of this creature. The floor was dirty, the mirrors untouched for years.

Winfried must have seen the look on my face as we met in the hallway.

"We can't stay here tonight," he said.

"What are we going to do?"

"You stay here with the stuff, and I'll call for some other hotel place."

With that, he left me sitting on my bed surrounded by our luggage. I put my purse right next to me and held on to Winfried's camera. The minutes passed painstakingly slow. I had no idea where we had ended up on our first day in the New World, and I was scared. Scared to lose our luggage and scared for Winfried out there in a strange neighborhood. I had read about the high crime rate in New York back in Germany and began to worry about what could happen to him out on the streets. What if they robbed him of his money he had brought? What would I do by myself? With each passing minute, my thoughts turned darker and darker. What if he got lost? I stared at my watch. The minutes ticked away. The eerie silence in the house began to twirl around me. I just sat there on the bed....

Finally, after 45 minutes, he came running up the stairs.

"Boy, what a mess. The phone booth at the comer was not working, I had to run to the next block. Then I tried to call this distant aunt of mine in Brooklyn, but she could not help me at all. Finally, I got a hold of our airline, and they directed me to a hotel in town where we can spend the night. They are sending a cab for us in a few minutes to pick us up at the comer downstairs."

I was so relieved to see him back alive that any plan seemed all right to get us out of this crack house. With all our luggage in tow, we slipped out of the house without saying anything, stood by the curb site until a yellow taxi picked us up and took us to the Hudson Hotel on 353 West 57th Street in Manhattan. I was so relieved to walk into a well-lit hotel with a smiling receptionist. The room on the 23rd floor was a welcome refuge that night. The window opened wide to let the hot and humid air inside. Rain had fallen by now, and the noise coming from the streets below was deafening. I was still shaking from our odyssey that afternoon in the "student house". Despite the hot and humid air, I was freezing cold and had to huddle close to Winfried all night. The sirens never stopped; the traffic never let up. We had arrived in a city that never sleeps. I feared several times, the Hotel was on fire!

> Henry Hudson Hotel
> New York, May 18th, 1966
>
> Dear Mutti,
>
> Your letter is still here—this way we can tell you right away that we arrived safely on land and after some wandering around, we found a nice place to stay. It is late at night, and the overwhelming impressions of the city twirl around in my head. The last few days on the ship were beautiful, sunny and entertaining. We land creatures though are glad to be back on land again. The entrance toward New York was spectacular. Some fog ahead of us suddenly revealed the silhouette of New York. Our boat had been decorated with many colorful flags. The whole experience was like a dream, too much to take in. We will stay here tomorrow and explore the city. The skyscrapers are so awesome to look at, and people of all different races walk the streets…
>
> As you can tell by my writing, I better get some sleep—

> May 19, 1966
>
> We slept quite well on the 23rd floor, somewhere below us the traffic roared. The city is wrapped in rain and fog, for us an opportunity to visit one of the big museums.
>
> We are having breakfast in a drugstore where you can purchase toiletry, cosmetics—similar to our Drogerien—but next to it is a section with a counter to sit at and eat. I have never seen anything like it before in my life.
>
> It is really warm here, humid, and foggy. We have been spoiled by the fresh air out on the ocean. Both of us got some tan, the exam- paleness is gone. Even my nose is sunburned … it looks suspicious.
>
> I will close for now. Greetings from your children,
>
> Maria and Winfried

CHAPTER TWENTY-SIX: 2020-21

Our sightseeing day in New York turned out to be a wet affair. We had trouble looking through the steamy windows as the rains poured down for hours. Water was gushing down the gutters everywhere. Later on did we learn that this was the wettest day they had in years! Everything looked gray over gray, even St. Patrick's cathedral was dark inside, the pale colors of the stain glass windows without shine. We spent the afternoon at the Modem Museum of Art which houses European and American masters. Picasso's sculpture of his goat stood in a beautiful, garden courtyard. The presence of paintings and avant-garde creativity made us feel more welcome and gave us a time of reprieve from the enormous noise of street traffic and the bombardment of language chatter. I tried so hard to understand—my head was spinning.

Early on May 20th, we left New York for Los Angeles by plane from JFK airport. Neither one of us had ever been on an airplane before. I was quite nervous about it and tried to sit quietly in my seat. The plane did not seem crowded as we roared down the runway. The noise was deafening, the ascent so steep. The plane tilted immediately to the side, flaring out toward the ocean. My heart sank. I thought the plane was losing balance and direction. I held on tightly to my arm rest and Winfried next to me. Once above the clouds, we soared on wings all the way to Los Angeles. Down below, the continent took on new dimensions, expansive country sides, endless fields, snowcapped mountains, and desert land. We arrived safely in Los Angeles that day receiving a warm welcome by Winfried's sister, Irmgard, by a number of our future parishioners, and the Rev. Dr. Richard Cain. Our life in the new World was about to begin.

"Just for two years?"

July 1, 1966

Dear family!

Thank you for your letters. Mutti, your second letter arrived today, and I decided to postpone all other activities in order to tell you how we are getting along. It is hard to believe that we are already working here for the last four weeks and live in this beautiful house.

In the meantime, we have gotten to know our congregation a little better. There must be a total of about 150 members, about 100 in worship on Sunday mornings. That is quite remarkable; maybe it will remain this way.

The congregation—may I say so—has grown into a somewhat aging club over the century. Everyone tends to the German tradition that they left some time ago. This is understandable, we will most likely do the same. The cultural mixture is quite interesting. The theological field resembles more a compost pile with many weeds and sour pickles, but it appears that the underlying soil could be potentially fruitful. Winfried compares his task to the sower with the four-fold field who is sowing freely with far reaching movements, in the hope that some seeds will fall on good soil.

The church music is not much to crow about. They sing and they have a choir including a men's choir. Most of the hymns Winfried asks them to sing are totally new for them—you should hear them sing! Many people are delighted about the new style and participate enthusiastically. Even the choir started to sing some classical pieces and some contemporary tunes. So much is going on in our lives.

Many members in the church seem to understand that as a Christian today you cannot remain in the Middle Ages. We are happy about their attitude and do not view our task as hopeless. Tasteful, Christian art has gotten lost here. It is their custom to have a printed program for each Sunday which includes church news, and the order of service. The pictures on the covers are usually decorated with sentimental images of our Lord Jesus portrayed with long locks and dusty feet. One of our first tasks became the search for a new bulletin cover—we were able to find them! There are so many details to think about in order to polish the image of a backyard congregation.

We spent one whole week at this year's annual conference of the Methodist Church at the University of Redlands. The location of the conference was close to the mountains, at the edge of the desert, and it was so hot during the first few days that we could hardly walk in the sun. It was our first opportunity to meet the Methodists in this country. The legislative sessions were frequently interrupted by entertainment. One person told the latest jokes; unfortunately, I could only understand one of many! Then a large choir from Hawaii sang and danced, (Hula dance, or something like that). People sang, danced, and performed skits—right in the chapel in front of the cross. The Bishop sat next to all this spectacle and seemed pleased.

CHAPTER TWENTY-SIX: 2020-21

We met many new people, or we got reacquainted with a few. We saw Dr. Williams, Bob Blaney, and friends of the Sawyers—who belonged to the Sunday school class in the 40's. We were so impressed that the church here does not only turn around itself but openly discusses current problems in society even problems among the membership of the conference and clergy. Of course, we felt quite insecure with our poor language skills and a whole week of English speaking was really helpful. We felt quite at home with our new colleagues and friends, and felt accepted by them. At the end of the week, Winfried was ordained a deacon, so that he can do his duties in the local church.

Sure enough, during the first week an old woman died in the congregation. We rushed to buy Winfried a black robe, and to his surprise the ceremony had to be held in English. Thank God, we did not know the content of the coffin. That would have been too much: all the bereaved, speaking in English, a new robe not to stumble over, half a flower shop as decor at the mortuary, and electronic, tremolo music. Well, for the first service—it went all right. We were both relieved when we were back in the car heading home. Winfried will be wearing this robe every Sunday to conduct services. In two weeks, he will conduct a wedding at our church, and a baptism will follow… You see, the work is going full force.

This following incident recently happened during a weekly Bible study. After the study part, everyone was invited to pray. This old Babushka, Hulda Meyer had listened attentively and started to pray,

"Well, dear God, we already know your Word quite well—but a professional gets still more out of it!"

At the next Bible study, she prayed again,

"Dearest God, we thank you. I think with the new preacher you sent us someone good again!"

I had to keep a straight face throughout.

Our main luggage has not arrived yet, our travel luggage was forwarded to us without extra cost although we came by boat only as far as New York. Therefore, I have my kitchen stuff. In the meantime, we have a new refrigerator with frost-free freezer, a vacuum cleaner with cleaning tools, new lamps and a round couch table. I am a comfortable housewife with

> washing machine and steam iron. Finally, today the previous minister moved his belongings out of the house. His family had left it here for the last 4 weeks—for the first time I saw the complete house empty. Winfried's study will be very nice and full of light after the bugs and the dirt have been removed. At this moment, he sits there and contemplates his next sermon. In the emptied study we found an ancient, green couch, heat. We had to unwrap it at the harbor and then transported it home in our VW. Since the instrument is less than one year old, the customs fee had to be paid.
>
> We started this morning to attend adult English classes at the Los Angeles city college for the next six weeks. Every morning between 8 and 10 o'clock, a conversational English class, we need it badly!
>
> We look forward to your next letter. It is not that far, and only takes about 4 days!
>
> Greetings,
> Maria and Winfried

"Just for two years?" ...

Maria and Rev. Winfried Ritter at The German Methodist Church, Los Angeles, CA 1966.

Epilogue: Temple City, 2014

My dear faithful readers, all of you, my children, grandchildren, family members and you,

Time had come to return the folder of mother's precious letters to the Temple City United Methodist Church in gratitude for the 64 CARE packages and money they had sent between those horrible years or war and survival. How could I ever say thank you for such kindness? The only way would be to tell the story and never ever forget the capacity of persons to have empathy and see beyond war and hate, reach out to feed the hungry, comfort the grief stricken, and help others in their need.

"We are looking forward to seeing you tomorrow and welcoming you in the service," Marcia had said a few days after the Christmas Holidays. "Afterwards, you can greet some people that remember the folks of the Artaban Sunday School Class and even know their names. Then, we want you to be our guest for lunch."

Marcia, of course, referred to the picture that my brother Klaus took of the Sunday School Class when he traveled in the US and visited them in 1957. He stands there in the middle, back row, smiling and surrounded by all the people that contributed to our family's survival. I do not know them all by name, but I know that each one of them had followed the calling of the 4th Wiseman, a true Saint in my mind. Likewise, all have finished their journey by now, except for one woman sitting in the front row. "She is in a nursing home," Marcia said.

I had carefully copied all the letters and other documents in the folder, the fragile papers carefully folded back into the plastic holders. Having had the folder in my home for quite some time made it hard to say goodbye to it. They represented such an important time in my family's history and the evidence of their letters connected me more so with my mother and her thoughts and feelings during that time, a homecoming of sorts. Maybe the letters were meant as a visit from the past not just in pictures, but in words written on bleached papers and run ink. Some letters had been written with a pencil. I am sure that was all mother had to write with. A small brown ring book among all the letters contained each line item written down by the Artaban Sunday School secretary of each food and clothing items sent. Each CARE package was documented on one page. It spoke so directly of the choice of purchases made, of each personal donation and the exact price. Why did the secretary document their actions with such diligence? The Artaban's mission and their records became a living document to tell the story. Maybe I will be able to keep the little brown booklet as a witness. It is a priceless treasure.

Traffic on the bumpy freeways on Sunday morning toward Los Angeles was light and flowed easily with the San Gabriel Mountains in clear view. There was time before the service to look around the town of Temple City. We entered several residential streets with familiar looking single homes so poorly maintained, lagging a fresh coat of paint, with half trimmed front lawns, and roughed up sidewalks. They had seen a much better time with lace curtains in windows, flower beds with blooming geraniums and birds of paradise plants, painted fences and inviting gates.

"I used to come here for a Bible study during the years when we lived in Los Angeles," Winfried mused.

I remembered those evenings, sitting in someone's living room with Winfried leading the study for mostly old, tired, yet dedicated Christian folks with long prayers to follow his theological explanations on the grace of God in our human frailty.

It all came back when I looked at the older, single homes on this quiet Sunday morning.

"It is like a time warp to me. Not much has changed in this neighborhood close to these mountains. I remember these homes so well, the avocado green and orange carpets, the narrow streets and all except the people's faces have changed. It reminds me of our trip to China a few years back and people walking on the streets."

EPILOGUE: TEMPLE CITY, 2014

Over the years, a large Chinese population had moved in and made this community their home. A new group of immigrants had arrived and was looking for a better future just like when we arrived in this country in 1966, and many German immigrants lived right here in the San Gabriel Valley.

Most signs on the small stores along the main road were in Chinese, a bridal store at the corner displayed gowns and accessories, a noodle shop further down the street still closed this morning. The display over the entrance, a large bowl of soup overflowing with noodles would invite any hungry soul, and I remembered the smell of warm steamy chicken flavored broth while cruising down the Yangtze River last year. On the left a 'German Piano' store sign seemed totally out of place but served as the reminder of previous generations and how us German immigrants tried to continue our musical heritage and teach the next generation.

"There's is no Starbuck's in sight," I muttered, looking for some coffee before making our way to church. "Maybe, over there at the Ralph's market."

But Starbuck's had not invaded the main street yet, not even inside the Ralph's Market which was open for business as usual. Across the street, the doors to the Clover Leaf Bakery and Café opened and closed with people returning to their cars. The sweet smell of cinnamon, freshly baked pastries welcomed us. Young people walked in and out, a woman picked up breakfast on a tray, and an elderly man sat at a table nearby, wearing a decorated cap which read, "WWII Veteran." Even after all these years, here too, we found reminders of war as he sat there and witnessed to the hardship and pride of service and survival. It seemed such a painful reminder on this special Sunday morning when I was here to remember the years after the war and the recovery efforts on the victors and the survivors' sides. The cycle of strife and stemming the tide never stops.

"The wallpaper over there has a picture of Sigmund Freud on it and a quote." Winfried pointed to the back wall of the coffee shop near the restrooms.

"What is he doing here?"

"Maybe to set an atmosphere of the Vienna Café houses," he grinned.

I walked over and quickly jotted down the following quote printed in Spanish, on the wallpaper of a Chinese owned coffee shop serving everyone in Temple City, California.

"Non siamo mai cosi prividi difese, come nel momento in cui amiamo."

RETURN TO LEIPZIG

"We are never so defenseless, as when we love." (1939)

I had to ponder this statement for some time to come and consider the risking act of loving as true vulnerability. Why are we defending against this special human ability?

Marcia's husband, Bob, waited for us in front in the church courtyard and greeted us with warm welcome. A woman joined us.

"I am Carol Daugherty, the one who put the folder together after I found all your mother's letters stuffed into a plastic bag." We hugged as if we had known ea other for a long time; in a way we did. She had read my book and knew all about my family's history.

"I can never thank you enough." That was all I could get out without choking on my tears.

We learned that the church housed a thriving Chinese congregation with two services and an English speaking, smaller congregation. The choir was rehearsing in the sanctuary the old familiar hymns. We were asked to sit up front like you would seat special guests. The singing, the smell of candle wax, the piano music and congregational singing seemed so familiar, yet they seemed to come from a time long past. Maybe, today I was here to honor all the persons not sitting in those pews anymore, the Saints of the church gone ahead of us who prayed,

"Lord, you deliver the needy when they call.

You take pity on the weak and the poor who have no one to help them...."

The faces had changed, the message was the same. Listening, praying, and responding is going on just like it has in ages past.

After Marcia introduced me, I presented the congregation with a framed picture of the Artaban Sunday School Class of 1957 below and read the following statement:

EPILOGUE: TEMPLE CITY, 2014

Back row: Clarence Parker, Norm Scott, Richard Boeck ?, Ed Sawyer, Klaus Schnädelbach, Marion Scott, Mrs. Richard Boeck, Wilma Vogt, Stan Vogt. Front row: ?, Victoria Shoemaker, Lotte Parker, Beth Armagost, Jean Schaeffer, ? Lillian Sawyer, Florence Waller.

My dear friends,

On this picture, my oldest brother, Klaus Schnädelbach, (2nd row center) visited the 'Artaban' or 'Caravaners' Sunday School Class at the Temple City Methodist Church in Temple City, CA in 1957.

Between 1946 and 1951, this Sunday School class sent 64 CARE packages to our family in postwar Germany.

Their acts of kindness saved our lives and serve as an inspiration to all of us.

The members of the Sunday School Class followed 'Artaban', the legendary 4th Wiseman, who helped the poor, comforted the grief stricken, fed the hungry, visited the lonely and cared for lost animals.

He never made it to Bethlehem to pay homage to the newborn King.

He was too busy helping others on the way.

> At the end of his life, he was comforted by Christ's voice saying to him,
>
> "Truly, I say to you, all that you ever did for your needy brothers and sisters, you did for me."
>
> What a discovery to have Marcia Galland and others to clean out your archives and find this red folder documenting the CARE packages project of the Artaban Sunday School mission project between 1946 through 1954, finding in return my mother's letters written in Germlish, pictures, and most of all, documenting a heartwarming story of friendship, care, and love for needy brothers and sisters, overcoming years of war, hate, grief, or bitterness. Maybe it is a good idea to clean out the archives in our homes, garages and in our minds. You might find your own treasures of stories, pictures, and items.
>
> It is with much gratitude that I return the folder to you today, having learned so much more about my own history 68 years ago. I am here to honor the passed-on members of your Artaban Sunday School Class, who kept a record of letters and wrote down every content item of the CARE packages sent to my family and others in need.
>
> May we follow their journey of kindness and forgiveness in our time.
>
> With deep gratitude,
> Maria Ritter
> Epiphany 2014

After I read my statement, I looked out into the congregation. I saw the smiles on the faces of people I had never met. Although the church was sparsely attended with many empty seats, I began to see all the pews filled by the Saints of the past like the Sawyers, the Bocks, the Slosson family, Rev. Dougherty, and many others I did not know by name. It seemed to me they were all sitting there in their pews filling the church with their witness. They had left a message on the minds of this current generation of Caravaners, of seekers on their journey. I felt a sense of homecoming as if they knew who I was and where I had been.

EPILOGUE: TEMPLE CITY, 2014

Temple City, California, 2014

A warm reception followed a traditional worship service with Rev. David Palmer's sermon on God's Life app. He thought about the use of i-phones we have become accustomed to, texting messages all day long to stay in touch if we wish to be connected. How the church and we listeners could hold on to messages of faith and never be alone when in need. The red folder filled with my mother's letters seemed in contrast to be a document of the old times, never to return. My mother's handwritten letters on thin papers had faded with time, sun and moisture, untouched for years stuffed in plastic bags, some hardly readable. Way back, they had traveled for weeks across the Atlantic and back to Germany by boats, stuffed in crates, waiting to be sorted out at a local post office and finally delivered by a postman to a mailbox in front of a home in Temple City, or at a mail slot at the door in Leipzig, and later in West Germany, in Bergzabern. The joy of opening a letter is the same as opening an email from a special person. It really does not matter so much at the end how long it took. It is just a matter of time. If we have an instant connection or wait for weeks, the message is what ultimately counts, those signs of peace to each other, of caring for others in need, of spending time to read, listen and respond in deed just like the 4th Wiseman, Artaban, had done all his life.

"Come, meet these women at the coffee hour," Marcia said as we left the sanctuary and put her arm around my shoulders.

A large poster displayed my book cover and the picture of the Artaban Sunday School Class of 1957. Names had been filled in. Lorraine Vogt, the daughter of Wilma and Stan Vogt, the couple on the second row, right side, greeted me. She had made an extra trip to be here. On the table nearby, coffee and tea were being served by women who had baked cookies and short bread. The green rice crispies reminded me of the many refreshment times after church during coffee hour, and I smiled as I complemented the ladies serving punch. I thought of the green or red Jell-O salad layered with marsh mellows and pineapples, apples and nuts next to green rice crispies and chocolate chip cookies, people's laughter and warm greetings with lime flavor or fruit punch in paper cups ….

We said goodbye and will never forget. Artaban is still alive among us. Maybe the Fourth Wiseman continues his journey. *"Truly I say to you, all that you ever did for your needy brothers and sisters, you did for me."*

EPILOGUE: TEMPLE CITY, 2014

> June 2021
>
> My dear readers,
>
> Thank you for having joined me on my journey from war to times of peace and grace, through hardship, losses, endings, and times of beginning. Through sadness and joy, through hate and famine, through loneliness and kindness but helped by the sounds of music and comforting words in letters and postcards—reaching out to each other in deeds of reconciliation. My journey is your journey. Be always hopeful on your journey and know I am there with you.
>
> With much love to you all,
> Your loving Mom, your Oma, your Maria, and all you friends.

I have added two of my poems, the first, *On the Path*, which I wrote after a visit to Spain in 2001, my experience in the pilgrimage town of Santiago de Compostela and reading Paulo Coelho's book, *The Pilgrimage*. The other poem, *The Pilgrim—Artaban*, was inspired by the name of the Temple City Sunday School name and the inspiration of reading, *The Story of The Other Wise Man*, by Henry Van Dyke (1896).

On The Path (2001)

*She had arrived that day at morning break
and rushed the last few miles along the rugged road.
The donkey huffed and grunted salty air,
while trotting faithful by her side,
avoiding slide and rocks on narrow paths.
He knew they had arrived at last,
her quickened steps had told him so,
her mumbled prayer turning louder with each new found breath.
She hushed into his ears,
"We're here, at last!"*

*His load had been so heavy many weeks ago
when rolled up bundles packed high on his back
and scents of spicy fish kept floating in the air.
A thick rope dangled from the wooden crates
marked by the painted scallop shell -
the sign of passage to a holy place.
Of all the donkeys in his quiet town
he pushed and shoved to get in line up front*

EPILOGUE: TEMPLE CITY, 2014

to volunteer his back and legs for her because
she was alone, her eyes so filled with wonderment and awe.
This was his chance to join her journey of a life
much like his brothers walked before in ancient time:
for Balaam's route, that special child to Egypt land,
and palms Hosannas through the Golden Gate.

They started off one early morn'
when dew dripped from the leaves above his head.
She said goodbye to all in town
"Santiago...tiago..." still ringing in his ears.
With a bunch of flowers draped around his neck
he soon forgot the piled-up load,
the unknown route, saw open road,
and listened to her voice reciting verse by verse,
chased flies and insects with his tail
the sing song lifted heat and strain.

One night, she stopped at sunset for a lodge and food
while he stood in the courtyard of the inn.
The sky streamed brightest blue above,
the Milky Way arched sparkles all night long
and crickets scratched their old familiar songs.
It was as if he dreamt of pastures green,
of lambs and lions lying side by side,
with fox and hare in joyful play,
lush trees bent gently to the ground
to share its sweet and heavenly fruit.
He'd never seen a world like this,
so clear and colorful in sight.
So peaceful, bright, like paradise -
while touched by angels' wings all through the night.

He woke at daybreak, stunned and blurry eyed,
the stone walls close, the sky all gray and white -
he thought he lost his sight that night.

RETURN TO LEIPZIG

Back on the road again when crossing bridge and brook,
his hoof got stuck among the tangled wood.
He fell, the load spilled over road and rocks.
She helped him up—bandaged his hoof,
brought water from the nearby brook,
shared apple, bread, soft-leafy hay
then offered touch, a healing praise.
From this day on he limped a bit,
held up his leg whenever he could -
remembered pastures green and peace
while she sang Mary's litanies.

They wandered weeks along the path,
saw pilgrims, thieves and charlatans.
In Calzada joined a wedding feast
with hens and roosters parade the street.
At Pilgrim's House they laughed and drank,
heard tales of wand 'ring, dancing saints,
sword-flying fights and shiny knights
to conquer beasts and gold alike,
and love and greed and suicide.
Sometimes they slept in caves at night
when she ignored the eventide
with creaky noises in the trees
drowned out by storms and rain on fields.
The scallop shell did lead the way,
a veil of gray stilled fogged his face.

They arrived that day at morning break
and rushed the last few miles along the rugged way.
The Tiago Road grown hard with cobble stones and slippery hills,
the pastoral silence broken by shrill horns
of buses, trucks, and wheels.
He barely noticed blinking lights and fumes
and people rushing by his side.
Heard someone yelling out the door

EPILOGUE: TEMPLE CITY, 2014

and felt the children touch his fur.
More pilgrims chatted next to him,
when ancient bells began to ring.

He waited outside the Northern gate
while she joined pilgrims at the Midday mass.
He sensed her kneeling by the open portal door,
heard chants and bells, long litanies and organ chords.
He'd never felt a harmony like this
with silence, peace and voices chiming in.
It seemed familiar now, he recognized her voice,
so peaceful, bright—just like in paradise.
A wave of pungent smoke swept passing by
so full of colors and luxurious spice.
It was as if the holy smoke refreshed the soul -
all burdens lifted—pain and his dark sight...

His eyes were opened when she hurried out the church
he saw her smile, her golden curls,
her dangling shiny shell with clearer vision
than he ever saw or dreamt before.
His nights were lifted to bright colors in the sky:
he saw the rolling pastures green,
still waters and "he leadeth me..."
lush flowers, birds, and fruits in trees.

She yelled, "We have arrived, ... received the gift of grace -
and you regained the gift of sight!"
Hail Mary, James, and all the Saints above
rejoice, and laugh for many years to come.
Remember stories of the Common Road,

"We're going home and gladly live with God."

The Pilgrim—Artaban (2014)

He saw the star one night, the bright one, he had been waiting for
To journey to the newborn King of Israel.
Vasda, his horse, and camels piled up high with tents, and cloth, and finest gems –
The shine of darkest sapphire, rubies, one glowing pearl and golden spoons -
Such worthy gifts to bring a King.

He followed the star, to meet friends near palms along the desert sands,
A place to join the Magi, Caspar, Melchior, and Balthazar.
In darkest night, along the path, Vasda heard deep groans aside the road,
A half dead man lay lost to plead for wine and bread –
Such worthy food to feed a King.

He missed the star and nursed the man to life until he walked,
Shared blankets, touch, and golden spoons.
Rushed on to desert's edge near palms and water well,
Found only parchment scribbled words: "We could no longer wait, you missed the hour...."
Such worthy time to meet a King.

He saw the star and rushed through desert storms and heat
To reach the gates of Bethlehem.
The troops of Herod had arrived to kill the young or newborn Kingling there.
A mother knelt and pleaded mercy for her son—his glowing ruby paid the ransomed sum.
Such worthy time to miss the King.

He lost the star and headed south to Egypt land
Where such a newborn Kingling must have fled, they said.
He wandered down along the Nile to Luxor Temple, Karnack, and even Aswan's shore.

EPILOGUE: TEMPLE CITY, 2014

Crossed marketplaces, desert huts, climbed into silent tombs and pyramids.
Such worthy time to search the King.

He missed the star for many years. His eyes grew dim and grey with Vasda leading now the way.
Arrived in Jerusalem at last, heard deadly rumors of a hated King.
At Damascus gate the shouting rose "to death with such a King of Jews!"
"I am a Parthian girl to now be sold," she screamed, "please, pay up for the debts incurred!"
Such wasted time to miss the King.

He held the star. With glowing pearl in hands, he bought her freedom on the street
To show a love much greater than his goal to find the Lord.
An earthquake shook, he fell on stony ground—she by his side to hear a sound,
"What you have done for them—you've done for me,"
the ancient voices rang out loud.
Such worthy time to find the King.

(Freely adapted from, *The Story Of The Other Wise Man*, by Henry Van Dyke, 1895.
A Ballantine Book, Random House Publishing House, Toronto, Canada 1984)

Conclusion

After the collapse of Germany in 1945, neither unending grief nor mountains of shame could ever suffice as a silent atonement. Maybe as survivors, we deserved the hunger and the suffering. I accepted this fact as a fitting punishment. More so, we all were hungry and cold during the winter. They called it die *Hungersnot,* the famine.

And then, a miracle happened. Starting in 1947, somewhere in America, a group of Sunday School members, by the name of Artaban, of a Methodist church in the Los Angeles, California area began to send us CARE packages, one at a time—all in all 64 packages over the next six years. These strangers in America saw us hungry, cold, and homeless and planned an organization to send us food, clothes, and blankets. How could they move through their own hate toward Germany and the Nazi destruction worldwide and look at us as suffering children in need? What changed their hearts to reach out while they still buried their sons and daughters?

The packages contained food and clothes to keep us alive and warm, basic items such flour, sugar, and milk powder as well as yarn, soap and even toys. Faithfully, Mother, in turn, wrote back many thank you letters, some in half English half German. Someone in that distant Sunday School Class took the time to translate some of mother's letters into readable English and saved all her letters in a folder. I remember my mother sitting at the table late at night, when we had gone to bed, "Dear Blanche, …"

These letters tell a story of human compassion, of survival and the power of faith. Gratitude is timeless and the Artabans are still among us.

A Word of Thanks

Composing and collecting memories cannot be done without the questions and encouragement of others, of family members, and friends. Finding documents such as folders of letters and loose pictures raise questions of time and place. I am grateful to my brothers, Klaus, Herbert, and Gerhard Schnaedelbach whose sharp memories of names, locations, and sequence of events helped me as the youngest in the family find my place and set me on my journey.

This document, Return to Leipzig, is not meant to be an accurate recount of history. It reflects my experience then, my subjective memories, and my association now. It is meant to be a gift to my children, grandchildren, friends, and all you dear readers. My heartfelt gratitude goes to Robert and Marcia Galland in honor of past and present members of the United Methodist church in Temple City, California who uncovered my mothers thank you letters for the Care packages we received during times of famine and hopelessness after WWII in Leipzig, Germany. We share a joint history with familiar names and pictures.

A completion of a journey acknowledges an end and encourages us to move forward with what has been discovered and learnt. The past is now behind us, and I can look forward with courage and strength. So can you!

To put my journey on paper requires much help and patience. My deep gratitude goes to David Wogahn and his staff who creatively and thoroughly found a way to put my small voice on paper, sorting through text and pictures while formatting it all into a book. Thank you!

I am so grateful to my daughter Lisa for all her patience and help to manage drafts and computer challenges. Grateful to my husband Winfried, to Peter, Julia, Michael, Matthew and Katherine, Luke and Andrew and their acceptance of their heritage and interest to know more. There are friends around me like Phyllis Tyson, Cal and Jean Colarusso, Warren Poland, Patricia Lindquist, Patricia Judd, Gay Parnell, Barbara Rosen, Mark and Jean Trotter, Richard and Alexa Kratze, and Melanie and Bill Silva, and many others who listened and encouraged my writing. No writing is meaningful unless it is read. Thank you!

Appendix

Some copies of the original letters.

LENI SCHNÄDELBACH
LEIPZIG S 3
LÖSSNIGER STR. 47

Leipzig, 22.1.48.

Liebe Frau Flossan,

vor ein paar Tagen kam zu unserer grossen Freude Ihr schönes Paket ganz unversehrt an, weil es so schön eingepackt war. Das war ein Fest als wir es auspackten, die Kinder und ich waren so glücklich und froh darüber, wie schön wäre es gewesen, wenn Sie hätten bei uns sein können, um diese Freude mitzuerleben. Ja, das wäre das richtige! wenn Sie dabei gewesen wären. Es war alles so wunderschön, wir können alles so gut verwenden, von Herzen besten Dank! Bitte geben Sie unseren Dank weiter an alle Frauen der Samstagsdrillklasse, die mitgeholfen haben uns zu erfreuen. Gott segne alle Lieben und Ihre Hilfsbereitschaft. Sie jeden würde ich jeden einzelnen die Hand drücken, das geht nun leider nicht, weil der Ocean dazwischen liegt. Aber wir sind auch so verbunden und wir spüren Ihre herzens wärme und

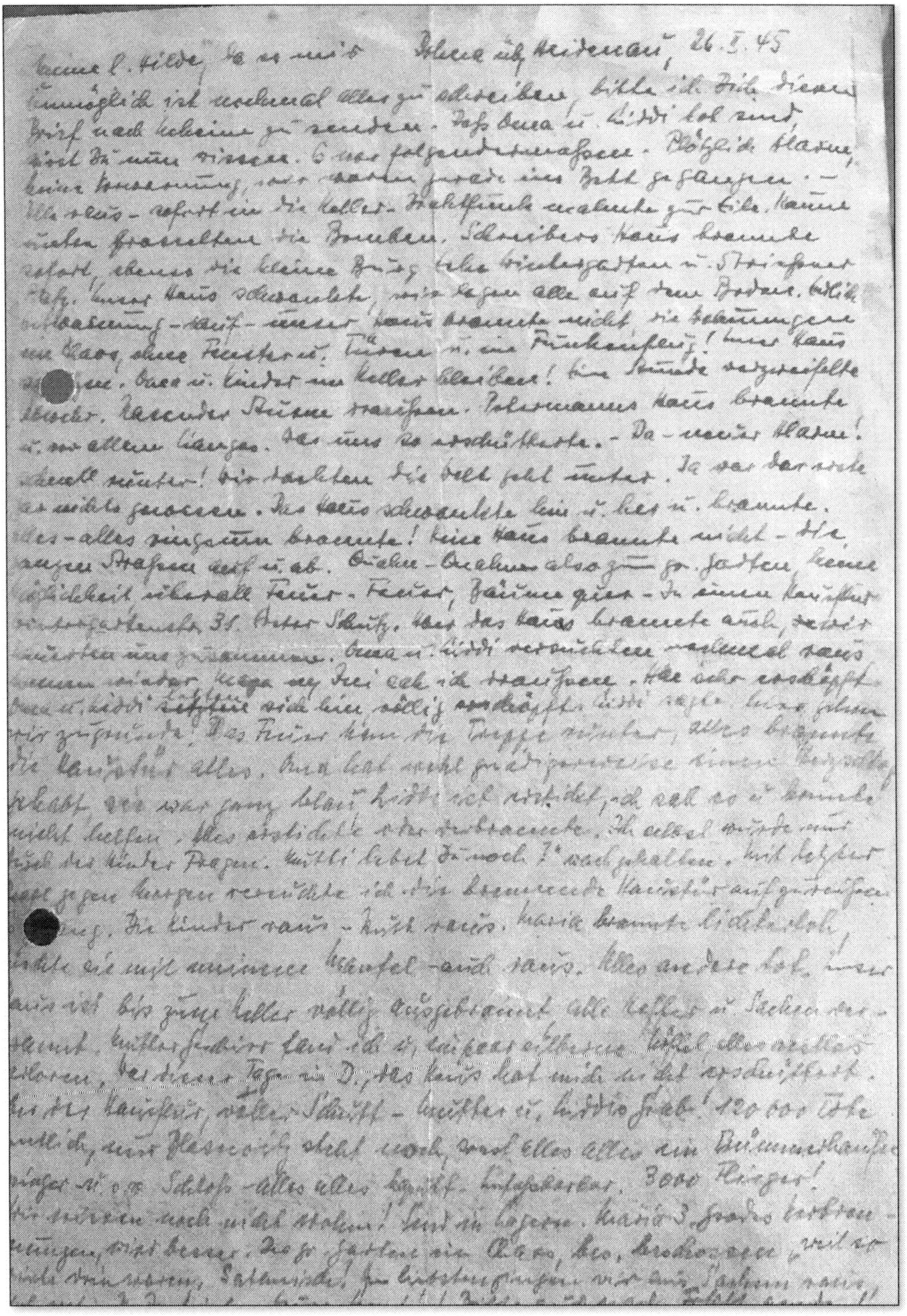

Package #18	sent 9-18-48	
#5 flour		.47
5 bottles novamin capsules 25 @		1.25
#1 dextrose		.75
#1 raisins		.16
1 used woman's corduroy suit		.30
1 used saddle shoes – boys		.15
2 girls skirts		.10
1 tooth brush		.10
2 used hankies		.05
2 used towels		.05
2 (pr.) shoe strings		.10
3 spools thread		.15
1 roll cotton tape		.10
1 card buttons		.10
1 tooth paste		.10
1 beef stew		.45
1 used rain coat + hat		.25
	Total value	4.63

APPENDIX

Hilde Alrutz (Wunderlich) mother's older sister.

Opa Schnädelbach's letter to me 1950.

APPENDIX

Levi Schmädelbach
Kinder- und Jugend-Erholungsheim
am Wonneberg
Luftkurort Bergzabern/Pfalz

Bankkonto: Bergzaberner Volksbank, Bergzabern
Postscheckkonto: Nr. 20431 Karlsruhe i. B.
Telefon 293

(22b) Bergzabern, 14.12.54
Wiesenstraße

Dear Mrs. Sawyer and all our friends of the Arthaban-Class,

we thank you very much for your fine letter, which came to us, in the beginning of november, the Bank draft was in and we have received the money in a short time, it was not so late just last jear, and we have had a great ? joy.
This at first, that you know, that your letter and the joy, you want to do to us, is in our hands just in the Christmas -time. We are very enjoyed about it and we want to give you our hands and our thank for all your love and friendship.
It is so fine, that we have friends who are children of Jesus Christ also. My heart (Herz) is happy to know, that in so many countries are people, who like Jsus Christ, and all this people are as like as a family. I believe ,when one of us come to you, or one of you come to us, we were brother and sisters, who know the name of the other and had aheart for the others.

I am very unhappy, that I can not tell you, Ilike to tell you, the words do not come. But I believe, you know I want to you.

Just in the last time often I think to you and your work you have done on my family.
In Leipzig at first you haven saved our life, specielly this of my children, I believe we did not live just, because we had so little need, that we could not live. Gerhard was so ill, his Lunge was very ill, and all your helpness had given us the life. Just now I think, it is not to understand, that people can live in such need, but in the greatest need was the Lord to next.

We are thankfull for this time, now we know, that The Lord did never come to late.

So often I hope, that we can see one of you. It was so fine, that Mrs. Williams was here and he can told you about our work and our family.

My children are now by good healthy, only Herbert, the second did not, his heart is not so well. He want to go at eastern to university, music and germanistik. Klaus study in Karlsruhe Technik and Gerhard und Maria aregoing to school in Bergzabern. Gerhard wannt to study Theologie in Frankfurt in the Theological Seminary.
Childrens-Home
Our Kinderheim is a work which give us many joy, but also many Sorgen. We have had many children last year and we hope, that the children XXXX get not only good healthy — that the name of the best friend of the children will rest in their hearts.
Infantile paralysis

Document report of the Dresden bombing in 1945
and the death of grandmother and mother's sister

APPENDIX

Leipzig, 11.3.48.

Liebe Frau Flossmann,

gestern kam von Ihnen wieder ein Paket bei uns an. Das Datum des Absenders konnte ich nicht genau erkennen, es war aber vom 30.?.1947! Es war ganz unversehrt und enthielt neben einer schönen Daunendecke, Weidenpfosten(?), die uns so sehr erfreuten. Gerhard war begeistert von dem schönen warmen Morgenrock u. der Hose, die ihm so gut paßt! Er bedankt sich ganz besonders! Ach, die schönen Sachen erfreuen mich so, wir wollen einen Überzug darauf machen, so wird sie uns gute Dienste tun. Zwei Tage vorher war ein Paket von Ihnen gekommen, das Sie vor am Jan. 30.48 abgesandt hatten und schon ankam. Auch dafür ganz, ganz herzlichen Dank. Ich kann Ihnen im Einzelnen gar nicht alles aufzählen, es war ja so viel u. Wertvolles. Auch dafür ganz lieben Dank, wir werden Ihnen so gern noch mehr unsere Freude zeigen, u. Ihnen herzlich die Hände drücken. Bitte geben Sie unseren Dank auch weiter

303

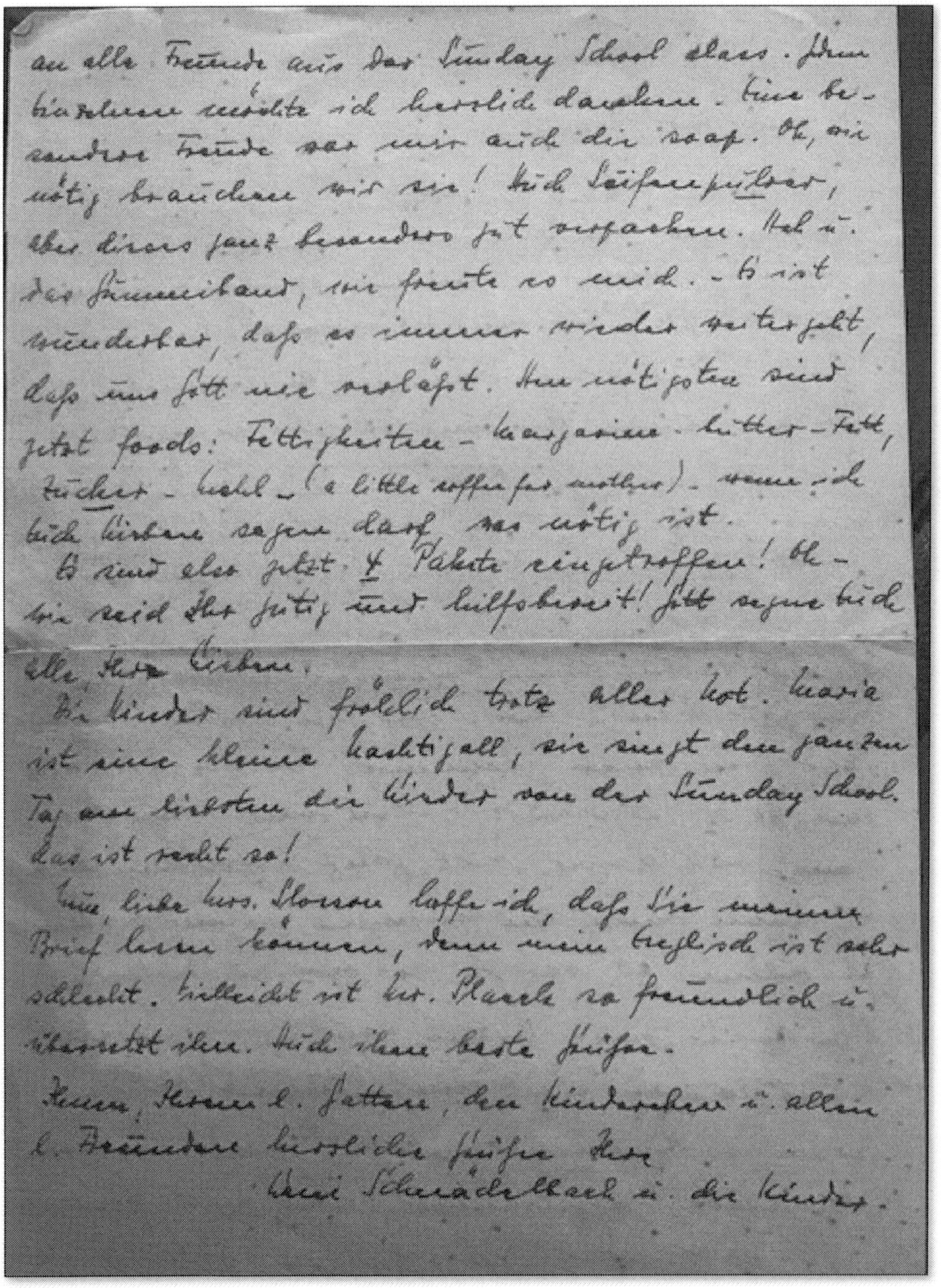

[Handwritten letter in German, partially legible]

an alle Freunde aus der Sunday School class. Ihnen
[...] möchte ich herzlich danken. Eine be-
sondere Freude war mir auch die soap. Oh, wie
nötig brauchen wir sie! Auch Seifenpulver,
aber dieses ganz besonders gut verpacken. Hab u.
das [...], wie freute es mich. – Es ist
wunderbar, daß es immer wieder [...],
daß uns Gott nie verläßt. Am nötigsten sind
jetzt foods: Fettigkeiten – Margarine – Butter-Fett,
Zucker – Kohl – (a little coffee for mother) – wenn ich
Euch [...] sagen darf, was nötig ist.
Es sind also jetzt 4 Pakete eingetroffen! Oh –
wie seid Ihr gütig und hilfsbereit! Gott segne Euch
alle, Ihre Lieben.
Die Kinder sind fröhlich trotz aller Not. Maria
ist eine kleine Nachtigall, sie singt den ganzen
Tag am liebsten die Lieder von der Sunday School.
Das ist recht so!
Eine, liebe Mrs. Slosson hoffe ich, daß Sie meinen
Brief lesen können, denn mein Englisch ist sehr
schlecht. Vielleicht ist Mr. Plaerle so freundlich u.
übersetzt ihn. Auch ihnen beste Grüße.
[...], Vater, den Kinderlein u. allen
l. Freunden herzliche Grüße Ihr
                Anni Schwadellach u. die Kinder.

About the Author

Maria Ritter is the author of four books, most recently *The Golden Cup* (2020), a modern folk tale about turning broken shards into golden opportunities. With vivid illustrations, *The Golden Cup* brings to life the story of Sieglinde, a young woman who embarks on an emotional journey to find her hidden gifts and her purpose.

In each of Dr. Ritter's three books she uses storytelling to help her readers make sense of the world around them. *The Adventures of Wilhelm, A Rat's Tale* (2018) is an allegorical coming-of-age travel adventure that inspires thinking about good and evil, tolerance and acceptance while helping readers learn about the importance of valuing other cultures.

Return to Dresden, (2004), an autobiographical reflection on her childhood in Germany during and after World War II, is a healing memoir that confronts national guilt for the Nazi past. *On the Path and Other Wanderings*, (2015), is a collection of poems and stories on people, animals, and encounters. These rhymes and musings, short stories and reflective memories can inspire others to search their own attics and archives of memory for keepsake treasures.

Dr. Ritter is a retired Clinical Psychologist and Psychoanalyst with a retired private practice for adults in La Jolla, California. She now lives in Austin, TX.

Made in the USA
Monee, IL
01 July 2022